FIERY FERMENTS

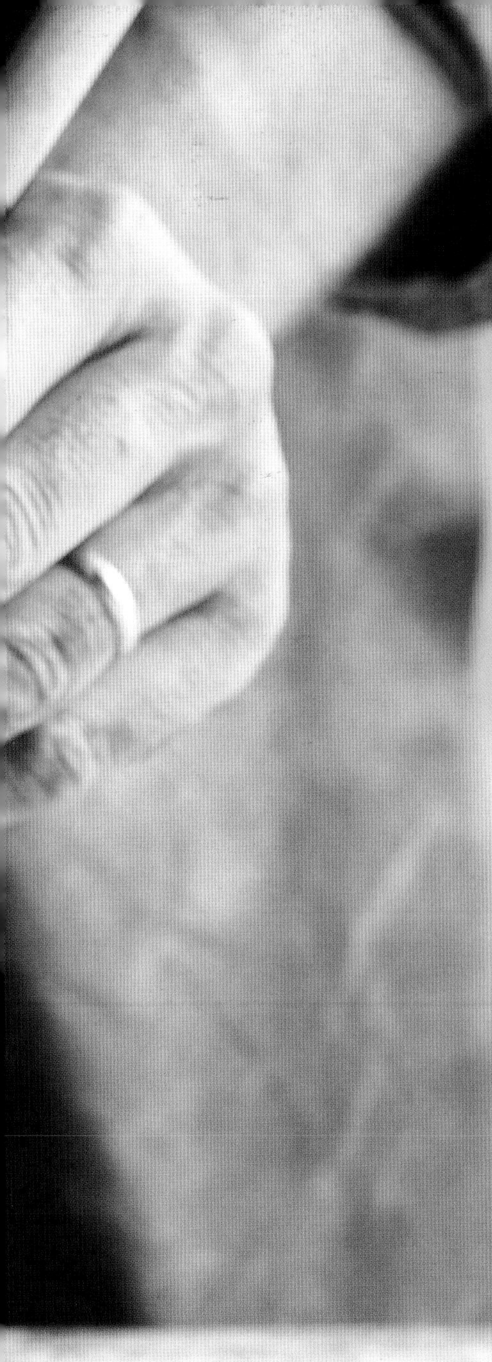

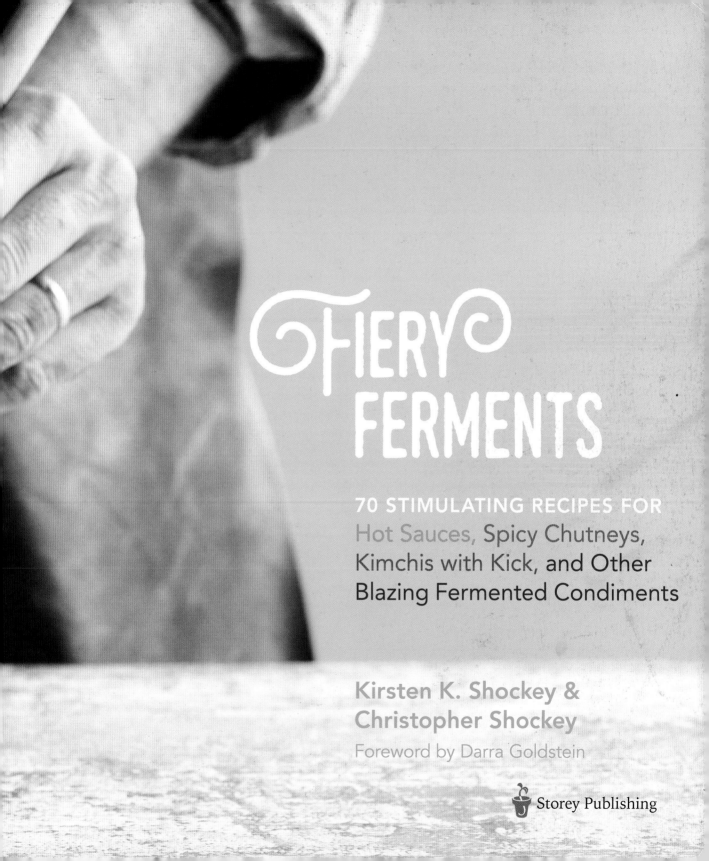

Fiery Ferments

70 Stimulating Recipes for Hot Sauces, Spicy Chutneys, Kimchis with Kick, and Other Blazing Fermented Condiments

Kirsten K. Shockey &
Christopher Shockey

Foreword by Darra Goldstein

Storey Publishing

The mission of Storey Publishing is to serve our customers by publishing practical information that encourages personal independence in harmony with the environment.

EDITED BY Margaret Sutherland and Hannah Fries
ART DIRECTION AND BOOK DESIGN BY Michaela Jebb
TEXT PRODUCTION BY Liseann Karandisecky
INDEXED BY Samantha Miller

COVER PHOTOGRAPHY BY © Lara Ferroni, except authors' photo by © Ariana Shockey
INTERIOR PHOTOGRAPHY BY © Lara Ferroni, except © Kirsten K. Shockey, 63, 67, 70 (right), 250–253; © Maja Smend/Getty Images, 48; © Dorling Kindersley/Getty Images, 54 (left); © Wildlife GmbH/Alamy Stock Photo, 54 (right)

ILLUSTRATIONS BY © Veronica Ballart Lilja

Be sure to read all instructions thoroughly before using any of the techniques or recipes in this book and follow all safety guidelines.

Storey Publishing
210 MASS MoCA Way
North Adams, MA 01247
storey.com

Printed in China by Toppan Leefung Printing Ltd.
10 9 8 7 6 5 4 3 2 1

Library of Congress Cataloging-in-Publication Data on file

Rund-Glas 100

CONTENTS

Foreword

Food is life, but as Kirsten and Christopher Shockey demonstrate in this marvelous book, it is also alive. That is, food ferments. It bubbles and churns, froths and foams, releasing compounds that benefit our health. But *Fiery Ferments* isn't primarily about nutrition (though that's a nice bonus). The Shockeys celebrate flavor, specifically flavor that zings, and they are excellent guides into the lively world of fermentation—the wonders of microbial action, the magical transformations it achieves.

And what magic! *Fiery Ferments* travels the globe as the recipes progress from familiar hot sauces and salsas to condiments other cultures enjoy: Haitian pikliz, Indian achar, Indonesian rempah, Yemeni zhug. And they're all presented in a spirit of experimentation and fun. Why stick to traditional kimchi made with cabbage when you can use nettles, green beans, summer squash, or rhubarb instead?

The late anthropologist Sidney Mintz wrote about the "core-fringe" pattern of eating in which bland, starchy staples—foods like rice, potatoes, cassava, even pasta—are enhanced by a "fringe" of condiments that stimulate the appetite by providing vibrant texture, color, and taste. No wonder the word *relish* refers to these condiments as well as to our pleasure in eating them.

These fringe foods and the pleasure they inspire is what *Fiery Ferments* is all about. After beginning with the basics of fermentation, the Shockeys usher us from kitchen to table with recipes for wonderfully innovative meals. Why season chili with a standard chili powder blend when you can use your own fermented green chili base and top the steaming bowl with homemade habanero carrot sauce? You'll also discover that jalapeño poppers really pop when you begin with fermented carrot-stuffed peppers. And don't forget dessert. What better way to end a tongue-tingling meal than with chocolate-cranberry mole ice cream or persimmon ginger sorbet?

Kirsten and Christopher are two of the most generous cooks I know, and the best kind of teachers. After sharing their carefully tested recipes and secret tips for success, they encourage us to experiment on our own. I'm ready to take the plunge. After all, as this book amply demonstrates, fiery ferments sustain both body and soul.

DARRA GOLDSTEIN

Editor in Chief, *CURED* (curedmagazine.com)

INTRODUCTION

Fiery Ferments is not just another hot sauce book.

Don't worry, there are plenty of delicious fermented hot sauce recipes in this book; if that is all you want, you will not be disappointed. However, we wanted to explore what it means to push the essence of pungency. As we researched and experimented, we discovered that there are many ways to wake up the tongue in that eye-popping, wow-what-did-I-just-taste moment. And there are a lot of people who love stimulating, flavorful food but prefer not to singe their mouths. This book is for them, too.

Humans seem to have always craved some spice in their lives and in their meals. Until very recently (if you consider the time frame of all of human history), our favorite spicy foods and condiments were likely preserved through lacto-fermentation, with all the flavor, nutrients, enzymes, vitality, and other elements of goodness that accrue from working with probiotic bacteria. Then methods of quick acidification with vinegar and pasteurization came along, and our traditional spicy foods lost their probiotic love. Yes, modern hot sauces can stand on grocery-store shelves waiting for you to buy them for a very long time and will remain safe and flavorful, but they are no longer alive.

We think it's time to bring that life — the fiery ferments — back into our own lives. We have devoted ourselves to researching ancient accounts of meals around the world, deconstructing hot sauces and rebuilding them with new custom vegetable ferments, and doing a lot of testing on the plate. We hope you enjoy these spicy characters as we give them their seats at the head of the table. They are fun, a bit crazy, and full of flavor.

THE ORIGINS OF SPICE

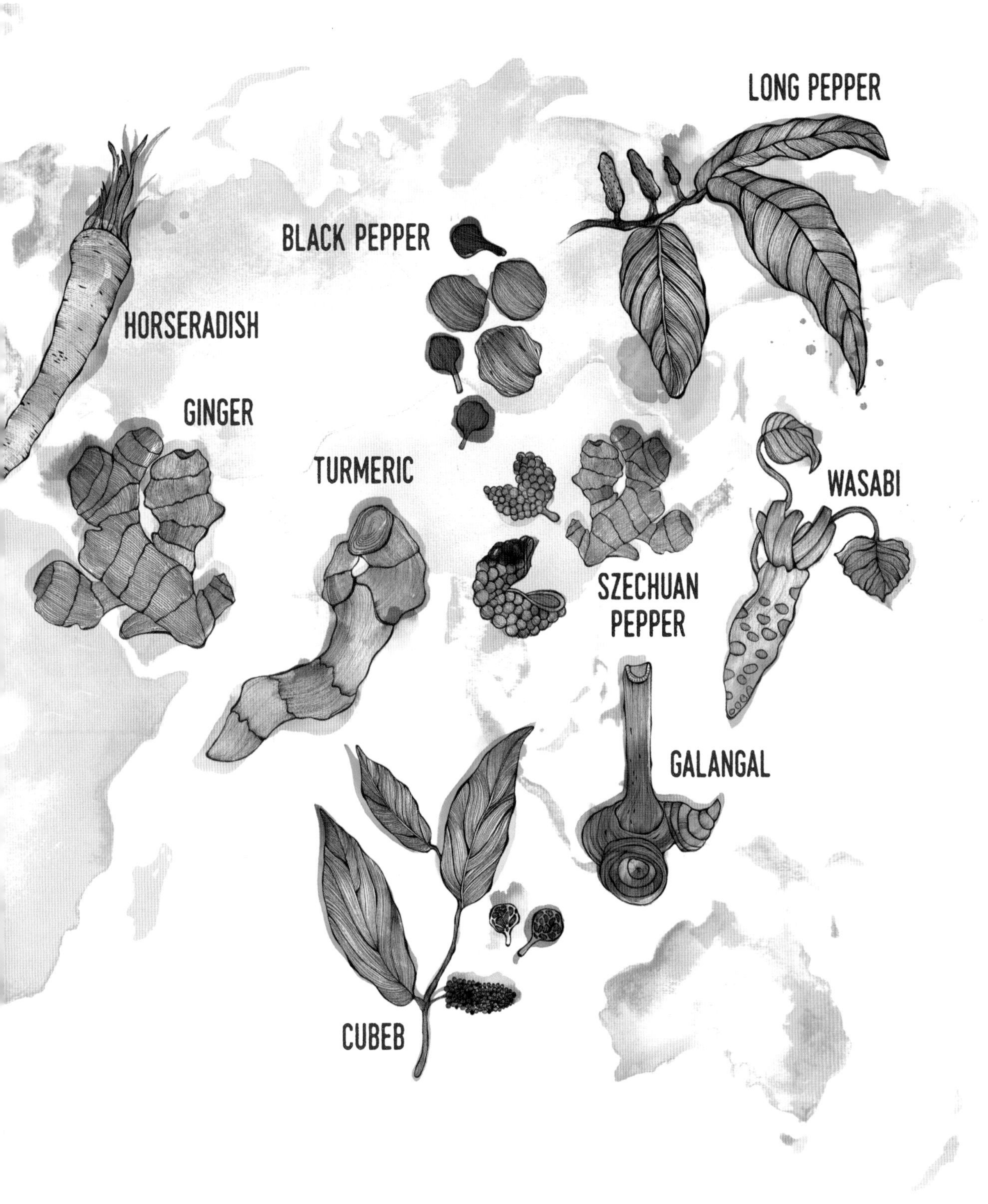
LONG PEPPER
BLACK PEPPER
HORSERADISH
GINGER
TURMERIC
WASABI
SZECHUAN PEPPER
GALANGAL
CUBEB

Some Like It Hot! (A Brief History)

It was once thought that spice was a modern invention, that our Stone Age ancestors had no time or appreciation for anything that didn't directly fuel their survival. But in recent years, with the help of some ancient dirty dishes, scientists have discovered a different story: this love for spice has been with us for thousands of years, and civilizations the world over have always cultivated a local version of something hot.

STONE AGE SPICE

When researchers from the University of York analyzed some 6,000-year-old clay pots from Stone Age dwelling sites in Germany and Denmark, they discovered that fish and deer were eaten with ground garlic mustard (*Alliaria petiolata*), especially fish. When they re-created the meals, the researchers agreed that the addition of the mustard, while adding little if any nutritional fuel, did improve the flavor.

Similarly, a team of scientists at the Smithsonian Institution has been able, through the analysis of starch grains housed in their vast reference collection, to date the presence of chiles to that same Stone Age period in at least seven sites stretching from southern Peru to the Bahamas. These chiles differ slightly from the wild chile, meaning they had been cultivated by humans.

Root crops that included turmeric, ginger, and garlic show up in the archaeological record about 4,500 years ago, again in some very old pots, this time found in New Delhi. Linguistic evidence suggests that turmeric and ginger were also important to the peoples of southern China during this period: The Austronesians had begun a massive migration of thousands of miles, all the way east to Easter Island, south to New Zealand, and west to Madagascar. The ancient languages of these areas all have a word for ginger, and it's the same word. Ginger was important enough to these people, who took only what they could carry, that it came with them and stayed with them.

Meanwhile, in India turmeric and native peppers were being used medicinally, as referenced in early Ayurvedic texts. This includes both black peppers and long peppers, and if you haven't heard of long peppers, you will soon (see page 54).

So up until a few thousand years ago, your choice of spice had everything to do with the continent you called home. If you lived in Europe, it was mustard and horseradish. If you lived in Asia, you used either black pepper and its relatives or ginger. We have some tasty recipes for these in chapter 4, our chapter devoted to recipes without chiles. If you lived in the Americas, your go-to spice was the chile. Chapters 5 and onward are devoted to recipes that showcase the versatility of this picante, mouth-singeing fruit.

THE ARRIVAL OF THE CHILE

For most of the world's populations, there is a distinctive Before Chiles (B.C.) period and an After Chiles (A.C.) period, which is the world we know today. The chiles of the Americas were not revealed to the rest of the world until Columbus and his gang left with a sampling of the Americas' menu of potatoes, tomatoes, corn, and chiles.

Although the chile was not the black pepper the traders were hoping for, they called it a "pepper" nonetheless (kicking off centuries of name confusion). The chile was pungent and a lot easier to grow than black pepper, which made it attractive to the Portuguese traders headed around Africa to India and farther east. Within a few decades the chile was dominating local cuisines in Africa, India, Japan, Thailand, Indonesia, and China. Trade routes headed inland from port cities further aided its spread, and chile quickly become the dominant global spice it is today.

What was it like for these traders to risk their lives in terrible conditions just so the royalty back home could dine well? Consider their personal space: 500 hardy souls, packed into the equivalent of a large two-story house, the majority of them crammed below with the cargo, kitchen, mountains of wood, and five months of provisions. At least for the Portuguese sailors, everyone on board got a cut in the form of their own "liberty chest," which they were free to fill with whatever they could procure and bring back (rather like the duty-free shops in the airports). If they survived the year at sea, and if they were not robbed on the way back, there was a chance that little box's contents would buy them and their family a new way of life. Like the gold rush in the West, a journey to the Far East called to the adventurous and the desperate.

What Is Fermentation?

All of our recipes in this book are fermented. But what is fermentation exactly? Just a few years ago it was a dirty word, as in scary and weird. Chocolatiers and cheesemakers (who create some of the sexiest fermented foods) did not talk openly about how the flavor and texture that make their products delicious are a direct result of the action of bacteria. *Bacteria!* Yikes! But that is so yesterday. In the last few years, working with bacteria to produce delicious fermented foods has become cool, and something to be proud of.

Fermentation is defined as the chemical breakdown of a substance by bacteria, yeasts, or other microorganisms, often resulting in effervescence and the release of heat. In lactic-acid vegetable fermentation, it is the members of the lactic-acid family of bacteria that transform the (often) low-acid vegetables into high-acid vegetables — a.k.a. pickled vegetables — by consuming the carbohydrates in the vegetables and converting them to acid. Like the before-and-after shots of a makeover, there are some significant, almost magical changes that turn these veggies into a long-lasting "superfood." Why "super"? (After all, "superfood" is an extremely overused word usually used to describe the next trendy green or berry.) They're super, in short, because these veggies, after fermenting, have more bioavailable vitamins because the carbs have been predigested by probiotic bacteria. But if that isn't enough — and it isn't, really — they just taste mighty good.

In fermentation, most of the taste comes from the action of the microbes, which act like billions of little chefs layering on flavor over the course of two stages of fermentation. This two-stage succession of bacteria comprises a whole assortment of different species that occur naturally in the soil and are therefore found on the plants. So whether you buy vegetables from the store or harvest them from your garden, they come to you fully inoculated with the bacteria needed to get things started. You just provide the environment (which we'll get into later).

We are still learning so much about the microorganisms that flavor our food and keep us healthy, but right now, broadly speaking, we know that four key species of lactic-acid bacteria are present in vegetable fermentations: *Lactobacillus brevis, Lactobacillus plantarum, Leuconostoc mesenteroides,* and *Pediococcus pentosaceus.* Several more species of lactic-acid bacteria have been found in cabbage-based fermentations. Each of these groups has its own specific niches and reactions and, we are finding out, flavors. You will hear most about *L. plantarum,* a second-stage fermenter, as it produces high acidity in all vegetable ferments. But honestly, you don't need to know or remember any of these guys' names to make great spicy ferments. You just need to know how to manage their homeplace, and they will do the rest.

People come to fermentation for a number of reasons. For some it is for the age-old reason of preserving the harvest into the cold, lean months. The acidification (or pickling, if you will) of vegetables — including peppers, the star of many of the recipes in this book — can hold off the forces of decay for months and sometimes years. But many more people come to fermentation for the health benefits (or to freak out their parents by eating foods with funk). These are all good reasons to make and eat fermented foods, but ultimately it is flavor that will keep you coming back for more.

So here we are at the core of why we ferment: flavor. It has to be flavor, because, ultimately, if you don't like these ferments you won't eat them, and then it really doesn't matter how long they last, or how digestible and full of vitamins, minerals, and probiotics they are. We hope to introduce you to some flavors that we find fantastic while encouraging you to invent your own.

It is an exciting time right now as we reinvent our fermentation foodways. Chefs and home cooks are experimenting with using microbes for flavors in ways previously unimaginable. Many feel we are just scratching the surface of possibility. And this possibility lies not only in the fermenting itself but also in how we use these foods, whether as condiments or as ingredients in interesting meals. One of the things that we have enjoyed most since our book *Fermented Vegetables* came out has been meeting both home cooks and chefs who are bringing these ferments to their dinner tables and menus in intriguing ways.

We invite you to enjoy all the advantages of fermentation, from flavor to health to preservation. And we invite you to play around with the recipes, using whatever vegetables are in season or at hand, as you create your own unique fiery ferments. Using chiles and other veggies that you buy from your local farmers allows you not only to create a truly local product — including local bacteria! — but also to support your local foodshed, and to play a small part in establishing your region's food security.

Spices were trendy for much the same reason in 1500 as they are now. Once again, people are looking to spices for the elixir of life or a ticket to paradise. And the future bodes well for people who study spices as well as for those who come up with new ways for us to consume them. . . . We are living in a new golden age of spice.

Michael Krondl, *The Taste of Conquest: The Rise and Fall of the Three Great Cities of Spice*

Part I
Getting Started

With fermented products there is no safety concern. I can flat-out say that. The reason is the lactic-acid bacteria that carry out the fermentation are the world's best killers of other bacteria.

Fred Breidt, USDA microbiologist

First of all: you've got this! Don't be daunted by fermentation. The worst that can happen is that you have a failed batch. You won't kill your family (cliché alert), but if we had a nickel for every time somebody came to us and said, "I want to do this, but I am afraid I will kill my family," we would be quite wealthy. After all, for a society that has grown up with germ theory and refrigeration, there is nothing intuitive about letting food sit on your counter for a few days or weeks, possibly having to remove a layer of yeast or mold, and then digging in.

Fermentation advocate and USDA microbiologist Fred Breidt is often quoted as saying that, as far as he knows, nobody has died from eating properly fermented vegetables — the operative word being *properly*, because this is where things can go south. The good news is that if they do, you will know. We like to remind people that our species is still around after thousands of years because we have five very capable senses. Okay, so you may not *hear* it go wrong, but you will smell it. The smell is not funky or pickle-y pungent, but bad — like something rotting, which is essentially what is happening at that point. Your eyes will see things that are off-color or otherwise unappealing. (The caveat is that sometimes the top layer of the ferment, the part that was exposed to oxygen, might look off-color — but you will remove that layer and find wonderful flavors underneath where the environment is far too acidic for pathogens to live.) It may feel slimy. Your survival brain will kick in and tell you, *do not put that in your mouth*. And if you do and it feels and tastes wrong, it probably is; spit it out.

Now that you have the worst-case scenario out of the way, don't be afraid to fail. Take the risk! Enjoy the process, even if it means you may sometimes feed your compost pile instead of your family. Even a failed batch is a wonderful opportunity to learn a little more about the process. We know, we hated to hear that when we were kids, and we still do. If it makes you feel any better, we couldn't write these books without plenty of yuck to keep us learning so that we can help you avoid those moments.

CH 1

TOOLS AND TIPS

VEGGIES + SALT / in a VESSEL + TIME = YUM

Fermentation is as humble as this formula. We humans have been processing our vegetables this way for more than a few years — we've been doing it for so long, in fact, that our first vessels were probably animal bladders and crude clay pots. In this chapter we will touch on the many ways to house and care for your ferment. We'll also go over the key elements of lacto-fermentation — salt and unchlorinated water, brine, and time — and how each affects our friends in the lactobacillus family. With a few management strategies, you'll find it an easy process, and your hot ferments will turn out delicious.

Be a Good Host

Let's talk quickly about how lacto-fermentation works. It starts with making the friendly bacteria comfortable — we want them to settle in, enjoy the ambiance, and (unlike most houseguests) to reproduce. They don't need much — just an anaerobic saline pool to swim in and plenty of fresh veggies to eat.

The key here is that lactic-acid bacteria are anaerobic — they don't need oxygen — but many of their competitors are not. The most important thing to remember, therefore, is this: keep everything under the brine, which keeps the process anaerobic. The good guys thrive in these conditions, and when they thrive they multiply and consume (or convert, if you will) the carbohydrates to create an increasingly acidic environment — the death toll for the bad bacteria. Spores, molds, and yeast simply cannot live in the conditions that provide us with preserved, safe, live, tasty food. How cool is that?

The Perfect Vessel

In the last few years, folks have come up with ingenious ways to manage the process of fermentation, not to mention stunning pieces of functional art. So what you need for a vessel is more a question of what will make this process enjoyable and successful for you. For some, that means having a crock that is a piece of art gracing their countertop; for others it means a hermetically sealed jar that discourages alien invaders in the form of yeasts or molds. The beauty is that with the wide range of possibilities available, you will surely find a fermentation vessel that works for you — your environment, your lifestyle, and your style of cooking.

When you're fermenting, all the bits of your fermentation mixture must be kept submerged in the (anaerobic) brine. While there are a lot of ways to do this, it is really very simple. (This process was perfected a long time before we could peer through a lens at the workings of microbes.) Must the entire inner environment of the vessel be anaerobic? It doesn't have to be — lots of the old-school crocks or pots used in fermentation have an open top and are meant to be used with just a weight (to keep the mixture submerged) and a towel (to keep out dust).

However, fermenting in a big crock can be daunting and unwieldy, and since most of the recipes in this book are for very small amounts (after all, a gallon of habanero sauce may be more than you could eat in a lifetime), you will likely be using jars. Fermenting in a jar is great for a number of reasons beyond the approachable size. The biggest benefit is you can see what is going on with your ferment, which is especially handy when you are first learning. For example, you may see a huge layer of brine on top of your veggies and think, "Cool, my ferment is making brine." However, if you look into your glass jar, you can see that what is actually happening is that the brine is getting pushed out due to the trapped carbon dioxide (CO_2); this is called a "heave" or a "surge." You'll be able to see the air pockets in the ferment where the brine used to be. If you are using an open fermentation method, it is critical that you press on your ferment to release the air and allow the brine to sink back down, submerging the vegetables.

Though crocks, jars, and other open vessels work great, many people prefer not to deal with the yeasts and molds that can take up residence on that exposed top layer of brine — hence the invention of "closed" systems and airlock systems that let the CO_2 push the oxygen out and don't allow new air back in. (Getting the oxygen out of the picture also helps retain the color of your ferment because it can't oxidize.) The first of these inventions was the water-seal crock, which has a moat in the rim that holds a bit of water and the lid; air can bubble up and escape but can't come back in. Many of the systems you will see still use water as the seal, including jar lids with the traditional brewer's airlock. The Ferment'n cap is essentially the same idea but has been redesigned to be less unwieldy on the counter and comes with a weight to keep your ferment under the brine. Kraut Source designed a trough system not unlike the water-seal crock; the stainless steel lid has a moat and a plunger to hold the ferment down.

Also gaining popularity are the waterless "one-way valves" or "expansion valves," which release air only when the pressure has built up enough to open the valve in one direction. The Pickle Pipe and the Sterilock are examples of lids that function this way. However, we have found that a Weck jar also works on this principle: the lid and rubber gasket are held in place by clamps that have enough give to allow built-up pressure to break the seal; the gas escapes and then the lid immediately reseals.

Because the pockets that form in a ferment within a closed system are generally just CO_2 and not oxygen, it is less crucial to press down on the ferment to eliminate them as you do with an open system. That said, the flavor can still be affected if the vegetables are not completely submerged in brine, so it is best to press everything back down regardless of the system.

As far as equipment goes, the simplest closed system is a jar with a lid. You pack your jar with the ferment (or, in the case of brine pickles, pour in the brine), leave an inch or so of headspace, and screw the lid down tightly. This does not allow the CO_2 to escape on its own, though, so you have to burp your jar manually during the fermentation process so that the CO_2 molecules have someplace to go. When the pressure is released and those molecules shake free, you actually get a burst of energy in the form of a fizzing sound as the millions of CO_2 molecules rush to get out the door. If you burp your jar regularly you will simply hear a hiss with the release. If you wait too long, you may have quite an eruption. Do you remember shaking a soda can as a kid? Same idea.

Remember, however, that not all ferments are made alike. Some will require more frequent burping — one or two times a day — while others may require little or none.

Fermentation works in many environments, which is part of what makes it so incredible. New choices in small home fermentation systems continue to appear on the market. In the chart on pages 16–17, we look at various kinds to help you understand how each system works and decide which one is right for you.

The instructions in this book assume you are using a basic jar method, but you can use any vessel or lid type you like, as long as you follow the instructions for that system.

Babysitting Small-Batch Ferments

Most of the recipes within these pages have mighty flavor and therefore are made in small quantities and require special attention during the fermentation, or curing, time. Let's just say they need babysitting. Because small-batch ferments have less brine, it is often impossible to weight them down enough to keep the CO_2 from creating air pockets. And remember, this whole thing needs to stay anaerobic. (Some of the new jar lid systems can help; see page 12.) To keep your ferment covered in brine, you will find yourself pressing gently on it or the weight often — even daily.

Fermentation Systems

HANDMADE WATER-SEAL CROCK
(HADAR IRON)
HANDMADE TRADITIONAL
ONGGI POT
(ADAM FIELD)
WATER-SEAL
JAR SYSTEM
(KRAUT SOURCE)
ONGGI POT
(ELIEFS)
WATER-SEAL JAR SYSTEM
(FERMENT´N)

Vessels at a Glance

FERMENTATION VESSEL + SYSTEM	DESCRIPTION	EASE OF USE
Onggi pots and straight-sided open crocks with followers and weights (Adam Field, Ogusky Ceramics)	The classic, time-honored system in which a plate (follower) is nested inside the crock on the surface of the ferment, with a weight on top to press it down.	Straight sides handy for pressing in ferment; finding the right sized plate for a follower can be a challenge.
Water-seal crocks (Hadar Iron, Harsch)	Ceramic crocks with a trough along the rim allowing lids to nest in water. CO_2 is able to escape. Usually have split ceramic weights.	Require less monitoring then a straight-sided crock. Split weights slip into place; water trough needs some monitoring.
Jars with gaskets, Fido-style, bail-style, or Weck jar	The vulcanized rubber gasket on bail-style and Weck jars works like an airlock. Unlike an airlock or valved lid, CO_2 needs to build up more pressure to lift lid momentarily and slip out.	Very easy to set up and monitor. The Weck jar releases on its own more readily than a clamped Fido-style jar. Pull the gasket at the tab to release air.
Just a jar, burping method	Ferment is pressed into a jar with 1–2 inches of headspace, and lid is tight. CO_2 escapes when lid is opened manually.	Very easy to set up. Check regularly to release CO_2 and press ferment.
Just a jar, ziplock method	Ferment is pressed into a jar to about ¾ full; ziplock bag full of water is placed on top to act as barrier and weight. CO_2 escapes through wrinkles between bag and jar.	Very easy to set up and monitor.
Just a jar with weights, another jar, or ceramic or glass weights	A waterfilled jar is placed on top of the ferment to keep it weigted down, similar to the ziplock; an open system.	Very easy to set up. Needs regular pressing to keep ferment under brine.
Brewer's airlock for mason jar lid (FARMcurious, Pickl-It)	Jar is topped with plastic lids fitted with a brewer's airlock; a closed system.	Very easy to set up. Needs minimal babysitting.
Waterless one-way valve lids (Masontops, Sterilock)	Jar is topped with a lid that has a bubble valve that lets CO_2 out.	Very easy to set up and monitor.
Systems using pressure (Kraut Source, Ultimate Pickle Jar)	Jar with a lid that uses mechanical means to keep the ferment submerged.	Takes a little finesse to get all the pieces in place the first time, but simple once you've done it.
Ferment´n Home	A weight and waterseal airlock system developed by a potter. Lid is designed to be used with a canning jar ring.	Intuitive, simple design: place weight on ferment and screw on lid. Virtually no monitoring.

WHAT IS GREAT ABOUT THIS SYSTEM	CHALLENGES OF THIS SYSTEM
Easy to find; come in many sizes, making it a good value for large batches.	May be hard to find a suitable follower. Weighting down soft, juicy ferments can be tricky. Open top can make ferment prone to yeast or mold growth. Small crocks are difficult to weight and less practical than the 1-gallon or larger. Managing weights can be unweildy.
Creates a closed system, which helps control scum. The crocks (especially handmade ones) are beautiful.	Can be quite heavy to manage, move, and clean. Water trough does require some monitoring as water can evaporate, causing the seal to break.
A clean system that has the ease of an airlock without all the pieces; you can have a number of different ferments going without making as much investment as crocks.	More expensive than a mason jar. Bails on Fido-style jars can corrode (but that doesn't affect the ferment). Weck jars may be hard to find.
All you need is a jar. Works especially well with very small, dry ferments (in very small jars). No start-up costs, and you can make ferments on the road without spills.	If you forget to release the pressure, you'll have a small mess. Make sure the ferment stays under the brine.
Works well with small ferments. No start-up costs. The waterfilled bag fills in all the airspace and lets very little new air in (almost like a waterseal).	Involves disposable plastic. Ferment must be monitored for airpockets if the weight isn't heavy enough.
Very little cost, convenient, no plastic.	Most likely to develop scum on top and must be monitored for airpockets if the weight isn't heavy enough.
Once it's set up, there isn't much fuss — the water doesn't evaporate rapidly.	Tall profile can be a little awkward on some counter spaces. Lots of little plastic parts to keep track of when not in use.
Self-sealing and low profile; no pieces to lose, rust, bend, or break.	Bubble valve is surprisingly tempting to pinch by passersby, which defeats the purpose and can cause scums. Silicon lids can stick to the jar and be difficult to open.
Ferments don't heave once they are anchored down. Kraut Source is entirely stainless steel.	Lots of pieces to keep track of. For plunger to work properly, jar must be filled to a specific level.
Ceramic weight is heavy and holds ferment in place, even for hard-to-weight tiny batches.	Some thinner paste-style ferments will try to sneak through the "donut hole" in the middle of the weight, so may need a thin follower of some sort, like a small round of cheesecloth or a piece of cabbage leaf.

Slicing, Shredding, Chopping, Grating, and More

Vegetable fermentation depends on brine, and in most ferments this brine is created by breaking down the cell structure of the veggie and drawing out its water with salt. This requires slicing, shredding, chopping, and grating. Here are some helpful tools and gadgets.

CUTTING BOARD AND KNIFE

Don't underestimate how much can be done with a roomy cutting board and a few good-quality sharp knives. We do most everything with an 8-inch chef's knife. It's perfect for general chopping, slicing, dicing, and mincing.

HAND GRATER

Many of the recipes in this book call for finely grated ingredients. We have found a microplane grater/zester to be invaluable for ginger, turmeric, and galangal root, as well as for garlic and citrus peels. For larger pieces, regular tower hand graters and slicers can be useful.

MANDOLINE

Mandoline slicers have a series of intimidating super-sharp blades. However, most come with a hand guard that, when used properly, makes them safer to use than a knife. If you have a mandoline without a hand guard, find a sturdy slash-resistant glove, available in kitchen stores.

PROTECTIVE GLOVES

When processing peppers, you can end up in a whole lot of pain if you don't take precautions to keep the spicy capsaicin off your hands.

SPICE GRINDER

Spices are so much more flavorful when they are lightly toasted and freshly ground. (See our guide on page 55 to getting the most flavor from spices.) A coffee grinder is a wonderful tool for turning your whole spices into a fine powder. For years we used the same one that we use for coffee, carefully wiping it out before and after each use, which worked well. (Worked well, that is, until our youngest son caught us — he believes that mustard or coriander in the coffee grinder is a kitchen foul. The next Christmas there was a new grinder under the tree, just for spices.)

VEGETABLE CHOPPER

Hand-operated vegetable choppers, also called onion choppers, are satisfying to use and can give you the same small chop as a food processor, which is handy when you are working with small amounts.

BLENDER

A blender is useful for the final step of turning your pepper pastes into smooth sauces.

STRAINER

A medium to large, fine-mesh, stainless steel strainer is important because some of the pastes have pepper skins that won't fully break down in a blender. You'll want a good-quality one, because it is going to take some abuse as you press the mashes through it.

STRAINER
HAND GRATER
HAND GRATER
WEIGHTS
WEIGHTS
FUNNEL
pH 1-14 Test Strip
No.114
pH STRIPS
PROTECTIVE GLOVES
SILICONE LID LINERS

MOLCAJETE
(MORTAR & PESTLE)
FOOD PROCESSOR
SPICE
GRINDER
VEGETABLE
CHOPPER
MANDOLINE
Made in FRANCE
Professional Stainless Steel Knife

MORTAR AND PESTLE

Thai pepper pastes, Indian chutneys and spice mixes, Indonesian sambals, Mexican salsas and moles, Andean hot sauces like Bolivian llajwa — all are traditionally made by grinding the spices and other ingredients between two stones. Whether you call it a mortar and pestle, *molcajete y tejolote,* or any other name, this tool was the first food processor. You can find mortars and pestles in a variety of textures and materials. Molcajetes are often made of porous basalt stone, and you must season a new one to fill in some of the gaps. Do this by grinding something like rice in it and then wiping it out with a dry towel.

FOOD PROCESSOR

For many of the recipes in the book, we find a food processor to be invaluable for finely chopping the ingredients that become pastes and sauces.

FUNNEL

A small funnel is very handy for getting your newly created hot sauce into a hot sauce bottle.

SILICONE LID LINERS

These lid liners by Mason Jar Lifestyle are a great new find for preventing corrosion to your metal lids from salt and acid. We have even used them without the lid, clamped down by the ring. They also fit under Ball plastic storage caps, making them leak-proof.

FERMENTING WEIGHTS

Some of the fermentation systems we talk about use weights; some do not. We, personally, like weights. You can get thick, heavy rounds of pottery or glass that fit right inside a canning jar. If we were to choose one luxury to invest in for simple jar fermenting, it would probably be some easy-to-use weights. In crocks, weights are not optional but a required part of the set-up.

Salt

Salt is pretty great. How cool is it that a little salt can preserve fresh vegetables, vitamins intact, for months or even years? This mineral is also important for flavor and for the health of our bodies. Our ancestors went to great lengths to get salt as well as many spices. In fact, some of the earliest armies marched across landscapes far from home just to be paid in salt (the word *salary* actually comes from the word for salt). There were times when salt was only for the aristocracy — ironic, considering that with the industrialization of salt mining and food systems, it now dominates our cheapest processed foods.

The first purpose of salt in fermentation is to give the lactic-acid bacteria the advantage they need over the forces that rot. Salt isn't the preservative — the acid created by fermentation is what keeps everything safe (that's right, there's no benefit to tossing in a little extra salt for good measure). However, a correct saline environment, while not inhibiting the lactobacilli, makes it uncomfortable for many other kinds of bacteria to set up housekeeping and reproduce. Salt also affects the cells of vegetables. It hardens the pectins (keeping the veggies crisp) and draws out the vegetable's water, which becomes the brine.

Salt inhibits the yeasts that break down sugars into alcohol (not the yummy kind) instead of lactic acid. A mere 0.8 percent ratio of salt weight to vegetable weight will prevent the type of decomposition you don't want. Standard ferments use anywhere from 1.5 to 3 percent, and sometimes more for commercial products. The recipes in this book tend to stay in the 1.5 to 2 percent range.

Another purpose of the salt is to keep fermentation moving along at a steady rate by slowing it down a bit. This can be particularly important when fermenting in hot climates, to keep the process and the flavors in check. If you live in a warm environment (and it is warm inside as well as out), you may have to add a bit more salt, bringing the ratio up to 2 to 3 percent by weight.

We prefer to use natural salts with trace minerals and lower sodium chloride content, such as Redmond Real Salt, a fine rock salt, or the gray Celtic sea salts. But as long as you stay away from salts with additives (most notably table salt and kosher pickling salt), any choice is acceptable.

We have always told folks to add salt slowly and taste often to avoid an oversalted ferment. Oversalting can happen so quickly and is often a new kraut maker's first fail (oh, the disappointment!). We stand by that advice, but with the powerful little condiments in this book, you may not be able to taste the subtleties of the salt over the heat. Therefore, it is not crucial that you taste for the salt. Condiments are potent and less overwhelmed by salt, and since they are used to enhance flavor, they are saltier by nature. Also, because of the bold flavor of the ingredients in most of the recipes, the measurements tend to be more precise than "one head of cabbage," which leaves less wiggle room when it comes to salt. In sum, just go ahead and use the amount of salt called for in these recipes.

Water

Some of the recipes in this book call for water — specifically, unchlorinated water. Be sure that it is, in fact, unchlorinated, as chlorine can inhibit fermentation.

The advice for removing chlorine from water used to be to let the water sit out overnight, or to boil it, which would cause chlorine to dissipate. You could also use a simple charcoal filter on your tap or in a pitcher system.

Can I Use Iodized Salts?

In refined salt, the amount of added iodine can be up to 300 percent more than the amount that occurs naturally in unrefined salt. Because iodine is antimicrobial, it is possible that using salt with added iodine could inhibit fermentation and cause discoloration. For this reason, we avoid using iodized salt in our ferments. We have never had a problem with natural salts containing trace amounts of naturally occurring iodine.

However, increasingly, municipal water systems are using a combination of chlorine and ammonia, called chloramine, that does not evaporate and is not removed by simple charcoal filters. To remove chloramine from water requires a more comprehensive system that uses first a carbon filter to remove the chlorine in the chloramine molecule and then a reverse-osmosis filter to remove the remaining ammonia.

Time and Temperature

Unlike so many of the culinary arts in which timing is clear — bake at 350°F for 30 minutes, simmer for 2 hours, marinate for 1 hour, chill for 45 minutes — fermentation calls for a murky zone of whatever timing is right for your conditions. If your home is warm, the ferment will go faster than the recipes indicate; if you live in a tropical climate where it is mostly *too* warm, you have to come up with strategies to keep your ferment cooler (like adding more salt and sticking the ferment in a cooler with rotating ice packs). Conversely, if your home is in the frigid north, perhaps you can hardly keep the bacteria awake (boy, do you need hot sauce!).

Use the recipes as guides when estimating the amount of time a given ferment will take. They assume average home temperatures of about 65 to 72°F (18 to 22°C), which is conveniently ideal for getting your ferment started. Of course, there are other variables too: the amount of sugar in the vegetables, the amount of inherent lactic-acid bacteria (or the types), and even the size of your batch. While this may make fermentation sound daunting, it really isn't. For one, there is great latitude in terms of what makes a finished ferment — your taste buds decide. This is no soufflé.

Your other senses will help you out, too. The first thing you will do is watch the color of the ferment (assuming you are using a glass jar that lets you see the mixture). You will notice that the vegetables turn a dull color compared to the vibrant color they sported when first pressed in with the salt. Many online photos of ferments are taken when the ferment has not fermented yet; they are clear and bright. When the ferment is ready, the brine will become cloudy. There is a caveat, though: bright red fiery peppers don't lose a bit of their vibrancy.

So now what? Use your nose. Brand-new ferments smell vegetal — like the vegetable you just cut up and salted. Finished ferments smell acidic and pickle-y. The intensity of the smell can vary; for example, an herbal ferment will give off only a subtle acidic aroma.

Taste is usually our first-choice method of determining when a ferment is done, but for some people, this concept can be as mysterious as one of us recognizing middle C out of the blue, for example. The tuning fork of ferments is simple pH strips. They are widely available but come in many variations (and prices). Select strips made for cheese making or fermenting. The ones we use have a pH range of 3.0 to 7.0, with gradations of 0.2 or 0.3 between each reading.

Sometimes we use the strips because we're monitoring a recipe for doneness at 8 a.m. and have no desire to mix the taste of fiery ferment with creamy hot tea. On that same note, it can be difficult to differentiate the subtle sour or acidic notes when the concentration of spices is commanding all the attention. Visually discerning any changes can be hard with some recipes as well. Compact, condensed pastes often show little sign of fermentation, like bubbles, for example (see Introverts vs. Extroverts, facing page). A pH strip makes it easy to ascertain the acidity. A finished ferment will have a pH below 4.6. We have tested the pH on many ferments and most of them are well below 4.6 as soon as they taste acidic, coming in at 4.0 pH or lower.

Managing the Brine

As mentioned, in many of the recipes in this book, the salt makes the brine by drawing out the juices of the vegetables; this is often called "dry brining." In some other cases, you will need to make a saltwater brine for your ferment (you'll read about that on page 34).

The key to success is remembering that brine is your best friend. Please don't think that puddle of salty, unfermented juice left at the bottom of your bowl after you've massaged salt into the veggies is a waste product — that's good brine, and you should pour it proudly on top of your ferment. Remember, the brine is what keeps your ferment anaerobic. Besides, once it is fermented, it is delicious — you will want as much as you can make.

As the lactobacilli do their thing (consume the starches), they produce acid and CO_2. The CO_2 bubbles need to work their way out of the ferment. Sometimes they do this on their own. Other times, especially with some of the thicker ferments, these bubbles can form air pockets. While the air pockets may or may not have trapped oxygen, we have found that ferments are more successful if we manage the air

The Two Stages of Fermentation

During the first stage of fermentation, the dominant species *Leuconostoc mesenteroides* and friends like a temperature range of 65 to 72°F (18 to 22°C). The process will get started at slightly lower temperatures, but if they get too low the friendly bacteria have trouble waking up and getting a foothold. A little higher also works, but to develop the most flavor it is better to keep the ferment within this range. Also, allowing it to get too warm too soon can lead to softer ferments. (Don't worry if your pepper ferments are soft; peppers tend to be softer anyway.)

During the second stage, the acid-loving bacteria *Lactobacillus plantarum* and friends are said to prefer a climate warmer than 72°F (22°C) but not much higher than a steady 90°F (32°C). In these higher temperatures, *L. plantarum* (responsible for the extra-tart acidic flavor) proliferate very quickly. However, we have found that starting our longer-aged ferments at room temperature and then transferring them to our fermenting cave, which maintains a temperature of 58 to 60°F (14 to 16°C), slows down the process and gives us the most interesting flavors.

pockets. This is so important that we say it a lot in this book. If you are fermenting in a jar, you will be able to look into the ferment and watch for air pockets. When you see them, simply get a clean utensil and press on the ferment until the air pockets are gone and the brine pools on top of the ferment. With some of the thicker pastes, you may need to run a clean butter knife along the edge of the jar to release the pockets.

Beware, and don't be fooled by copious amounts of brine forming on top of the ferment. You think it means your ferment is submerged, right? Not necessarily. Often this is a sign that a lot of air pockets have pushed the brine out. Press down slowly, and you will see the brine settle back into the ferment, where it should be.

Burping Your Ferment

When you use a closed system (as suggested with mashes, pastes, and mustards), there is no air exchange with your ferment, in or out. Therefore, the CO_2 builds up and must be released, and this is where the "burp" comes in. Just like burping a baby, it will keep your ferment healthy (well, in the ferment's case, it will keep it from exploding . . .).

You may use a closed system with any type of ferment, not just pastes. This system works well with mason, bail-style, or Weck jars (which can release a bit on their own; see page 13). The only trick is that you will need to periodically check your ferment to see if it needs to be burped. If the lid is taut or slightly bulging, you know it's time.

The lid in a closed system is sealed, and you will be briefly breaking that seal to let out the CO_2. In a mason jar, this is just a quick twist: listen for the CO_2 escaping and then tighten the lid again. If your ferment is under a lot of pressure, it may be difficult to break the seal, or the brine may bubble out all over the place when you crack the lid. To avoid this, burp your active ferments often, even as much as once or twice a day.

For bail-style or Weck jars, simply pull on the tab of the rubber gasket. The CO_2 will escape and the gasket will pop back into place.

Introverts vs. Extroverts

Watching a ferment actively bubble is very satisfying, and many ferments offer plenty of effervescence to satiate that need to know something is happening. Beets and peppers, for example, usually don't disappoint. You can think of them as extroverted: they are working and they want you to know it.

The introverts, on the other hand, are quiet. Any ferment can behave quietly, but in general it's the herbal pastes that show you less action. Our little bacteria processors are hard at work, but we can't see or hear a thing. Just like it is okay when your ferment is bubbling out of the container, it is also okay if you don't see or hear a single bubble. Use your other senses to evaluate how your ferment is progressing and when it is ready to eat. Has the color of the brine or ferment changed? Does it smell pickle-y? Does it taste fermented? If you still are confused you can test the pH. If there are no signs of something gone awry, likely nothing is wrong. It's just quiet.

CH 2

MASTER THE TECHNIQUES

Never made lacto-fermented vegetables before? No worries! In this chapter you will become a master of the techniques used to create flavorful pepper mashes, pastes, and brine-based pickles and sauces. Every lacto-ferment uses the same process — veggies of some kind + a little salt + anaerobic conditions. However, a spicy pickle is a very different ferment from a fiery herbal paste, which is, again, different from a sauce.

Each recipe in this book will tell you which fermenting technique to use and detail the specifics that apply to that particular recipe. Think of this chapter's step-by-step visual guides as a reference to consult not only before you begin, but also when you are standing in the kitchen looking at your ferment and wondering, *what do I do now?*

You Can Have Your Mash and Eat It Too

Pepper mash is a fermented pulpy gruel of mashed hot chile peppers and salt, and it is the base of the hot sauces we know and love, from the vinegary Louisiana-style sauces (like Tabasco) to the unique flavors of Latin American and Caribbean sauces to the thick pungency of Asian-style sauces.

In a large-scale hot sauce plant, pepper mash is made by crushing whole red chiles with a hammer mill and adding a 5 to 8 percent salt ratio. This mixture is then put into barrels.

Traditional Louisiana-style sauce makers procure the charred white oak barrels previously used by Kentucky whiskey distillers. The barrels' wooden lids are fastened with stainless steel hoops and blanketed with a thick layer of salt. Tiny holes in the lids allow CO_2 to escape. The salt blanket hardens due to humidity and seals the barrel fully after the active fermentation process stops.

During the aging process the fermenting mash continues to develop complex aromas. At the same time, some of the liquid is lost through the porous wood, concentrating the flavors. It's the same thing that happens with fine wine or great cheese: time = delicious. Interestingly, science shows us that capsaicin compounds (responsible for the spiciness in chiles) decrease slightly in the early stages of fermentation, right after salting. After that they stay steady, which is to say, the length of fermentation does not affect the spiciness of your product.

Beyond flavor, a long fermentation period gives the product stability and thus a long shelf life; it also benefits the producer by breaking

The Salt Blanket: Sealing Your Mash for a Long Winter's Sleep

If you're feeling adventurous, you can seal a crock (of a gallon or more) for a long aging process by covering the mash with a blanket of salt. The salt will soak up some of the brine, which will help thicken and concentrate your final product, but, more importantly, after the fermentation is done and you remove the salt blanket, you can dry this briny salt with the sun or a dehydrator, yielding a delicious, spicy, pepper-infused salt. You should be seeing cute jars and holiday gifts right now — if you are willing to share.

STEP 1: Make enough mash for at least a gallon-sized crock. A crock is best suited for this, as the straight sides make it easier for you to add and remove the salt. To keep the mash under the brine, use a ceramic weight; you can also use a plate (close to the diameter of the crock) followed by a jar of water to weigh it down. Allow the mash to ferment for about 2 weeks.

STEP 2: Carefully remove any scum that may have formed on top of the mash. If you are using a plate followed by a jar for a weight on top, remove the jar and leave the plate; if you used a flat ceramic weight instead, leave it. Place a piece of muslin or cheesecloth across the top of the brine.

down the pulp in a way that keeps it from separating or layering in the bottles. When the mash is ready, the barrels are opened and the oxidized top layer of mash is removed. The rest is filtered and mixed with vinegar to produce the hot pepper sauce.

Though often aged for as long as 2 or 3 years, pepper mash can be fermented in just a couple of weeks or months. This means that you have flexibility. If you are very patient and relish the idea of a long-aged ferment, go for it — your taste buds will reward you. If you are more of an instant-gratification type, do a quick ferment. It will still be delicious, and you will enjoy it soon. After all, Maunsell White, creator of what would become McIlhenny's Tabasco sauce, started his sauce by fermenting the mash for only 30 days. Or you can do both — we are giving you permission to have your mash and eat it too. Make a large batch, use some or even most of it, and stash some away to age.

STEP 3: Pour a 2-inch layer of sea salt over the entire top of the ferment, letting the excess muslin or cheesecloth stick out around the edges.

STEP 4: Fold the excess cheesecloth over the top of the salt. Cover the crock and ferment for 6 months to 2 years.

STEP 5: When you are done aging the mash, lift the cloth with the brine-soaked salt and you'll find your mash underneath. The part that was in contact with the salt will be a bit saltier than the rest. Either mix it in or scoop a bit out and add it to your pepper-infused salt for more heat. Dry the salt by spreading it on a plate and leaving it in the open air, or use a dehydrator.

STEP 3

A Step-by-Step Visual Guide

Basic Pepper Mash

A pepper mash can be made with any type of pepper, from sweet to fiery hot, or a combination of peppers. The process is the same no matter which varieties you choose — with so many options, you have a lifetime of spicy experimentation ahead of you.

Weighting a pepper mash is possible (you could try it with a water-filled ziplock bag), but the mash is soft and lacks structure, so it is difficult to get a traditional weight to stay in place, especially in small, jar-sized ferments — the weights tend to sink. In the steps below, we suggest using a closed system for this ferment, such as a simple closed jar or an airlock system.

The trickiest part of fermenting a pepper mash is keeping it submerged and anaerobic. Unlike other ferments where the brine tends to float above the vegetables, the pulpy flesh and seeds of the mash tend to float to the top of the brine. If you have not fermented mash before, you will find that a little careful attention to setting up this ferment will go a long way.

1. Mash any type of fresh pepper. Use a mortar and pestle, food processor, or food grinder or simply dice with a knife.

2. Mix in the salt. A lot of brine will form immediately.

3. Press the mash into a jar, leaving at least 1 inch of headspace if you're using a pint jar, and more for a larger vessel. You may not see a lot of brine above the pepper pulp, but with a closed system that will be okay.

4. Screw the jar lid down tightly, or use an airlock.

5. Set the jar on a plate in a convenient place that is between 55 and 75°F (13 and 24°C). Monitor it daily, and if you are using a plain lid, burp the jar often (see page 25). Do this over the plate to catch any brine that bubbles out; discard that liquid. Look for floating pulp and air pockets (see Curing Notes, next page), and shake the jar as needed to encourage the pulp to settle under the brine.

6. After 1 to 2 weeks, or when your ferment calms down, move it somewhere out of the way for a longer fermentation, if desired.

7. After fermentation, store the mash in the refrigerator in an appropriately sized jar or bottle so that there is little or no headspace.

A Kahm-mon Problem

Ferments containing a lot of peppers often develop a white bloom of Kahm yeast on the surface (for a photo, see page 253). We have seen this happen even in carefully monitored airlock systems. But rest assured — it's harmless, and as long as there's enough brine, the peppers will be safe and tasty beneath it. Don't bother removing this layer during fermentation, as it will only bloom again across the top of the brine the very next day. If you keep removing it at the rate it appears, you will lose that all-important top layer of brine.

When your ferment is finished, you can ladle out the yeast, which takes finesse and patience, as you will chase the buoyant yeast particles across the surface. Use the sides of your vessel to help you catch them. Once you have scooped out as much as you can with your ladle or spoon, lay a clean paper towel on the surface to catch more of the yeast. Wipe the sides of the vessel with another clean paper towel before you empty the container. Most importantly, don't worry if you don't get all the yeast — it's likely you won't (and remember, it's harmless). We find that once the ferment is moved into a new jar or bottle, the yeast does not come back.

TO MAKE A SAUCE: After fermentation, spoon the mash into a stainless steel strainer over a bowl and press with the back of a wooden spoon until all that remains in the strainer are the tough skins and seeds. These can be discarded or set aside to dehydrate for seasoning (see the facing page). Scrape the underside of the strainer to get the last of the sauce.

CURING NOTES

Pepper mashes will need some monitoring, especially in the early stages, for the dreaded floating pulp. The ground pulp holds tiny air pockets that make it float on top of the brine (see page 252). As the ferment settles, it becomes easier to keep the pulp down and the brine on top. With a small, jar-sized batch where you can keep the lid tight, just shake up the jar when you see separation. Burp out the CO_2 as needed (page 25) by momentarily loosening the lid. If you're using an airlock, there is no need to burp. There is also less need to shake, but we like to anyway, to mix the brine and pulp together for flavor consistency; be gentle, shaking from side to side, so as not to plug the airlock with mash.

HOT TIP

Does the Hot Get Hotter?

Unlike some kinds of vinegar-style hot sauces that get hotter as they sit, fermented sauces tend to mellow out a little. This slight tempering seems to occur when the ferments are first chilled in the refrigerator. After this initial change, however, they retain their heat — for weeks, months, even years.

What about the Seeds?

For most sauces, it is all right to ferment the mash without removing the pepper seeds, which add a little more heat (and some chewiness). After fermentation, they will get strained out along with the tough skins for a smooth mouthfeel in your final product. You don't have to throw them out, though, even at this point. Instead, turn the fermented skins and seeds into a flavorful probiotic seasoning: Spread them on dehydrator trays and dehydrate at 105°F (40°C) for 8 to 12 hours, until dried. Pulse to a coarse powder in a blender and store in an airtight container.

On the other hand, if you are making a sweet pepper mash or using a very thin-skinned pepper that won't require straining (Fresno or habanero, for example), removing the seeds from the fresh peppers is worth the effort. You will get a nice, thick, ready-to-use mash. Finally, a few paste recipes call for including the seeds and never get strained, like the rempah base for sambal (page 159).

Remember to wear gloves when working with spicy peppers (see page 43.)

A Step-by-Step Visual Guide

Brine-Based Sauces and Pickles

There are as many opinions on how to achieve a perfect pepper sauce as there are pepper sauces. Some prefer the pepper mash method (page 30), which, while it has its challenges, is pure pepper power. Others prefer fermenting the peppers whole in a salt brine and then puréeing. We use both. Brining is the best method when you're using dried hot peppers, and sometimes dry is the only way you can get the chile varieties you desire for a specific sauce. We use this brining method not only for peppers that will become sauce but also for a handful of zesty recipes.

HOT TIP

Grape Leaves

Placing a grape leaf or two on the top of a brine-based ferment as a follower will not only help keep the ferment crisp but will "hold" any developing yeast above and away from the ferment. When you are ready to eat the ferment, the leaf can be easily removed and discarded, taking the yeast with it. See page 39 for alternatives to grape leaves.

WARNING *We recommend gloves for working with hot peppers. (See "Warning!" on page 43.)*

1. Prepare the brine, the vegetables, and any dried ingredients according to the recipe directions.

2. Pack the ingredients tightly into a crock or jar. If you're using whole fresh vegetables, wedge them under the shoulder of the jar so they will stay submerged in the brine.

3. Pour in enough brine to cover the vegetables completely. In a jar this may mean that the brine tops out quite close to the rim; in a crock you'll need to leave room for a follower. The follower can be anything that is close to the diameter of the vessel and will help keep the ingredients from floating, such as a plate or large cabbage or grape leaves. Store any extra brine in the refrigerator for up to 1 week. Discard after this point and make fresh brine if necessary.

4. If using a crock, place a weight, such as a sealed water-filled jar, on top of the follower. If using a jar, the tightly wedged vegetables usually stay in place. If they do not, place a follower and/or weight on top of the ingredients to hold everything down. Screw on the lid.

5. Set the jar or crock on a plate in a spot that is between 55 and 75°F (13 and 24°C). Let it ferment for the time indicated in the recipe, burping the jar as needed (see page 25). Note: As it ferments, the brine may bubble out. The plate will catch any spills; discard that liquid.

6. During the fermentation period, monitor the brine level and top off with reserved brine, if needed, to cover the vegetables. Veggies peeking up out of the brine will quickly get soft and spoil. If you see even a tiny bit exposed, poke it back under with a utensil, unless it has been out for a while and has softened or has yeast on it. In this case, pluck it out.

7. Following fermentation, store the pickled vegetables, in their brine, in the refrigerator. You can keep them in the same jar, providing there is not a lot of headspace. If your fermentation vessel is large, you may want to divide the pickles into smaller jars. After a day in the fridge, check to be sure the pickles are still completely submerged in their brine, topping off with the reserved brine, if necessary.

TO MAKE A SAUCE: Pour the entire ferment, including the brine, into a blender and blend to the desired consistency. Strain if needed. Store in the refrigerator.

CURING NOTES

Generally, air pockets do not develop in a brine ferment. Your monitoring will be more about making sure the vegetables stay under the brine. Remember to press any recently discovered floaters back under the brine, adjusting the weight as needed to keep the vegetables submerged. If you think that the incriminating veggie may have been sticking out above the brine for a while, it should be removed, as it could become a vector for mold or yeast, rendering the entire batch of pickles soft.

The most common issue with these ferments is a harmless Kahm yeast bloom (see page 31) on the surface of the brine, especially in ferments that have a many-months fermentation period. Remove all the yeast before refrigerating your ferment, topping it off with fresh brine if needed. For a sauce, be sure to remove all yeast or any other scum before blending.

Making the Perfect Brine

Making a great pickle starts with a good brine. Here are some tips:

- Brine begins with water. Make sure your water is unchlorinated (see page 22), as chlorine can inhibit fermentation.
- Use a high-quality salt. There's no need to use kosher pickling salt, which is highly processed and contains unnecessary (and less healthy and tasty) anticaking agents.
- The salt-to-water ratio varies depending on the type of pickle. For example, cucumber-based pickles require a higher ratio of salt to keep them crunchy. Most of the pickles in this book use a 3 percent brine made with ¼ cup salt to 2 quarts water.
- Always make a little more brine than you will need, as sometimes, especially during the most active first few days of fermentation, your brine may bubble over and you'll need to top it off. Store the extra, unfermented brine in the refrigerator; it will keep for about 1 week.
- Don't add vinegar to the brine until after fermentation, as indicated in the recipes. The salt solution is perfect for promoting lactic-acid fermentation, but acetic acid (vinegar) too early in the process can impede fermentation.

A Step-by-Step Visual Guide

Pastes and Mustards

The food traditions of many cultures worldwide are based on thick, robust sauces or pastes, and many of them are spicy. We have explored quite a few of these traditional flavors and have put our own spin on them with fermentation. The following technique is used a lot in this book for ferments that are much drier and thicker than your average juicy, briny ferment. Often pastes function as a seasoning base on which to build a meal, but they can also be used as condiments. These types of ferments have become a convenience food for our family and are very useful to have on hand in the refrigerator.

Often the pastes rely on dried spices with only a few wet ingredients. While the rules and techniques of lacto-fermentation remain the same, these ferments tend to feel just barely moist enough to create brine. We have found that we have much greater success with this type of ferment if, when tucking in the ferment, we *cartouche* it. Great word, right? (See page 39 for an explanation.)

1. Use a food processor or mortar and pestle to blend the ingredients, including the salt, to the consistency indicated in the recipe. Since you're breaking down the cell walls of the ingredients, the mixture will become moist right away.

(continued on next page)

HOT TIP

Opening the Stubborn Lid

These rich condiment pastes are, by nature, strong concentrated flavors. You might not use them daily, or even weekly. While this little jar waits quietly in your refrigerator, the ring that holds down the lid may begin to stick, rendering the jar seemingly impossible to open. We have done some unmentionable things to jars trying to open them. The gentle method that works every time is holding the jar upside down over the sink and running very hot water along the underside of the ring. Then dry it off and open. Voilà.

2. Pack the mixture into a jar that is just the right size for your ferment, pressing out any air pockets as you go. Leave about 1 inch of headspace. The small amount of brine will be thick, sometimes syrupy, and it may be hard to distinguish from the rest of the ferment. Don't worry if it "disappears" between pressings. As long as the ferment is moist and you are able pack it tightly, you have enough brine.

3. Place a piece of plastic (or other cartouche) against the surface of the ferment, smoothing with your finger so as not to trap any air beneath it. Screw the lid down tightly.

4. Set the jar in a corner of the kitchen, in a spot that is between 55 and 75°F (13 and 24°C). Let it ferment for the time indicated in the recipe.

5. During the fermentation period, watch for air pockets forming in the ferment. If you see any, open the lid and press the ferment down to push out the air. If the lid starts to bulge from the pressure of gas building up inside, simply crack it open for a moment to burp the ferment (see page 25).

6. Following fermentation, store the jar in the refrigerator. While it's in storage, the less headspace above a ferment, the longer it will last, so transfer the ferment to smaller jars as you use it. For dry paste ferments, place a new cartouche directly on top to help keep it moist.

NOTE: When you taste-test a paste, be aware that it will be somewhat saltier than some of the other vegetable ferments, because it's meant to be a concentrate, like bouillon. For mustards and condiments, the salt should be noticeable but not overwhelming.

CURING NOTES

Paste ferments don't usually show a lot of (if any) activity in the way a juicy batch of pepper mash might, but things are happening. This is because a lot of the paste ingredients, like the herbs, just don't have the high-carb content that excites the lactobacilli. When you are used to active ferments, this inactivity can make it seem like the fermentation isn't working. Don't worry, it is. Watch for other signs of doneness — a change in color, a slight acidic smell, a well-balanced flavor — and if you are unsure, use a pH strip (page 23).

Cartouche Your Ferment!

What? Isn't a cartouche the Egyptian oval that encloses the name of royalty? It is, but in cooking terms it is a round piece of parchment paper placed on the surface of food, often under a saucepan lid to reduce evaporation. In the case of fermented pastes, we use a cartouche to reduce evaporation as well as air exposure. It can take many forms:

- A cabbage leaf, grape leaf, horseradish leaf, or other vegetable leaf
- A circular piece of parchment paper cut to fit the surface of your ferment
- A piece of plastic cut from a ziplock bag (more inert than plastic wrap)
- A small circle cut out of a silicone mat (reusable)

While plastic is the most accessible material to use, we have read conflicting information about its safety. Whether or not to use it is, we think, a matter of personal preference.

A Step-by-Step Visual Guide

Kimchis, Relishes, and Salads

This "dry brine" method is the basis for some of the juicier ferments in this book that have more texture because their vegetables are cubed, grated, or sliced. Some of the kimchi-type ferments use this technique, though the traditional kimchi method requires a two-step process (see facing page).

This very simple, bare-bones fermentation strategy uses any jar (no matter the size or shape) and a ziplock freezer bag. However, you can use the general technique with any of the myriad fermentation setups out there.

> **WARNING** *We recommend gloves for working with hot peppers. (See "Warning!" on page 43.)*

1. Use a knife, mandoline, or food processor to prepare the ingredients as indicated in the recipe. Add the salt, massaging it in to develop a moist ferment. Some ferments will have a scant brine, while others will be downright juicy.

2. Pack the vegetables carefully into a jar, pressing out any air pockets as you go. Leave the top quarter of the jar free.

3. Press a ziplock bag against the surface of the ferment, fill the bag with water, and zip it closed. (See All-in-One Simplicity, page 42.)

4. Set the jar in a corner of the kitchen, in a spot that is between 55 and 75°F (13 and 24°C). Let it ferment for the time indicated in the recipe.

5. During the fermentation period, watch for air pockets forming in the ferment. If you see any, adjust the ziplock, pressing it gently on the ferment until the pockets disappear. Or remove the bag, press the ferment down with a clean utensil, rinse the bag, and replace.

6. Following fermentation, screw on the lid and store the jar in the refrigerator.

KIMCHI'S EXTRA STEP

For some people, kimchi is synonymous with fiery ferment. Though kimchi is often hot and spicy, that is not what defines it. Kimchi is simply the Korean word for pickled or fermented vegetables. There are hundreds of varieties of traditional kimchis and even more individual takes on the theme. Many of them are made with a two-step process.

We like to explain this process as a hybrid of brine pickling and dry brining. The napa cabbage, or whatever vegetable you're using, is left to soak in a brine solution for 6 to 8 hours. During this time (as with brine pickling), the vegetable soaks up brine; salt penetrates it by osmosis and dehydrates it. The soaked vegetable is now set up for fermentation from the inside out.

At this point, the soaked veggie is removed from the brine and mixed with plenty of pungent flavors — gochugaru, garlic, and ginger — as well as other vegetables that have not been soaking. These ingredients begin to

All-in-One Simplicity

Using a water-filled ziplock bag to seal and weight down a ferment works well for everything from very small to very large batches. We know folks who use this method (with a much bigger, tougher bag) for 55-gallon drums of kraut. This system works so well because the water in the bag seeks the lowest point and therefore covers the uneven top of the ferment while also providing that all-important weight. At the same time, the wrinkles in the bag act a bit like an airlock: brine travels up them, sealing the ferment while allowing a path for the CO_2 to bubble out as needed.

The important thing to remember is to leave room in the jar when you pack it. A good rule of thumb is to leave the top quarter empty for the bag. Open the bag and place it in the jar on top of the vegetable mixture, pressing it onto the surface and around the edges. Fill the bag with water; you will see it seal the ferment with its weight. When the water is at the level of the top of your jar, zip the bag closed.

(Note: The heavier freezer-style ziplock bag is preferred; it's sturdier. Plastic concerns? Yep, we hear you. We stay away from plastic as much as we can, for ecological as well as food-safety reasons. However, the rigid-type plastic that these bags are made of does not contain BPA.)

break down and release their own juices, rather like dry brining. The mixture is then packed into a jar, submerged in its own brine (no soaking brine is added), and left to ferment for the appointed time.

The extra time and planning that go into making traditional kimchi are worth it for the flavor. We use this two-step method for greens- and cabbage-based kimchis but have also included a few kimchi recipes that are made like a simple relish, with no extra step.

CURING NOTES

Be sure to watch for air pockets. The thicker ferments may or may not show a lot of "heave" as the CO_2 tries to escape. The thicker the ferment, the harder it can be for the CO_2 to wiggle its way up and out. Sometimes, when air pockets have been developing in the ferment for a few days, a bitter flavor develops. If this happens, press out the air pockets and allow the mixture to ferment for another week or more, keeping an eye out for more air pockets. Often the flavor will right itself.

Conversely, these ferments, especially if they have a lot of fresh peppers in them, can be exceedingly dynamic, heaving and surging and hard to control the first few days. Even with an airlock system this can happen (the swelling ferment can fill your airlock and keep spreading right on out if it is that active). This is nothing to worry about; it is normal. You can plan for energetic fermentation by leaving extra headspace at the top of your vessel to accommodate the movement. If it is too late and you are staring at a mess all over your counter, don't worry — everything inside the vessel is just fine. Open the vessel, press everything down, replace any weights, wipe off the inside walls with a clean cloth or paper towel, and put everything back to ferment. These initial over-the-top "explosions" may happen once or twice, but usually the ferment will then calm down enough to stay contained.

Warning! Take Care When Working with Fresh Chile Peppers

Working with fresh hot chiles can be a full-body experience if you are not careful. Since capsaicin is an oil, it is not easy to wash it off your hands, and that burning sensation can spread to any skin you touch. Before you cut any of the hot peppers, put on a pair of thin protective gloves, or rub a small amount of cooking oil on your hands; either acts as a barrier. When you are processing large quantities of peppers or even a few superhot chiles, we recommend gloves. And it is important to note that we have had the capsaicin penetrate the gloves (with no perceptible damage to the glove), leaving a trace amount on our fingers. It's not a big deal; just keep in mind that you are working with a powerful oil.

A great strategy when working with the small chiles is to hold the stem and use kitchen scissors to cut the chile into small slices. The seeds will end up in your ferment, but there are very few, and this way you never touch the capsaicin. When you've finished handling the peppers, wash your hands in hot water with dish-washing liquid or an oil-cutting soap. If you still feel a burning sensation, rinse your fingers in lemon juice or rubbing alcohol, then rub in a little aloe vera or milk. The casein protein in milk, and in products made from it, such as buttermilk and yogurt, neutralizes the capsaicin (see Extinguishing the Fire, page 90).

The lungs are even more vulnerable than skin; airborne capsaicin irritates the mucous membranes, and inhaling it can cause breathing problems. You'll feel it as a tightening in the lungs, or you'll start to cough. Use caution if you suffer from any breathing problems, particularly asthma. Be sure to seed, chop, or grind raw peppers in a well-ventilated area, and remember to be aware of lingering capsaicin during cleanup. We have on occasion managed to sail through the preparation process without feeling the effects of this devilish compound, only to be struck with a coughing fit when the dishwater hit the utensils.

CH 3

THE HOT STUFF: YOUR INGREDIENTS

This chapter will introduce you to the ingredients that make your fiery ferments, well, fiery. We've divided it into two sections: first, an exploration of the spicy ingredients used in many parts of the world before chiles came along; second, a full investigation of the now ubiquitous, go-to ingredient for burning heat — chiles. In chapter 4 we'll offer a handful of unique pre-chile recipes before we dive into all things chile!

HOT AND SPICY B.C. (BEFORE CHILES)

Humans have been seeking flavor and spice for a long, long time — for many thousands of years before trade brought aromatic and tasty gifts from far and wide. Before chiles found their way out of South America as the collective burn of choice, humans across the globe relied on a number of different spices. In this section, we want to introduce you to some of these lost and found flavors.

I think ginger has a heat, a warmth that is often not fully understood because I think people use a small amount. And if you use quite a lot, you really see that it's like reaching for another form of pepper.

NIGELLA LAWSON, FOOD WRITER AND HOST OF *NIGELLA KITCHEN*

Ginger

Cultivated in tropical Asia for over 3,000 years, ginger (*Zingiber officinale*) is perhaps one of the oldest fundamental spices. Its origin is ambiguous, but it was used extensively in the cuisines and medicine of ancient China and India. Because ginger is a rhizome and easily transported fresh or dried, it was a good candidate for early trade, which might explain why it was one of the first Eastern spices to reach the Mediterranean. From Rome, it traveled to northern Europe.

Ginger's warm, woodsy flavor is pleasingly hot with rich, sweet notes — what's not to like? The world seemed to be in agreement. Arab traders introduced ginger to East Africa, and the Portuguese brought it to the other side of the vast continent. Meanwhile, Spanish explorers took it with them to the West Indies. Eventually ginger found its way into savory dishes and sweet confections everywhere.

Ginger is available year-round, but like all produce, its freshness waxes and wanes due to harvest times, shipping, and storage. The other factor affecting flavor is how long the rhizome was allowed to grow. Ginger is most pungent and fibrous when harvested after 8 to 10 months of growth. At this stage the skin is thick and papery and the roots do not appear plump. (This may also be the case if it has been stored a long time.) This older ginger is better for recipes in which the ginger is grated, like any of the kimchi recipes. The flavor is wonderful, but the fibers can get in the way of a pleasing sliced-ginger pickle.

During the ginger harvest season (generally fall and winter), you can find younger fresh ginger that is plump with thin, moist, almost translucent skin. This ginger slices well; it's the best choice for making the fermented ginger pickles on page 78. (Then again, if the ginger feels older and fibrous you can make the same recipe as a grated paste.)

Galangal

There are two varieties of galangal root. The lesser (*Alpinia officinarum*), native to China, is more pungent and is preferred for medicine. The greater (*Alpinia galanga*), native to Java, is sometimes called sand ginger or cekur. We will concentrate on greater galangal, since you are more likely to find it in the West. A common ingredient in the cuisines of Indonesia, Thailand, Malaysia, Vietnam, Laos, and Cambodia, galangal is used in soups, sauces, stir-fries, and — most relevant for our purposes — pastes and sambals.

Though a relative of ginger, galangal is not a substitute for it, or vice versa. Its flavor has more pepper notes and is a little fruitier than that of ginger; some find it hotter.

GALANGAL

In appearance, it is much thicker than ginger and lighter in color, with pink hues on the shoots. It is also much denser and more fibrous and must be ground or grated to be used in ferments. You can find it both powdered and fresh in many Asian markets, and you also often see it in co-ops and natural foods markets. Make sure the pink shoots are fresh-looking and unbruised.

Warm Medicine

Ancient healing traditions, folk remedies, herbal medicine, and traditional Chinese medicine use ginger liberally for conditions that require warming the body. It is believed to improve circulation, aid digestion (from stimulating saliva and bile production to moving food through the gastrointestinal tract), reduce nausea, ease the symptoms of colds, increase energy, and reduce inflammation.

Turmeric

Turmeric (*Curcuma longa*) does not pack a heat punch but is considered a pungent spice. A peppery, bitter quality complements its otherwise dusty flavor and woodsy fragrance. Fresh turmeric is sweeter and more delicate than its dry, powdered counterpart. (And we must add that this fresh root is amazing when fermented.) From the outside, this rhizome looks a bit like a skinny, finger-sized, dull orange version of its cousin ginger. Inside the skin, its brilliant golden-orange hue has made it a popular food coloring and dye for a millennium. In fact, Marco Polo compared turmeric, which he met in China in the thirteenth century, to saffron — and sure enough, it became a "cheap" substitute for saffron in Western cuisine.

However, turmeric's history runs much deeper. The plant is native to southern India, where it has a 4,000-year-old medicinal and culinary history. Since it does not propagate by seed, its spread across China, Asia, and Africa was brought about by people who carried and traded it from one place to the next. Turmeric shows up in Egyptian writings dating as far back as around 1500 BCE.

Most people know turmeric in its dried, powdered form, but it is increasingly common to find fresh turmeric rhizomes in the produce section of the market. In recent years it has become widely available, in part due to the stellar antioxidant, anti-inflammatory, and other health benefits of its active ingredient, curcumin. Look for roots that are firm, with good color and no pockmarks in the skin.

And, we repeat, fresh turmeric is an awesome ferment ingredient. We encourage you to try this root in any ferment. It adds beautiful color and is tremendously healthy (remember, fermentation boosts the good stuff by increasing the bioavailability of the nutrients in all our foods). For the full anti-inflammatory benefits, combine it with black pepper (see Turmeric + Black Pepper, page 145).

Horseradish

Horseradish (*Armoracia rusticana*) is thought to be native to central Europe and western Asia. It is in the brassica family, a large, distinguished group of veggies, and shares with its cousin mustard a particular nose-twitching vaporous burn, thanks to their constituent allyl isothiocyanate. This compound, like the capsaicin in the chile, is what makes horseradish and mustard hot. The difference is that allyl isothiocyanate is light and volatile, so when you take a bite it heads up and out your sinuses and nose. Capsaicin is heavier, sinking into your tongue and making its way down through your system.

Fresh horseradish roots can be found in the produce section of some grocery stores and at farmers' markets, though you have to watch for them — they are not a regular item. Their outside is a khaki-earthy color; they can also be a bit gnarled. Look for roots that are firm and free of blemishes. When you peel or slice a root, it should be creamy white. The whiter the root, the fresher it is.

Is Your Wasabi Horseradish?

Probably. Most people have never tasted real wasabi — even in Japan, where botanical texts tell us it has been on the menu since 794 CE. True wasabi (*Wasabia japonica*), which has a thick, root-like stem, has fairly particular growing requirements and takes around 3 years to mature. Horseradish, on the other hand, can be almost weed-like in the garden and is therefore more available commercially and a lot cheaper. The nose-tingling green wasabi paste is usually made from a combination of horseradish, mustard, starches, and green coloring.

As far as flavor goes, real wasabi is said to offer a much more delicate heat, but it is also quite volatile: the flavor dissipates and is lost only 15 minutes after the root is grated. This does not make it a good candidate for fermenting (assuming you got a hold of it in the first place). Nor does commercial "wasabi" powder — I've dumped a lot of it into various ferments, only to lose the flavor. Use fresh horseradish as a substitute; everyone else does.

Long-Lost Cousin Zedoary

In our readings about the spice trade, zedoary was mentioned often. Zedoary (*Curcuma zedoaria*), also called white turmeric, is highly aromatic and has a flavor reminiscent of rosemary. It was brought to Europe in the sixth century and topped the food trend charts in the Middle Ages before slipping back into obscurity. While it not generally available here in the West, it is still used in Asia for condiments that might also use ginger or turmeric.

Mustard

Mustard is thought to have been one of the first — if not *the* first — piquant spice. History tells us that some of our earliest ancestors chewed mustard seeds with their meat. The fermentation of mustard seeds (especially the white variety) also goes way back. Early on, when the concept of "antimicrobial" was thousands of years away, someone noticed that these seeds have outstanding preservative qualities and added them to some of the first pickled foods. Mustard in Latin was called *mustum ardens*, meaning, roughly, "burning wine." This is because ground mustard seeds were mixed with must — the freshly pressed juice, skin, and seeds of wine grapes — to make a condiment.

Nutrient-dense mustard seeds are high in antioxidants and selenium and boast a quality protein. They are also known to have anti-inflammatory properties. On the Indian subcontinent they are pressed into a high-quality oil, an important ingredient in the traditional ferments of that region (see the achar recipes in chapter 6). On our plates, that tasty squirt of mustard is known to stimulate the appetite and, in moderation, is a digestive aid because it increases the action of our salivary glands eightfold — it's truly a mouthwatering condiment.

You will see four names for mustard seeds: yellow, white, black, and brown. Each of these types releases a slightly different mix of compounds that affect the flavor. "Yellow" and "white" are two names for the same seed (*Brassica alba*), and they are actually light brown or tan in color. These light-colored seeds are the most common type of mustard seed and release a milder, nonvolatile compound. "Black" mustard seed (*B. nigra*) is a bit spicier and less common (since it's hand-harvested) than "brown" mustard seed (*B. juncea*), but these names are often used interchangeably despite the difference. Many recipes for prepared mustard mix white and brown seeds to provide complex flavors and control heat levels.

When you get the hang of making mustard, keep inventing — it's easy, and you may realize that you never want to buy prepared mustard again.

Mustard Medicine

Mustard seed wasn't always reserved for use as a condiment on our plates. In ancient cultures, its role was often medicinal rather than culinary, with some superstition mixed in:

- In Greece in the sixth century BCE, Pythagoras used mustard as a cure for scorpion stings. (No idea if it worked.) A century later, Hippocrates used it to make poultices.
- Egyptians used mustard to treat gastrointestinal disorders. They also used it to combat food-borne bacteria and pathogens.
- In India, where mustard cultivation is believed to have begun in 3,000 BCE, it has been used for gastrointestinal disorders, as well as ulcers, respiratory disorders, and diabetes. It also was believed that spreading mustard seeds around one's home would keep away malicious spirits. (Good to know.)
- The Romans reputedly brought mustard to Britain, where it was used to treat chilblains (a skin condition). Meanwhile, German brides would sew the seeds into their wedding dresses for domestic success; the seeds were thought to guarantee that the bride would be the authority in her household. The Danes felt that mustard seeds mixed with mint and ginger would stimulate a healthy desire and passion.
- Many a congested patient in all corners of the world through the centuries has had a poultice made of mustard, called a mustard plaster or mustard pack, applied to his or her chest to stimulate healing.

Peppercorns: Black, Green, and White

There was a time when a satchel full of peppercorns meant you had some spending money — rent, taxes, a night out. This stuff was worth its weight in gold and was even used as currency in the Middle Ages. Black peppercorns are the sun-dried, fermented, unripe green berries from the vine *Piper nigrum*. Green peppercorns are the same green berries, but they are not fermented before they are dried. They have a wonderful, light, milder taste, and in Asia they are often used fresh and pickled instead of dried. White peppercorns are the ripe berries soaked in water to remove the outer skin, then dried.

The pretty red or pink peppercorns (*Schinus molle* or *Schinus terebinthifolius*) are not in the pepper family and are considered slightly toxic — but don't worry, you'd have to eat a lot of them to do any harm.

The Other Peppers

Ships did not sail around the globe only for black pepper. There were a lot of options to bring that peppery tingle to your plate. Each of the following "peppers" was once in high demand in the West but was lost through the ages of trade due to clever marketing, competing prices, or even laws forbidding their use (see cubeb). However, these spices never went away in their native lands, and thanks to global trade and creative chefs, many are being retrieved from obscurity.

GRAINS OF PARADISE

For many centuries spices were the most expensive household items in both the East and West. In the West they were kept in locked cupboards and used as medicine, perfumes, and preservatives, as well as flavorings. Grains of paradise (*Aframomum melegueta*), however, one of the cheaper substitutes for black pepper in the Middle Ages, may not have been locked up. After all, it came from West Africa — a lot closer to Europe than India.

This medieval spice, along with cubeb and zedoary, is nearly lost to us, though chefs are slowly rediscovering it. The flavor is a great combination of black pepper and cardamom, but more woodsy and lighter than both. The heat is slow and lingers nicely. In keeping with the region from which it hails, we use this spice in our fermented harissa (page 155). You will also find it in a pickle mix based on Bartolomeo Scappi's spice blend (page 185).

CUBEB

Cubeb (*Piper cubeba*), native to Java, is a member of the same family as black pepper and is still used in Indonesian and Moroccan cuisine. Imported by Arabic traders, it was once a common spice in the West in both sweet and savory dishes. Its decline began in the seventeenth century when the king of Portugal forbade the sale of cubeb to promote the sale of black pepper. Otherwise we might all have cubeb mills on our table with the salt shaker. This spice has medicinal qualities, and its warm flavors are more in line with those of allspice than black pepper. Today's global market now makes it available with the click of a mouse.

LONG PEPPER
GRAINS OF PARADISE
SZECHUAN PEPPER
BROWN MUSTARD
YELLOW MUSTARD
BLACK MUSTARD
BLACK PEPPERCORN
GREEN PEPPERCORN
WHITE PEPPERCORN

▲ Berries and red-green leaves of *Zanthoxylum simulans*, one species of Szechuan pepper

▲ Flowering spikes of *Piper longum* are dried to make long pepper.

SZECHUAN PEPPER

Also called Sichuan pepper, Chinese prickly ash, fagara, and Nepal pepper, Szechuan pepper (*Zanthoxylum simulans, Z. bungeanum*) is one of China's oldest known spices and is also used extensively in the cuisines of Nepal and Tibet. This spice is the dried berries (sans seed) of the Chinese prickly ash, a small shrub-like tree. It is sharp, tingly, numbing, somewhat bitter, and lightly citrusy, but not hot in the way that black pepper or chiles are. This buzzy tingle changes the way you taste, so in pickles and dishes, when Szechuan pepper is combined with the heat of chiles it can set up your mouth for quite an experience.

We have a number of recipes inspired by traditional Nepalese *achars* (pickles) that use Szechuan pepper and chiles. Be sure to pull out any of the tiny black seeds that are still floating around with the husks, as they are bitter.

LONG PEPPER

Long pepper (*Piper longum*) had its day in the sun. At one point in time, it was one of the ancient world's most popular spices. As with many aromatic spices, it was used in the apothecary as well as the kitchen. The Romans preferred it to black pepper and paid up to three times more for this spice. In medieval Europe, long pepper was used interchangeably with black pepper, a botanical cousin.

Long pepper comes from the dried, brownish-black flower spikes of a perennial flowering vine, harvested before the tiny berries (the size of poppy seeds) are fully ripened. These minute fruits are embedded on a strand resembling a dried immature hazel or alder catkin. In fact, some speculate that this long, skinny pepper could be the very pepper that Columbus was thinking of when he mistakenly called the chiles he encountered in the New World "peppers."

When you open a jar of long pepper, you will not smell that familiar pepper scent. This pepper does not have much scent at all, nor that distinctive black pepper flavor, though it is indeed pungent and actually a little more intense. Its heat lingers on the tongue with a warm tingle, combined with a wonderful sweetness (while it doesn't taste like ginger, it is somehow reminiscent of gingerbread). When you bite into the pepper spike, you feel a slightly sticky, almost resinous consistency, in contrast to the flaky dryness of crushed peppercorns.

Long pepper is used in many traditional Indian achars and has been an important player in the human quest to wake up our tongue's pain receptors for that little endorphin rush. It is still used in Southeast Asia and is common in Ethiopian and Moroccan spice mixes. If you like discovering new flavors, we encourage you to play with this spice. It is available on the Internet and often stocked by Indian grocery stores, where it is labeled *pippal*.

Getting the Most from Your Spices

A spice is usually defined as a pungent or aromatic substance that comes from a plant — but not the leaf (those are herbs). When we use the word *spice* we are talking about roots, berries, seeds, or barks. These different parts of a plant vary in the ways they hold on to or release the volatile oils that we taste and smell. Two tips about spices:

BUY WHOLE SPICES IN SMALL QUANTITIES. Whole spices last about twice as long as ground spices, and when they are freshly ground you are releasing the flavors and aromas at that moment and not subjecting them to the gradual deterioration that comes with life in a jar. As soon as the spice is ground, the volatile oils are released, and with them go the bold aromas as well as the subtle ones. The flavor and aroma compounds that remain are the more stable ones, which can give the spice a flatter flavor.

TOAST THEM. Now that you have whole spices, you'll want to release the full potential of their flavors. For many spices, this is done with a little heat. Most of the spices we use in this book can be toasted in a dry pan over medium-low heat; shake or stir them with a wooden spoon to heat them slowly and thoroughly without scorching.

Of course there are always exceptions. Case in point: Don't toast your peppercorns. Piperine is the pungent, spicy compound that makes black pepper peppery. When toasted, however, it mellows out and the pepper loses its bite. (Surprisingly, this is not true for its cousin long pepper, which we do recommend toasting.)

THE CHILE: QUEEN OF HEAT

Nearly all hot sauce cookbooks exclusively feature the chile — after all, she conquered the world with her fiery spice and everyone wants to invite her to the dance. We prefer to mix it up a little bit, with lots of other spices contributing fire to our ferments, but certainly chiles play a vital role. Let's take a look at the virtues of the most common chile varieties and the subtle flavor profiles of a few uncommon varieties.

Where Does the Fire Come From?

What makes peppers hot and spicy is capsaicin. All peppers have it to varying degrees except the bell pepper, a variety that, while a member of the *Capsicum annuum* species, carries a recessive gene that eliminates capsaicin. Capsaicin is an alkaloid that does not contain any of the flavor (or color) of a pepper but holds all of the heat. This compound is potent! So much so that it withstands extended periods of freezing, drying, and heating without losing its punch. We have noticed that the curing time of fermentation can take it down a notch, but once fermented, this substance stays stable.

Our mouths have the ability to feel even the smallest amount of capsaicin, which we experience as painful burning and short-term inflammation. One person's pain is indeed another person's pleasure; for fiery food enthusiasts, this pain is exactly what they seek.

The common belief is that the seeds are where the heat of a chile lurks and that removing the seeds will keep the heat tolerable. This is true in part — removing the seeds helps, but their guilt lies in that they are tucked into the pith, the innocuous-looking spongy white part that makes up the core and ribs inside the pepper. Capsaicin is produced in the cells of the pith, not the flesh or the seeds.

If you have very hot peppers and want to do some damage control, carefully take out all the pith (also called the placenta) with gloved hands. Set it aside, and remember to taste your creation before you tuck it in for fermentation. If you want a little more heat, put some of the pith back in. Keep in mind when tasting your ferment that the heat often mellows a little as the fermentation proceeds.

Mind-Altering Pain: Capsaicin and Your Brain

As soon as a hot pepper's capsaicin hits your tongue, the pain receptors in your mouth, nose, and throat send SOS messages to your brain — PAIN, PAIN, PAIN . . . HELP. Your brain responds by releasing endorphins, our own natural (and addictive) painkillers, which give us a rush of relief — relief that comes with feelings of euphoria akin to what you get from a "runner's high," sex, coffee, or marijuana. Chiles do, after all, come from the psychotropic plant family. Maybe John Mellencamp was actually singing about chiles when he crooned, "It hurts so good."

HOT TIP

Tasting the Flavor of Extremely Hot Chiles — Safely

KIRSTEN WRITES: I enjoy spicy food, I enjoy some heat, but I am not a bona fide hothead. There, I said it. I love the flavors of chiles, and I do want to know what the super-hots actually taste like (after all, we are told the hottest pepper on record, the Carolina Reaper, is extremely sweet). However, I don't want to be taken out by the burn for 20 minutes. Fortunately, my preference can be accommodated — very carefully. The white pith usually isn't present at the very bottom tip of the pepper, and I have found that if you bite the tiniest piece of that tip, you can taste the pepper without getting bit yourself. Or you can use Christopher's method . . .

When we were writing this book we grew dozens of pepper varieties. Christopher helped care for them, admired them, and asked me regularly, "Now what pepper is this?" So when a bush of the tiny, mighty chiles pequin had finally, finally ripened (to be fair, we asked it to grow in Oregon), he did not remember this chile's character. I picked a pepper and held it up as he passed by. Before I could say *that-is-super-hot* he took it and popped the whole thing in his mouth. He said, "Cantaloupe," and then went quiet . . .

CHRISTOPHER WRITES: I remember that little pepper was so bright it looked like an exotic sweet fruit, and I just ate it. I swear I tasted cantaloupe before my peripheral vision turned dark. There was a fire in my mouth, I was sure of it. All I could think of was getting up the hill to the farmhouse, to the refrigerator, and to the milk. Just three things, in that order, nothing else. I don't think I have ever been so clear and focused in my life.

HOT ANATOMY

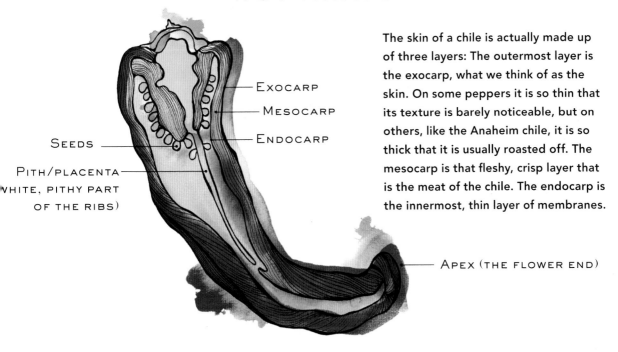

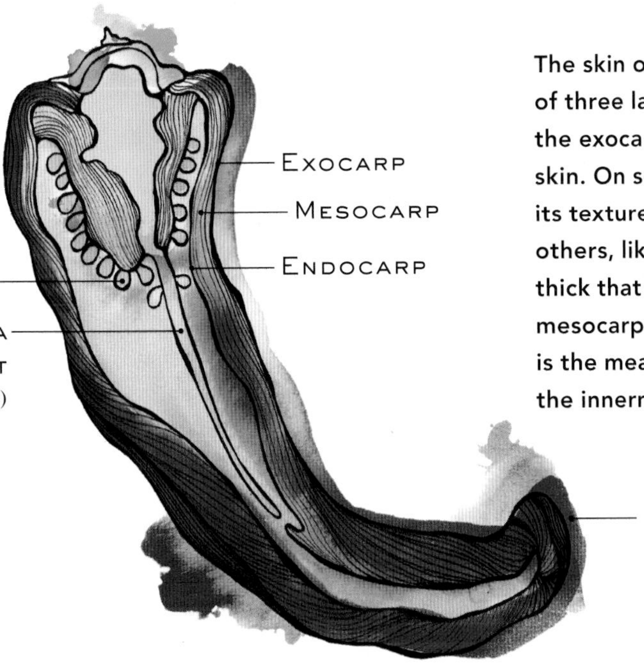

The skin of a chile is actually made up of three layers: The outermost layer is the exocarp, what we think of as the skin. On some peppers it is so thin that its texture is barely noticeable, but on others, like the Anaheim chile, it is so thick that it is usually roasted off. The mesocarp is that fleshy, crisp layer that is the meat of the chile. The endocarp is the innermost, thin layer of membranes.

How Hot Is Your Pepper?

The pungency of individual chiles, even of the same variety, can vary quite dramatically from one to another. We have grown jalapeños that are as mild as Anaheim green chiles, and we have also grown jalapeños hot enough to put habaneros to shame — for example, that year we had unprecedented heat and forest fires that kept our world smoky for over a month. We mention this because one thing that affects pungency is plant stress. Chiles grown under the pressure of arid hot climates produce more capsaicin. Contrary to urban myth, size doesn't indicate heat — smaller chiles are not necessarily hotter.

While there will be some variation, your best bet in managing the heat factor is to consider the general pungency traits of the diverse varieties of chiles and choose ones that will generally match your tolerance level. To help you out, a pharmacologist named Wilbur Scoville developed a measuring standard called the Scoville heat unit (SHU) in 1912. This standard is still used today to indicate a chile's heat, though now a machine analyzes the amount of capsaicin in the chile rather than subjecting it to a brave panel of tasters.

At this point you would expect a chart, produced and confirmed by leading testing laboratories around the world, that pinpoints the exact Scoville heat unit ranking for each pepper. We don't think such a chart is possible, and here's why. There is no single version of any pepper, as any gardener knows. Plants at one end of a row that received regular watering will likely produce a milder heat than the plants at the far end, where the drippers stopped or the overhead sprinklers didn't quite reach. Heat also varies among cultivars. So in the chile descriptions on the following pages, you'll find a range of SHUs, pulled from the best resources we could find. And the hottest chile? It will certainly have changed by the time you are reading this — the much coveted and contested "hottest pepper in the world" title has changed hands many times just in the last ten years (see page 73).

Meet the Chiles

The list of chiles in this chapter does not represent even a fraction of the thousands of varieties of peppers that spice up our planet. Chiles come in every shape, color, and size. The flavors range from vegetal to fruity, herbaceous to citrusy, nutty to smoky — often changing as the fruit matures. Some have soft skins, while others have thick skins that get tough with fermentation. Some have juicy, meaty flesh and make a bunch of brine, and others seem like dried peppers even when they are fresh from the vine. Our list is meant to give you a sense of some of the varieties and how they ferment so you can then apply your knowledge to any peppers that may cross your path.

In general, it's best to choose the freshest ingredients. For sweet or hot chiles, this means they should be firm and have taut, glossy skin, with no wrinkles. However, there is a caveat: we have found that partially dehydrated peppers (wrinkled and leathery) can make a wonderful addition to a ferment. They should be not degrading — no soft spots, dark spots, or mold — but simply drying out. As the pepper flesh dehydrates, the flavors become more concentrated. Sometimes there is still enough moisture with which to create a brine. Thick-walled chiles like Fresnos and jalapeños might create a salsa more watery than you would like; using partially dried ones will make a thicker condiment.

Then there is the heat — capsaicin expresses itself differently in different pepper varieties, but it is not as simple as mild, medium, hot, or insanely hot. Some peppers grab ahold of your tongue immediately and render it a burning, flapping appendage. Others seize your lips. Then there are the peppers that start slow, giving you just enough

When you start really getting into chiles, you break them down into groups. There are the everyday chiles. The strange chiles, shoved to the back of the pantry, you bought that one time to make a foreign dish that you enjoyed but have yet to revisit. The chiles to strike fear in the hearts of your enemies. And then there are the chiles so fascinating, so strangely complex, that you can't stop buying them.

Max Falkowitz, seriouseats.com

Same Chile, Same Plant, Different Heat

KIRSTEN REMEMBERS: When the kids were young, our neighbor Tina and I tried to consolidate our efforts and grew our vegetables together. There were many summers that we cultivated long rows of green chile peppers. In the fall we would harvest the peppers, then roast, peel, and freeze them. I don't know how chiles that head for a can are rated hot, medium, or mild, but it must be a better system than we had. The Shockey family didn't mind hot chiles; Tina's family wanted mild chiles. Before each chile — and there were hundreds — went into a freezer bag, it was taste-tested. Our middle son or I would pinch a small bit off the stem end (the hottest part) and try it. Hot to the Shockey pile, mild to Tina's pile. It was striking how much the heat varied from pepper to pepper — and from the same plant!

time to think, "Oh, this isn't so bad," and all the while the heat is sneaking to the back of your throat and you realize that you are in for a long, slow burn.

This vast (and at times bewildering) collection of peppers has developed across all regions of the world from five domesticated species (and 26 wild species). So many regions and so many peppers have made the classification and nomenclature of varieties a bit slippery. Even the spelling confounds — chile, chili, chilli (all from the Aztec Nahuatl word *xilli*). You can get lost going down that path, as entire books have been written on the subject, but for our purposes, the quick guide that follows focuses on varieties that are featured in this book and, more importantly, how they perform in a ferment.

We have tried to use readily available varieties but have also dabbled with some lesser known ones that are pretty incredible — grow some if you are a gardener, or seek them out at a farmers' market or specialty market. And every recipe will work with the usual suspects, so feel free to substitute with what is available or what is simply your favorite.

Of the Species *Capsicum annuum*

Most of the peppers you know are part of this clan, from bell peppers to the tiny, fiery chiles pequin. They are some of the easiest to grow, and while the species name *annuum* suggests that they are annual plants, in places with mild winters they are perennial and can live and bear fruit for many years.

ALEPPO

This is the principal hot spice of the Mediterranean region. You can find it at the market dried, powdered, and sometimes fresh. A fermented fresh Aleppo pepper has a very distinct fruity, almost citrusy flavor, with some earthiness. Interestingly, we made two pastes the same day with the same batch of Aleppos, and the one that had been fermented with garlic and lemon juice held much more heat. Ancho powder is a good substitute for Aleppo powder, and Fresno peppers are a good substitute for fresh Aleppos. If you are a gardener and you want to try this pepper (or have trouble finding it for sale), the seeds are readily available and it is easy to grow. **10,000–23,000 SHU**

ANAHEIM (GREEN CHILE)

If you live in the American Southwest, you might know the Anaheim as the Hatch chile, coined by the New Mexico town of the same name to draw hotheads to their festival. You might also know it as the New Mexico chile, or just plain green chile. Regardless, this chile owes its existence to Fabien Garcia, a 1904 graduate of the New Mexico College of Agriculture, who realized that for the larger Anglo market to embrace chiles, they would need to be consistent in flavor, heat, and structure. Eventually the New Mexico No. 9 was born. Consistently mild in flavor and long in form, with thick and fleshy walls, it is perfect for stuffing or roasting and peeling. **500–2,500 SHU**

BELL PEPPER

This branch of the family has many varieties in all the colors of the rainbow, but the common varieties are green, red, yellow, and orange. They are the only chiles that do not produce capsaicin and therefore are never hot. We have found that you can use them as a base for a mash when you do not have enough hot pepper to ferment. We also use this strategy when fermenting powdered pepper varieties (see page 93). **0 SHU**

BULGARIAN CARROT

The Bulgarian Carrot pepper is aptly named. It is brilliant orange and looks a lot like a baby carrot. This gives it a deceivingly innocent look. For some reason, its heat level is inconsistent on Scoville charts. In our experience, this pepper is fire. Every time we've grown it, we've found the heat to be up there next to that of habaneros. Besides being beautiful, it is a fruity pepper that ferments well, making a striking golden hot sauce. The skin is quite tough and should be strained out when you're making a sauce. If you are a hot-pickle-lovin' gardener, we recommend this chile, as it is easy and prolific. **5,000–23,000 SHU**

CAYENNE

Ground cayenne is the most common hot powder spice, and old jars of it linger in cabinets across the country. It is also the pepper of choice for herbal remedies, though that may be simply because of its ubiquity. The powder you can buy at a grocery store is not always pure cayenne; sometimes it includes a variety of chile peppers. Cayenne is also commonly the basis of "crushed red pepper" or "red pepper flakes." Long, skinny, and striking crimson, the fresh pepper is grown in many gardens. Dried cayenne pods are a perfect ingredient in brine pickles. We have found that powdered cayenne must be used liberally to increase the heat in a ferment. A mash made from the fresh chile is very seedy and must be strained; once strained, it is a thin, tart sauce that, on our own heat index, achieves a ranking of about 2 to 3 (see page 72). **30,000–50,000 SHU**

CAYENNE

CHERRY BOMB

This pepper is an excellent choice for fermenting. It has a thin, palatable skin and thick, sweet flesh, and it produces a comfortable heat. Good for an all-purpose pepper mash, cherry bombs also make excellent whole pickles and can be stuffed. They are often available in grocery stores. **3,500–5,000 SHU**

CHILE PEQUIN

This semidomesticated North American chile, also known as chile tepin, chiltepin, or bird pepper, still grows in the wild. It offers a peek into where all the peppers began — as a little fruit for the birds. Literally — birds see red and are drawn to the red upright fruit of the chile pequin. In a convenient biological exchange, the birds get nutrition while sending the seeds unharmed out the other end, chemically modified by their digestive systems for better germination. As humans selected bigger, fleshier fruits, the chile began to morph from its wild version into the many regional variants of chiles seen throughout the Americas today. The heat of the chile pequin comes in at a fiery **60,000–265,000 SHU** — but the birds don't even taste it.

FRESNO

This cherry-red pepper is often confused with the jalapeño, and to be fair, the heat level is similar; however, they are not the same. This is our hands-down go-to pepper for an all-purpose pepper mash. We make a gallon of it every year and use it liberally straight from

Any Time's the Right Time

All chiles start out green and, as they ripen, turn color— anything from yellow, orange, or red to purple, nearly black, or even white. You can eat the members of this family at any time in their development, but some peppers become a different ingredient at various stages of growth. Green jalapeños perform in dishes very differently than their mature, red, smoke-dried counterpart, the chipotle. That said, fully ripened peppers tend to have a more complex aroma and are more nutritious because the flavor compounds, sugars, and vitamins become more concentrated in the final stages of ripening.

the jar. Fresno peppers have few seeds, and their thin skins and walls make a nice, smooth mash — no straining. In fact, when strained, the sauce is very thin. **2,500–10,000 SHU**

GOCHU

Gochu means "pepper" in Korean. You might find this pepper under the name gochu pepper, Hong Gochu, Korean kimchi pepper, or Korean hot pepper when you are at the market or shopping for seeds. There is a hot and a mild variety. However, when purchasing seeds we have only found the milder variety. These are the peppers of gochujang (Korean pepper paste), and the most common one, the mild variety, lends kimchi its fantastic orangey-red hues but not much heat. Sweet, it lands at just around 3,000 on the Scoville scale. If pushed to choose a similar pepper, we would have to say paprika comes closest for the sweet, thickening quality it brings to a dish, but the flavors are very different.

Our farmer friend Mary grew a row of gochu peppers for us to try, and we will be growing them from now on. If you are a gardener who loves kimchi, we can whole-heartedly recommend this variety. Freshly grown, dried, and ground gochu has an intoxicating aroma and unbelievable flavor. You can ferment the fresh peppers, but they are not nearly as interesting in texture and flavor as they are when dried. The commercially available powders also ferment beautifully. However, the English translations on the labels can be off or confusing. If you are at an Asian market or online shopping, be advised that *maewoon gochugaru* means you are getting very hot, spicy pepper flakes, and *deolmaewoon gochugaru* means milder. For powdered gochu (rather than pepper flakes), which we call for in our gochugaru pepper paste recipes (see page 146), look for *gochujangyong gochugaru*. Try to find powders without sugars or other additives, though many of the plain ones still contain a bit of salt. **500–3000 SHU**

The Plot Thickens

Research published in the *Journal of Ethnic Foods* in 2014 throws a wrench in the idea that the first peppers to leave the Americas left in 1492 with Columbus. It is widely believed that the Japanese introduced peppers to the Korean Peninsula when they invaded in 1592, but findings now show that the gochu pepper is biologically different from those in the Americas and in other Asian countries. In fact, it may have been brought by birds millions of years ago. Historical documents show that Koreans have been growing, harvesting, and fermenting gochu for at least 1,500 years.

▶ **1.** Tabasco **2.** Gochu flakes, peppers, and powder **3.** Aji panca **4.** Ancho **5.** Cherry bomb **6.** Piri piri **7.** Casabel **8.** Scotch bonnet **9.** Criolla sella **10.** Thai dragon **11.** Aleppo **12.** Chipotle **13.** Chile pequin **14.** Chilhuacle negro **15.** Paprika **16.** Cayenne **17.** Guajillo

1
2
3
4
5
6
7
8
9
10
11
12
13
14
15
16
17

GUAJILLO

This pepper's dried, thick, leathery pods are readily available in the Mexican food section of most grocery stores. They are often soaked and puréed; we've found that fermenting them in a brine, then blending and straining them, makes a flavorful, medium-heat base for a sauce. We use these peppers for our Tunisian harissa (page 155). Fresh guajillo peppers have a tart flavor that ferments into a smooth sweetness. We've found that they develop a richness of flavor that our tasters agree is hard to describe. The paste must be strained, but the resulting pulp is thick and delicious — like ketchup with a kick. **2,500–5,000 SHU**

JALAPEÑO/CHIPOTLE

When all else fails, use a jalapeño. It is versatile, ferments deliciously, and is available year-round. The walls of the pepper are juicy and thick, and the skins disappear in the ferment. The mash does not need to be strained for a sauce, if it was made without the seeds. The downside is that the mash from the more common green jalapeños is a dull green color that isn't as inviting as the similarly flavored but fire-engine-red Fresno mash.

The smoke-dried red jalapeño gives us the delicious, smoky chipotle. A little goes a long way, so for a chipotle relish type of ferment, you may want to use another pepper as the base and chipotle as a seasoning. However, if you are making a chipotle sauce, use the brining method for dried peppers on page 34, then puree, and enjoy its full, glorious smoky heat. **2,500–8,000 SHU**

MARIACHI

This hybrid pepper showed up in a 10-pound pile in our test kitchen as a gift. It is an unusual variety, so we hesitated to put it in the book, but the results were fantastic. It has a wonderful fruity flavor. The pepper holds up well in sliced relishes and makes one of the best all-around mashes — like the Fresno, but fruitier, milder, and lighter. Plus, the apricot color of the ferments is terrific. Good substitutes for similar heat and flavor are pimento or cherry bomb. **600 SHU**

PAPRIKA

Paprika is a powered spice made from sun-dried chiles. There are many varieties of paprika made from different varieties of chiles. The heat ranges from very mild to hot. In this book, we use the Spanish smoked paprika to round out flavors and add a hint of smoke to some of the ferments. **100–500 SHU**

PEPPERONCINI

Although pepperoncini are the quintessential pickled peppers, we have yet to have a flavorful success with a lacto-fermented brine-pickled version. Over the years we experimented with various varieties of pepperoncini and a number of methods. While our batches are technically good — as in properly fermented with the right pH — they are not good as in tasty (we have found them to be somewhat acrid). We have enjoyed them best seeded and cut open, then dry-salted and fermented with generous amounts of oregano and no added brine. Yet they are still a bit bitter, and that recipe did not make the cut for this book. We have yet to grow all the varieties of pepperoncinis, though, and we invite you, dear reader, to share successful experiments. Meanwhile, we continue to grow these little peppers every year because they are prolific, ripen early, and are delicious when pan-fried in generous amounts of butter. **100–500 SHU**

POBLANO/ANCHO

The poblano is a deep, glossy green, mild chile. Short and fat, it looks similar to a bell pepper and ferments well, as the thin skin virtually disappears in the texture of a salsa or mash. We have found that the modest heat of a poblano disappears in the ferment, making it an ideal pepper for a salsa starter that has the flavor but not the bite.

Anchos are red-ripe poblanos that have been dried. They have a sweet, mild flavor and are one of the fleshiest of the dried peppers; they are often toasted and soaked before use. Anchos can be brined for a fermented hot sauce or ground and added to a ferment. **1,000–2,000 SHU**

SERRANO

The serrano is hotter and smaller than a jalapeño, but the flavor is very similar, and both are often used green. The serrano is a great choice for bumping up the heat. The mash, if made without the seeds, is an all-around good, hot daily-use green mash. The dried red serrano is called *chile seco*. **6,000–23,000 SHU**

THAI

We are generalizing here with the name "Thai chile," as we have run into naming mix-ups among these related peppers. But they are all small and fiery! The three that we use are Thai dragon, Thai bird's eye, and Thai volcano. The volcano is short and grows facing the sun, while the dragon pepper is long and skinny and grows downward, and the bird's eye is tiny, at just 1 to 1½ inches long. Thai peppers are often small, thin-walled, and quite seedy. We use them seeds-and-all in ferments throughout the book. The tiny Thai bird's eyes are great in small quantities but also work nicely when they are the dominant pepper, like in our Piri Piri Sauce (page 98). A good substitute for their heat is the dried Japón peppers that can be found in the Mexican food section of most grocery stores. For recipes that call for green Thai chiles (like the Thai Dragon Mint-Cilantro Paste, page 152), you can substitute a serrano pepper. **50,000–150,000 SHU**

THAI VOLCANO

Of the Species *Capsicum baccatum*

Baccatum means "berrylike," though it's not clear to us if this refers to the shape or the sweetness of the peppers of this species. The ones we have encountered have had a fruity flavor. This group of peppers has many cultivars similar to the *annuums*, with fruits that range from nonpungent to fiery hot.

AJÍ PANCA AND AJÍ AMARILLO

We read about *ají panca* and were captivated by the descriptions of its flavor: the burgundy-brown panca has a very sweet fruitiness (think blackberries), smoky overtones, and mild heat. It is usually found dried or as a paste — even in its native Peru it is rarely sold fresh — so we decided to grow it in our garden. We ate some fresh, fermented some as a fresh pepper mash, and dried it and pickled the pods in brine to blend into a sauce. It didn't disappoint. Grown along the coast of Peru, this pepper is used extensively in Peruvian cuisine, as is the *ají amarillo* (the slighter, more common, hotter variety). Both are thought to be remnants of the Incas — the ají amarillo is depicted on ancient pottery. You can use the powdered form of ají amarillo with yellow bell peppers to make a sauce (page 93).
1,000–16,000 SHU

MALAWI SWEET PIQUANTÉ, A.K.A. PEPPADEW

The story goes that this sweet cherry pepper was discovered growing on an itinerant pepper plant near a garden in South Africa. It hit the culinary world as the trademarked Peppadew variety, which is also a brand of pickled sweet piquanté peppers. There is controversy surrounding the validity of seeds labeled "Peppadew," however, right down to the question of whether the Peppadew variety is any different from the sweet piquanté. A little rarity, intrigue, and mystery are always good for any marketing campaign. We grew these peppers, which are the size of cherry tomatoes, in our garden and found that they make an

Bonus: Chiles Are Healthy

If you need to explain that eating fermented hot sauce on everything is actually part of your health regimen, here's your backup: Fresh chiles are quite high in vitamin C, and fermenting vegetables increases the vitamin C content and makes it more bioavailable. Chiles also boast loads of potassium, and they have flavonoids, antioxidants, and vitamins A, B, and E. Capsaicin is said to benefit circulation (and therefore heart health), aid in headache or congestion relief, treat chronic pain, reduce blood pressure, and boost metabolism and mood (there's that psychotropic thing again).

Hot Myth: You Get Used to It

MYTH: Like elite athletes, heat aficionados can "build up" their tolerance for the burn.

FACT: Not quite. The pain doesn't ever lessen — you just get tougher. One study points out that extreme pepper-eaters don't rate the bonfire in their mouth as any less painful. (But why do some people want ever hotter peppers? That could have something to do with the dopamine squirt, like runners who need to run ever farther to get the high.)

outstanding fermented whole pickle with mild spice and great texture. They were very similar to cherry bombs in everything except heat. The fermented paste is mildly flavored with a thick consistency. It is best strained, as the skins are noticeable. **1,000–2,000 SHU**

Of the Species *Capsicum chinense*

In a case of mistaken identity, Dutchman Nikolaus von Jacquin christened these peppers "Chinese" in 1776. Like all the others, however, these peppers are native to the Americas, where they are used extensively in the cuisines of the Caribbean and the Yucatán Peninsula. This group is perhaps the most infamous for its fiery clan members, which include the over-the-top ghost pepper and the Carolina Reaper, the current titleholder for the world's hottest.

CAROLINA REAPER

This world-record pepper looks devilishly hot because its bright red skin actually appears blistered (see Smokin' Ed Currie, page 73). If you want a crazy-hot ferment, you can grow this pepper — seeds are available. For the purposes of research, we found that we could blend Carolina Reaper purée into a ferment to get the Reaper flavor and raging heat — but blend at your own risk. **1,500,000–2,200,000 SHU**

GHOST PEPPER

The fiery ghost pepper, known in India as *bhut jolokia*, is a previous record holder and current darling of the culinary world. A naturally occurring hybrid of *Capsicum chinense* and *Capsicum frutescens*, it is now finding its way onto the menus of boutique restaurants (ghost pepper ice cream!) as well as those establishments that dot the strips and highway off-ramps, where it's served on burgers, fries, burritos, and chicken sandwiches. Why is it called the ghost pepper? The easiest explanation is that in the language of Assam (the Indian state from which this pepper hails), the word *bhut* means "ghost." It's often thought that this is to suggest that the fire you feel will make you see a ghost. However, pepper breeder Ed Currie explains that people didn't traditionally eat this pepper in India — instead it was relegated to the shamans for curative uses. The

DRIED GHOST PEPPERS

HABANEROS

remedy was designed to cure by exorcising the sick person's "ghosts." To accomplish this, the dried bhut jolokia peppers were thrown onto a fire and the patient's head draped with a cloth to capture the smoke. Upon breathing in this capsaicin-laced dragon breath, the patient turned red, coughed, released tears and mucus, and vomited, thus expelling the ghosts that ailed him. **855,000–1,041,427 SHU**

HABANERO

Easily obtained in the summer and at some markets year-round, the habanero (once the Guinness World Record holder for heat) is becoming America's go-to super-hot pepper. The heat isn't immediate. Often you taste the citrus sweetness and have time to think, "This isn't so bad . . . ," then the burn builds (and builds . . .) and lingers on for quite some time. Make a small jar of habanero mash during the harvest season, and you will be able to enjoy its bite for months to come. This is a thin-walled pepper and lends itself to a smooth mash (no straining), if you've removed the seeds. **80,000–600,000 SHU**

SCOTCH BONNET

This pepper is often associated with the habanero, and while it is similar in texture and heat index, the flavors are different. This pepper has a more apricot-like aroma compared to the habanero's citrus. It is used extensively in Caribbean cuisine and gives pikliz (page 191) and other condiments their special flavors. All that said, you can still substitute habanero for the Scotch bonnet. **100,000–350,000 SHU**

The Tabasco Pepper

Tabasco sauce derives its name from a pepper of the species *Capsicum frutescens*. The Tabasco pepper came from the Mexican city of Tabasco, which happened to be a trading partner with New Orleans in the 1850s. Maunsell White, a banker at the time, introduced the seed, which he shared, along with a sauce he had made from it, with a friend, Edmund McIlhenny. The rest is history. Perhaps the most interesting thing about this pepper is that it is not considered a fully domesticated variety, even though it has been farmed for Tabasco sauce on Avery Island, Louisiana, since 1869. We have not fermented with this variety, but it cannot be left out of the American story of fermentation. We suspect that it ferments similarly to the Thai volcano pepper (page 67). 30,000–50,000 SHU

Playing with Fire

While our title is *Fiery Ferments*, the truth is, not every ferment is going to be fiery. We realize that different palates have different opinions on what's hot (and not). Aiming to offer a little something for everyone, we've included a range of flame, from a pleasant warm smolder to a raging bonfire. And, armed with a little knowledge, you can turn the heat up or down and adjust the flavors as you see fit.

CONTROLLED BURN

As we created flavors, we tested our recipes with various tasters to come up with a heat index to help you decide how you want to approach the recipes (see page 72). The beauty of fermentation is that everything acidifies equally, so you can easily modify the ingredients. Here are a few tips to help you navigate to the perfect heat in your ferments:

- Heat levels are relative to individual tastes. We have tried to be consistent, but our taste for heat will be different from yours. So explore a few recipes and get an idea of how your personal heat level compares to the one in this book.
- The fire in your fresh pepper will be diminished a bit in the first stages of fermentation. This is good to know, whether you hope to tone it down or want to make sure you have full fire. (For the latter, add some dried pepper flakes to your ferment to bring up the heat.)
- If a recipe has caught your eye but the heat index does not match your desires, you can turn it up or down simply by choosing a different pepper. If the recipe calls for habaneros but you want less heat, substitute a "cooler" pepper. If you want more heat, you have two choices: use the same pepper (to retain the flavor profile of the specific variety) but add some dried pepper powder or flakes to bring up the heat, or substitute a hotter pepper variety.

Guide to the Heat Index

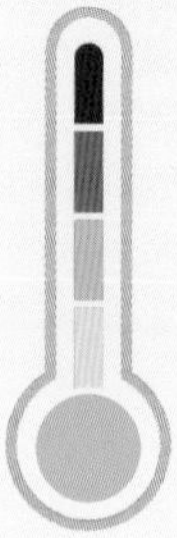

5 Self-preservation has kicked in. I am not thinking about the good endorphin rush until I know I am going to survive this.

4 Spice is the dominant flavor and causes a burn that brings on sweat.

3 The heat is pleasant. I can take another bite right away because I can taste all the flavors and am not looking for copious amounts of ice to chew.

2 The heat is a player in the flavor profile but doesn't steal the show.

1 I know the heat is there, but it doesn't really show up. This is mild.

If it's only about heat, what's the point? Is it a macho game? Is it a bar game? Or is it something that really tastes good on your food?

David Rosengarten, chef and host of *Taste*

MEET A HEAT MAKER

Smokin' Ed Currie, PuckerButt Pepper Company, and the Carolina Reaper

FORT MILL, SOUTH CAROLINA

Ed Currie of Fort Mill, South Carolina, holds the Guinness World Record for cultivating the world's hottest pepper — the Carolina Reaper, clocking in at an average of 1.56 million Scoville units (one individual pepper has been rated at 2.2 million SHU). He is just one denizen of the cutthroat world of competitive chile breeders, in which you can find drama and spectacle on par with professional wrestling. Pain-seeking fans enter brow-sweating, eye-popping, gut-wrenching contests. It's a world of irreverently named hot sauce brands and crude jokes about the hazards of touching hot peppers before touching the male anatomy.

For Currie, however, there is much more to the story. Beyond the fun of PuckerButt's storefront and extreme pepper sauces is a passion for health. His company's hot sauces are created with whole food nutrition in mind, and he and his family themselves grow all the peppers and fruit for the PuckerButt sauces. And the world's record-holding hot pepper wasn't bred for the record. He bred it for chemotherapy patients.

Currie's mission is to breed pepper strains that have high levels of capsaicin for fighting heart disease and cancer. He sees the hot sauce business as the high-profile front end of the much more interesting undertaking of breeding peppers for medical research, which is where most of the tens of thousands of peppers he grows end up.

The Carolina Reaper came about when Currie was working on a pepper with a sweet flavor for chemotherapy patients. These patients lose most of their taste receptors but can still taste sweet. He said that more complex sugars tend to make these patients sick, so he was looking to breed a sweet pepper that they could eat. "And it worked," he said, adding, "The capsaicinoids kill the cancer cells, and for circulatory heart health, the fat cells bind with the fats and take them through the liver before you piss them out. Excuse the language."

Part 2

Fiery Ferments

There are approximately 12,572 other hot sauces besides sriracha — try another one.

Sean Timberlake, punkdomestics.com

CH 4

SPICY PRE-CHILE RECIPES

We had fun using our imaginations to come up with flavors that turned up the heat without a chile. The recipes in this chapter are often based on historical research. Some of the ingredients are familiar, like ginger, while others really have been lost to time and trends, like the long pepper. You'll find other pre-chile ingredients, such as grains of paradise and Szechuan pepper, throughout this book in condiments that contain chiles as well.

YIELD: About 1 pint

TECHNIQUE: Kimchis, Relishes, and Salads (page 40)

HEAT INDEX: 2

FERMENTED GINGER PICKLES

In early winter the produce section of markets can be loaded with newly harvested ginger, galangal, and turmeric roots; they are full, succulent, and fresh. This is the time to preserve them. If you are lucky, you might find varieties beyond the widely available yellow ginger, such as the milder baby ginger, labeled "pink," "young," "new," or "stem" ginger, or the zestier blue Hawaiian.

This recipe can be used for any kind of ginger, turmeric, or galangal, though galangal is more fibrous and better suited for a grated paste. We use these slices throughout the year to flavor meals or to put in other ferments to give them a head start (for example, when starting a hot sauce with only dried chile pods).

- 1 pound fresh ginger root
- ½ teaspoon salt

1. Prepare the ginger by peeling off the skin and slicing the root as thinly as possible — think of the pickled ginger that's served alongside a plate of sushi. Place these slices in a bowl.
2. Mix in the salt.
3. Pack the mixture tightly into a pint jar, pressing out any air pockets as you go. Leave the top quarter of the jar free.
4. Press a ziplock bag against the surface of the ferment, fill the bag with water, and zip it closed.
5. Place the jar on a plate and set aside, out of direct sunlight, to ferment for 7 to 14 days. During the fermentation period, monitor for air pockets, pressing down the ginger if needed. As the ginger ferments, the color will change slightly. The brine will become milky.
6. When the pickles are ready, transfer the jar to the refrigerator. These pickles will keep, refrigerated, for 12 months, provided the ginger is kept under the brine.

VARIATION: Ginger (or Other Rhizome) Paste

Roughly chop the ginger. Blend in a food processor with the salt until you have a smooth, even paste. Ferment according to the instructions for fermenting pastes and mustards (page 37).

HOT TIP

Should You Peel Ginger?

For sliced pickles, we generally peel the ginger root for better aesthetics and mouthfeel. When we are planning to grate the ginger and combine it with many other ingredients, however, it is simpler to wash the skin and leave it on. Plus, the skin is where our friends the lactic-acid bacteria hang out. Try to use organic ginger, however, since conventional ginger is often irradiated, which can kill the bacteria.

YIELD: About ½ pint

TECHNIQUE: Pastes and Mustards (page 37)

HEAT INDEX: 2 (or 3 with chile paste)

HORSERADISH FERMENT, HOT OR HOTTER

This ferment is amazing, but it can be a little tricky because you don't have the luxury of waiting for the lactic acid to develop. As soon as the cells of the horseradish root are damaged by grinding or chopping, enzymes immediately begin breaking down the heat-making volatile compounds. The sooner acid is introduced to stabilize it, the sharper the flavor.

You can acidify your ferment by using some fermented brine from a previous ferment as the acid. Or you can get crazy and inoculate it with an already fermented pepper paste to get hot compounds from all directions. If neither of those options work for you, you can use lemon juice. In any case, make sure the roots you get from the store are fresh — roots that are drying out will not be hot and may taste quite bitter. Lastly, this ferment will continue to mellow over time. We recommend making it in small quantities, often.

- ½ pound or so horseradish root (to make about 1 cup grated)
- 1 teaspoon salt
- 2–3 tablespoons sauerkraut brine, fermented chile mash, or lemon juice

WARNING *If you haven't worked with fresh horseradish root, be aware that it can bite — as in sting your eyes and sinuses. Be cautious and don't get your face too close to the root when working with it.*

1. Peel the horseradish and cut it into small chunks. Combine them in a food processor with the salt and brine, and process until the mixture reaches a paste consistency.
2. Pack the paste carefully into a jar that is just the right size for your ferment, pressing out any air pockets as you go. Leave about 1 inch of headspace. This ferment is exceedingly dry; just keep packing — it will work even though you won't see liquid forming.
3. Press a piece of plastic (or other cartouche) against the surface of the ferment, being careful not to trap any air beneath it. Screw the lid down tightly.
4. Set the jar in a corner of the kitchen to ferment, and watch for air pockets forming in the paste. If you see any, open the lid and press the paste back down. If the lid starts to bulge, simply open it for a moment to burp the ferment.
5. Allow to ferment for 7 to 14 days. It is difficult to see any obvious changes, but when it's ready, it will taste acidic and pungent, like prepared horseradish.
6. When it is ready, remove the cartouche and place a clean small round of plastic or parchment paper directly on top of the paste. Tighten the lid, then store in the fridge, where this ferment will keep its full flavor for 3 months.

YIELD: About 1½ cups

TECHNIQUE: Pastes and Mustards (page 37)

HEAT INDEX: 1

HORSERADISH MUSTARD

This is spicy mustard, a hands-down favorite at our house. If you like the spice but want a milder version, try mixing it with mayonnaise or aioli.

- 2–3 tablespoons grated fresh horseradish root
- ¼ cup brown mustard seeds
- ¼ cup white mustard seeds
- 2 cloves garlic, grated
- 1 teaspoon grated fresh turmeric root or ¼ teaspoon powdered
- 2 teaspoons salt
- 1 cup unchlorinated water

TO ADD AFTER FERMENTATION:

- 1 tablespoon raw apple cider vinegar
- 1 teaspoon brown sugar or honey

1. Place the horseradish root in a blender with the mustard seeds, garlic, turmeric, salt, and water. Blend until smooth. As the mustard seeds break down, they act as a thickening agent, and the mixture will become creamy. Keep blending until it achieves a uniform paste.
2. Spoon your mustard into a pint jar, pressing out any air pockets as you go. When it is all in the jar, you may need to use a butter knife to work out any remaining pockets. Then screw the lid down tightly.
3. Set the jar on your counter to ferment for 3 days. This ferment will not create air pockets or release much in the way of CO_2, so you will not need to burp it.
4. Following fermentation, open the lid (it may pop slightly as a little CO_2 is released) and stir in the vinegar and the sugar or honey. If you're using sugar, it will take a little while for the sugar crystals to melt into the mustard. Let sit for about 10 minutes, stir again, and your mustard is ready to serve.
5. Store this mustard in the refrigerator, where it will keep for up to 3 months.

Spicy Fun Legend

Myth has it that the Oracle at Delphi told Apollo, "The radish is worth its weight in lead, the beet its weight in silver, the horseradish its weight in gold." Well, yeah — the Greeks thought horseradish was not only a pain reliever but also an aphrodisiac. Need we say more?

YIELD: About ½ pint

TECHNIQUE: Pastes and Mustards (page 37)

HEAT INDEX: 1

GREEN PEPPERCORN MUSTARD

This mustard has a wonderful kick; it is spicy, but in a very different way from the heat of chile or the sinus-invigorating horseradish. The ground green peppercorns give it a fun, flecked appearance.

- 2 tablespoons green peppercorns
- ¼ cup brown mustard seeds
- ¼ cup white mustard seeds
- 1 teaspoon grated fresh turmeric root
- 2 teaspoons salt
- 1 cup unchlorinated water

TO ADD AFTER FERMENTATION:

- 2 tablespoons white wine vinegar
- 1 teaspoon brown sugar or honey (optional)

1. Combine the peppercorns, mustard seeds, turmeric, salt, and water in a blender. Blend until smooth. As the mustard seeds break down, they act as a thickening agent, and the mixture will become creamy. Keep blending until it reaches a paste consistency.
2. Spoon your mustard into a pint jar, pressing out any air pockets as you go. When it is all in the jar, you may need to use a butter knife to work out any remaining pockets. Then screw the lid down tightly.
3. Set the jar in a corner of the kitchen to ferment. Watch for air pockets forming in the mustard. If you see any, open the lid and press the mustard back down. If the lid starts to bulge, simply open it for a moment to burp the ferment.
4. Allow to ferment for about 7 days. Mustards are ready to eat immediately, but the fermentation time gives them a nice, smooth acidity and brings them to a lower pH, which improves preservation.
5. Following fermentation, open the lid (it may pop slightly as CO_2 is released) and stir in the vinegar and the sugar, if using. If you're using sugar, it will take a little while for the sugar crystals to melt into the mustard. Let sit for about 10 minutes, stir again, and your mustard is ready to serve.
6. Store the mustard in the refrigerator, where it will keep for up to 12 months.

YIELD: About ½ pint

TECHNIQUE: Pastes and Mustards (page 37)

HEAT INDEX: 1

GREEN PEPPERCORN PASTE

This recipe was inspired by a list describing the likely cuisine of thirteenth-century Thailand. The meal consisted of glutinous rice with vegetables (sometimes fermented), meat or fish, soup, and a paste of shallots, galangal, and green peppercorns. Of course those long-ago Thai cooks would have used these green peppercorns when they were still soft and fruity instead of dry. We claim no authenticity in terms of thirteenth-century flavor!

This sweet paste, and its variation with turmeric, has become one of our go-to ferments for adding subtle flavor to everything from a cucumber salad to chicken meatballs (see our recipe for chicken sausage meatballs on page 204).

- ¾ pound shallots (about 7 medium), chopped
- 6 cloves garlic
- 4 tablespoons chopped lemongrass
- 1 tablespoon whole green peppercorns
- 1½ tablespoons grated galangal root
- 1 tablespoon dulse flakes
- 1 teaspoon salt

1. Combine the shallots, garlic, lemongrass, peppercorns, galangal, dulse, and salt in a food processor. Process until the mixture reaches a paste consistency. This ferment will be nice and juicy due to the shallots.

2. Pack the mixture carefully into a jar that is just the right size for your ferment, pressing out any air pockets as you go. Leave about 1 inch of headspace.

3. Press a piece of plastic (or other cartouche) against the surface of the ferment, being careful not to trap any air beneath it. Screw the lid down tightly.

4. Set the jar in a corner of the kitchen to ferment, and watch for air pockets forming in the paste. If you see any, open the lid and press the paste back down. If the lid starts to bulge, simply open it for a moment to burp the ferment.

5. Allow to ferment for 14 days. This ferment has a wonderful flavor, and you will know it is ready when it has a nice sourness. You may certainly enjoy it immediately, but it truly benefits from another month in the refrigerator, during which time the flavors will mingle to create a rich complex taste.

6. To store, remove the cartouche and place a clean small round of plastic or parchment paper directly on top of the paste. Tighten the lid and place in the fridge, where it will keep for 12 months.

VARIATION: Green Peppercorn Paste with Turmeric

Turmeric blends nicely with the flavors of this paste and gives it a bright yellow color. If you are trying to add more anti-inflammatory foods into your diet, this is a tasty way to do it, and this recipe provides the benefits of the combination of curcumin and piperine (see Turmeric + Black Pepper, page 145).

Follow the instructions for Green Peppercorn Paste and add 1½ tablespoons chopped turmeric (about ½ ounce) to the mixture.

YIELD: About ½ pint

TECHNIQUE: Pastes and Mustards (page 37)

HEAT INDEX: 1

LONG PEPPER CURRY PASTE

This recipe was inspired by jalfrezi curry paste, though it took some twists and turns and doesn't resemble a traditional jalfrezi paste at all. Traditional jalfrezi is an amalgamation of Indian and Chinese cuisines. It is a thick, spicy sauce served with fried meat (often chicken) or vegetables, peppers, and spices. While our variation isn't very hot — we were aiming to highlight the long pepper — with the addition of chiles this curry paste can be quite fiery.

- 1 bunch cilantro
- 3–4 cloves garlic
- 1 ounce ginger (a 2-inch piece)
- 1 ounce turmeric root (a thumb-sized piece)
- ½ teaspoon salt
- 1 tablespoon toasted and ground long pepper
- 1 teaspoon toasted and ground coriander seeds
- 1 teaspoon toasted and ground cumin seeds
- 1 teaspoon toasted and ground fenugreek seeds
- 1 teaspoon toasted and ground mustard seeds (any variety)

1. Combine the cilantro, garlic, ginger, and turmeric in a food processor and process to a paste consistency.
2. Sprinkle in the salt. Since the cell walls of the ingredients are already broken down, the paste will become moist right away. However, this type of ferment will not look juicy. Add the long pepper, coriander, cumin, fenugreek, and mustard seeds and pulse a few times to mix well.
3. Pack the mixture carefully into a jar that is just the right size for your ferment, pressing out any air pockets as you go. Leave about 1 inch of headspace.
4. Press a piece of plastic (or other cartouche) against the surface of the ferment, being careful not to trap any air beneath it. Screw the lid down tightly.
5. Set the jar in a corner of the kitchen to ferment, and watch for air pockets forming in the paste. If you see any, open the lid and press the paste back down. If the lid starts to bulge, simply open it for a moment to burp the ferment.
6. Allow to ferment for 7 to 14 days. You will know it is ready when the ferment changes to a deeper color and any brine turns a cloudy brownish color. There will be a tang to the flavor that wasn't there when it was fresh.
7. Place a clean small round of plastic or parchment paper directly on top of the paste. Tighten the lid, then store in the fridge, where this ferment will keep for 6 months.

HOT TIP

Toasting Long Pepper

Toasting long pepper on a dry pan over medium heat brings out the kick. Stir frequently, as you toast it, you will see the color change from dark brown to a lighter shade of brown. At the same time, the peppers will soften as they warm, which makes them easier to grind with a mortar and pestle. If you are using a coffee grinder, allow them to cool a bit before grinding, as the same softness that helps with hand grinding can make them a bit tacky for the grinder.

CH 5

SAUCES

Hot sauce is wonderfully simple and magnificently complex all at the same time. Each one begins with five elements: fire (chiles), mineral (salt), sour (acid), spice (aromatics), and sweet (fruit or vegetal sugars — think carrots or pineapple). Then the fun begins. What chile pepper will you choose from among the hundreds of varieties? Will the pepper be dried or fresh? Will you choose to accentuate the savory notes or the sweet? Will you change the ferment's acidity by adding vinegar to the final product? Truly, there are as many hot sauces as there are people — and, as it turns out, it is pretty easy to make one that is good, if not downright fantastic.

Getting Saucy

Most of the hot sauces in this chapter are blended sauces, meaning that ultimately everything gets puréed together, whether for a thinner sauce like Tabasco or for a thicker, ketchup-consistency sauce or paste. However, we also include barbecue sauce and some fermented salsa starters for fresh tabletop sauces.

There are two basic ways to make a sauce: fermenting a mash or brine-pickling your peppers. If your sauce is based entirely on dried peppers, you will need to brine-pickle your fermented base, but for most sauces you have a choice. In general, we usually prefer a mash-based sauce for its richness and complexity. We've included recipes for both methods, though, and invite you to experiment and find your own hot sauce bliss.

Check out the chile guide in chapter 3 (page 57) to get an idea of how some different peppers perform in a mash. Remember, most mashes need to be strained for a smooth, velvety sauce that will also let the flavors stand out more.

Finally, you'll find that many hot sauces throughout the world are cooked. We tend to keep our own sauces raw, but we have included some recipes from folks making amazing flavor by cooking their sauces.

Extinguishing the Fire

By our definition, any recipe with a heat index of 5 means that very soon after putting it in our mouths we had a full-body urge to put out the fire by any means necessary. Everyone is a little bit different, so it might be that for you a heat level of 3 puts you in this same place. The important thing is to know your limits and to know how to get relief, quickly, when you step over that line. We went through just about everything in the kitchen, so here are our dos and don'ts for neutralizing the effects of capsaicin.

Dos

- **ACIDIC JUICES** provide some relief. Straight-up lime or lemon juice will at least give you something else to pay attention to. Tomato juice is nice; just remember not to choose the spicy kind!
- **DAIRY** proteins help break down the bonds of capsaicin. Milk, yogurt, and, in a pinch, huge spoonfuls of sour cream (or ice cream) have all proved effective.
- **FATTY FOODS** can make a real difference. A favorite of ours is a tablespoon of peanut or almond butter. If you are in serious pain, chomping the end off a stick of refrigerated butter should (theoretically) do the trick — if you can stomach it.
- **A STIFF DRINK** (of the hard stuff — it is the high alcohol content that has the neutralizing effect) on the rocks will provide relief, though it's probably not appropriate for daily fire suppression. Room-temperature booze does not work, so plan ahead.
- **SUGAR** helps more than the medicine go down. We have found sugar, honey, and ripe bananas to be effective, honey having the most pleasing, smooth, coating effect in the mouth.

Don'ts

- **COLD WATER** is quick, it's convenient, and it just makes sense — but it doesn't put out the fire. As soon as you swallow, the burn is back.
- **COLD BEER OR HARD CIDER** also lets you down as soon as you swallow.
- **STARCH,** such as rice or a hunk of bread, always seems like it *should* work, but it never does. It does make a fine vehicle for fats like butter or nut butter, however.

YIELD: About 1 pint

TECHNIQUE: Brined-Based Sauces and Pickles (page 34)

HEAT INDEX: 3

SIMPLEST HOT SAUCE EVER: HAWAIIAN CHILE PEPPER WATER

Traditionally, chile pepper water is made with the Hawaiian red chile, which has heat and flavor similar to that of a Tabasco pepper. The chile was introduced to the islands in the nineteenth century. Some sources credit its importation to Don Francisco de Paula Marin, an amateur horticulturist who brought many plants to the islands, while other sources say it was American cowboys who were ranching on the Big Island around the same time.

Pronounced in the local pidgin as "chile peppa watah," this sauce is as ubiquitous in Hawaii as Tabasco sauce in a diner or sriracha at an Asian food cart. In researching this hot sauce we found many variations, but in its most basic form it is chiles, salt, and water. Nowhere did we find a lacto-fermented version, so we've created our own.

We tried one method that described placing the chiles in a bottle with the brine and mashing them with a chopstick. Turns out that trying to catch the buoyant chiles as they dodge the chopstick is like fishing for minnows with your hands. We recommend lightly crushing the ingredients on a cutting board before putting them in your jar.

- 4–10 small hot chiles
- 2 slices ginger root
- 1 clove garlic
- 2 cups brine (2 cups unchlorinated water with 1 tablespoon salt)
- 1 tablespoon rice vinegar

1. Crush the chiles (more or less depending on the heat you desire), ginger, and garlic with the back of a knife. Put them in a 12- to 16-ounce bottle.
2. Fill the rest of the bottle with the brine, leaving 1½ inches of headspace. Screw the lid down tightly.
3. Allow to ferment for 1 to 2 weeks (no burping required).
4. When the brine turns cloudy and develops a pickle-like acidity, add the rice vinegar. Store in the refrigerator, where this ferment will keep for a year.

Bottomless Burn

Puerto Rican *pique* sauces are not blended (or fermented). Instead, they are made by bathing the ingredients — which vary, but traditionally include whole fiery chiles — in vinegar. The vinegar is often topped off a number of times, making this a hot sauce that keeps on giving . . . sort of like that bottomless cup of coffee.

YIELD: ½ gallon

TECHNIQUE: Basic Pepper Mash (page 30)

HEAT INDEX: Depends on the chile variety

BASIC GO-TO MASH

If you love having a little something spicy to liberally toss into a recipe or dollop on food, make a half gallon of this — or more — when peppers are in season. It is the mash pictured in the step-by-step guide on page 30 and the building block of many a good sauce. It's even a great starter for making fiery ferments during the off-season (for example, Rhubarb Kimchi, page 171). Our favorite pepper for an all-purpose mash is the Fresno, but use any pepper you are lucky enough to have in abundance. Jalapeños, habaneros, and other thin-skinned peppers make a good mash that doesn't need to be strained if the seeds are first removed.

- 3½ pounds peppers, stemmed and seeded
- 1 tablespoon plus ½ teaspoon salt

1. Process the peppers in a food processor until evenly chopped to a salsa-like consistency. Sprinkle in the salt. The chopped peppers will become juicy immediately.
2. Pack the mash into a half-gallon jar, pressing out any air pockets as you go. Leave about 1 inch of headspace. You should see some brine above the pepper pulp. Screw the lid down tightly.
3. Set the jar aside to ferment, out of direct sunlight, for anywhere from 14 days to many months. You may want to set it on a plate during the first 2 weeks to catch any escaping brine while the ferment is at its most active. For the first week or two, check daily to make sure that the mash is submerged in the brine (see Curing Notes, page 32).
4. Start tasting the ferment on day 14. It's ready when it has an acidic vinegar-like quality. The color of the peppers tends to stay vibrant, so you may not see as much color shift as you would in other ferments.
5. Store this ferment in the refrigerator, where it will keep for 2 years or more.

VARIATION: Dry Chile Powder Mash

Once you are addicted to the wide world of peppers, you will be drawn to unusual varieties but may only be able to find them in the form of dry powders. We have found a good solution to this conundrum. Follow the instructions for the Basic Go-To Mash (opposite) using bell peppers (usually red or yellow) as the pepper base. When the peppers are in the food processor, add 1 tablespoon of powdered chiles for every ¾ to 1 pound of bell peppers. We use yellow bells with ají chiles for a wonderful ají amarillo sauce.

YIELD: Almost 1 pint

TECHNIQUE: Brine-Based Sauces and Pickles (page 34)

HEAT INDEX: Depends on the chile variety

BASIC BRINE MASH

Some fermentistas prefer to sink their peppers in brine before mashing them, as it can be simpler to manage than dry salting and fermenting the mash (as is done for the Basic Go-To Mash, page 92). We use the dry-salting method whenever we have enough liquid because it creates a richer, tastier final product. However, many pepper varieties are only available dried, and the brine helps draw out their concentrated flavors.

This method is also a good strategy for dried peppers or thin-walled peppers that have very little flesh (cayenne, for example) and therefore do not work well in a dry-salted mash. Try dried peppers like ají panca, chilhuacle negro, and guajillo. The instructions below are for dried peppers, but the process is the same no matter whether you're using fresh, dried, or a combination of the two. Note that with dried peppers, it may take 3 weeks until the brine turns acidic. To speed things up, simply add a tablespoon of brine from another fermented vegetable to kick-start it.

- 1–2 cups brine (1 quart unchlorinated water with 3 tablespoons salt)
- 3–4 ounces dried chiles, enough to fill a pint jar when stuffed tightly

1. Pack your chiles into a narrow-mouthed pint jar. Wedge them under the shoulder of the jar to so they will stay submerged in the brine.
2. Pour in enough brine to cover the chiles completely, pressing as you go to release any air from inside the dried peppers. Screw the lid down tightly. (Reserve any leftover brine in the fridge. It will keep for 1 week; discard thereafter and make a new batch, if needed.)
3. Place the jar on a plate and set aside to ferment, out of direct sunlight, for 2 to 3 weeks. Burp the ferment as needed. Always open the jar over the plate, as some of the brine may fizz out. If needed, top off with reserved brine solution to keep the chiles covered.
4. As it ferments, the brine will turn orange and cloudy. You will know it is ready when it tastes acidic. Place the mixture, brine and all, in a blender and purée until smooth.
5. Use a sieve to strain out the seeds and skin. The mash is ready to use as is, or you can use it to make a sauce.

HOT TIP

Adding Flavor to Brine

If you like, you can infuse the brine with flavor before fermenting. For example, replace regular salt with smoked salt or add a bundle of herbs that you will pull out before blending. We have also used salted coffee, tea, or light, unsweetened fruit juice to make our brines.

YIELD: 1 quart

TECHNIQUE: Basic Pepper Mash (page 30)

HEAT INDEX: Depends on the chile variety

MIXED-MEDIA BASIC MASH

Onions are standard hot sauce ingredients, so why not ferment them right alongside the chiles? The added bonus is that the moisture in the fresh vegetables gives the mash more brine for fermenting. This basic recipe can be adapted for use with any fresh veggies.

- ¾ pound fresh chiles, 3–4 ounces dried chiles, or a mix of the two
- 1 large onion, coarsely chopped
- 3 teaspoons salt

HOT TIP

Barrel-Aged without the Barrel

Brewing suppliers carry oak cubes and spirals made to give your brew that barrel-aged flavor. This is a great way to bring a lot of depth to the flavor of your hot sauces. Simply drop some of the blocks, or a piece of the spiral, into your pepper mash or brine-based ferment during the fermentation period.

1. If you're using dried chiles, remove the seeds and break the chiles up into pieces. For fresh chiles, remove the stems and seeds. Combine the chiles with the onion and salt in a food processor and process to a salsa-like consistency. It will become juicy immediately. Don't worry if the dried pepper doesn't break up much more — it will ferment in the onion's juices.
2. Pack the mash into a jar, pressing out any air pockets as you go. Leave about 1 inch of headspace. You should see some brine above the pulp. Screw the lid down tightly.
3. Set the jar aside to ferment, out of direct sunlight, for anywhere from 14 days to many months. For the first week or two, check daily to make sure that the mash is submerged in the brine (see Curing Notes, page 32).
4. Start tasting the ferment on day 14. It's ready if it has an acidic vinegar-like quality to the flavor. The onions will mellow and take on the heat. Purée into a smooth, thick (ketchup consistency) sauce. Use for a sauce blend, or store in a jar or bottle that is the right size to use as is.
5. Store this ferment in the refrigerator, where it will keep for a year or more.

VARIATION: Mixed-Media Basic Mash with Garlic

This garlicky variation is a starting point for all kinds of sauces. For example, for a wonderful base for enchilada sauce, make it with dried pasilla and guajillo chiles. Follow the instructions above, using the following ingredients:

- 1 pound fresh chiles (or red bell peppers)
- 3 ounces dried chiles
- 1 full head garlic
- 1½–2 teaspoons salt

MEET THE MAKER

Marcus McCauley, Foremother Foods

BOULDER, COLORADO

When we contacted Marcus to ask for an interview, he suggested either walking the fields of his farm or meeting at his processing plant. While we love a good farm tour, we jumped at the chance to see a hot sauce operation in full swing. It turned out to be a cold, rainy day, so when we ducked out of a downpour through an open loading-dock door, the warmth and pungent air were very welcoming.

Marcus's path to becoming a professional hot sauce maker begins with the familiar story of having farmer friends with a surplus of produce. His friend and farming mentor, Rich, called one day with a proposition — if Marcus could do something with a ton of peppers, they were his. Marcus was a busy chef at the time, his wife pregnant with their son, and yet he couldn't pass up the opportunity. He decided to ferment them — almost all of them. Bubbling 5-gallon buckets and scavenged jars of all sizes quickly filled their garage. Concerned friends would come by and ask, "What are you doing?"

"I don't know," was his honest reply.

Marcus knows what he is doing now. His sauce, Picaflor Srirawcha, is a combination of five peppers: Hot Portugals, Rellenos, jalapeños, Jimmy Nardellos, and cayennes. The garlic comes from his family farm. What we think makes Foremother Foods' flavors unique is Marcus's insistence on keeping the sauces alive and raw, using innovative ways to thicken and stabilize them. The srirawcha, for example, uses organic applesauce and Colorado honey. The golden-colored Picaflor Boulder Sol has lovely citrus notes and is made with Criolla Sella peppers thickened with fermented cantaloupe! We know what you might be thinking, but believe us — it works.

YIELD: About 1½ quarts

TECHNIQUE: Basic Pepper Mash (page 30)

HEAT INDEX: 3

SRIRAWCHA

Marcus McCauley's Srirawcha recipe (sriracha sauce made with *raw* ingredients) is a two-part process: first you ferment the pepper mash, then you mix the mash with garlic and sugar. You can depart from this recipe to use any type of peppers you like, but remember that your choice will affect the taste, consistency, and heat level of the sauce.

- 5 large red bell peppers
- 6–7 red jalapeños
- 2–3 fresh red cayenne peppers
- 2 tablespoons salt
- ½ cup evaporated cane sugar (or other sweetener to taste)
- 3 cloves garlic

PART 1

1. Remove the seeds and stems from the bell peppers, jalapeños, and cayenne peppers. Chop the peppers coarsely.
2. Add the salt, mix well, and let sit for about 1 hour.
3. Blend the pepper mixture to a smooth paste.
4. Pack into your favorite fermenting vessel, and let the paste ferment on your countertop for 4 to 5 days. At this point you can either move right to the next stage or, if the paste is in a fermentation vessel with an airlock, transfer it to the fridge, where it will keep for up to 12 months; in the fridge it will continue to age and evolve until you are ready to convert it to a finished sauce.

PART 2

Blend the pepper mash, sugar, and garlic into a smooth paste. Adjust the salt to taste. Store in the refrigerator, where the sauce will keep for 12 months.

YIELD: ½ pint

TECHNIQUE: Basic Pepper Mash (page 30)

HEAT INDEX: 4

PIRI PIRI SAUCE

Also called pili pili, this sauce is made with a chile of the same name — meaning "pepper pepper." (Our guess is that saying it twice equates to "it's hot!") This fiery little chile, landing between 50,000 and 175,000 SHU, is in the *Capsicum frutescens* species and grows both wild and domestically. It is also called African bird's eye chile, and if you can't find it, Thai bird's eye chiles will give you good results as well. Try to use fresh chiles, as they make an amazing sauce, though dried whole pods will work.

This sauce is used extensively in African and Portuguese cuisines. The recipes we researched varied (none were fermented), but they all had an olive oil component. In our version, the vegetables are fermented in a mash (which has an almost fruit-leather flavor under the burn), and then the oil is emulsified into the sauce post-fermentation.

- 20 piri piri chiles or Thai bird's eye chiles, de-stemmed
- 8 large cloves garlic
- ½ teaspoon salt
- ¼ cup fresh lemon juice
- ⅓ cup olive oil

1. Combine the de-stemmed chiles and garlic with the salt in a food processor and pulse until well chopped. With the processor running, drizzle in the lemon juice and process until the mixture reaches a paste consistency.
2. Pack the mash into a jar, pressing out any air pockets as you go. Leave about 1 inch of headspace. You should see some brine above the pulp. Screw the lid down tightly.
3. Set the jar aside to ferment, out of direct sunlight, for 10 to 14 days. This mash pulp tends to stay mixed and, with a tightened lid, doesn't need as much monitoring as some.
4. Start tasting the ferment around day 10. It's ready when the flavors have mingled and have taken on an acidic vinegar-like quality.
5. Return the fermented mash to the food processor and blend while slowly drizzling in the olive oil.
6. Store this ferment in the fridge, where it will keep for 3 months.

YIELD: ½ pint

HEAT INDEX: 2–3

VIETNAMESE DIPPING SAUCE (NUOC CHAM)

This is a light, refreshing dipping sauce for just about anything starchy that needs a little bling — spring rolls (fresh or fried), for example. You can serve it as is, or you can add garnishes, like sliced scallions, minced garlic, or minced cilantro, just before serving.

- 1 cup fresh lime juice
- ⅓ cup water
- ¼ cup fermented fish sauce, soy sauce, or coconut aminos
- 4 tablespoons evaporated cane or palm sugar
- 1 tablespoon pepper mash of choice

Combine the lime juice, water, fish sauce, sugar, and pepper mash in a bowl and stir together. Store the sauce in a sealed jar in the refrigerator, where it will keep for a few months.

HOT TIP

Palm Sugar

Palm sugar is made by boiling the sap of the sugar palm tree (also called date palm) to make a paste or cakes. You can buy it in most Asian markets. We buy the cakes (this solid form of sugar is also called "jaggery") and grate it by hand to add to sauces.

YIELD: 1 pint

HEAT INDEX: 2–3
(assuming Fresno chiles)

SWEET CHILE SAUCE

This recipe uses the Mixed-Media Basic Mash and works especially well with the garlic variation. It is a general-purpose, Asian-inspired, thick, sweet chile sauce for pouring on just about anything.

- 2 cups fermented Mixed-Media Basic Mash (page 95)
- ½ cup tamarind water (see Hot Tip) or rice vinegar
- ½ cup palm sugar or coconut sugar
- ¼ cup fermented fish sauce, soy sauce, or coconut aminos

Combine the mash, tamarind water, palm sugar, and fish sauce in a blender and blend to a smooth sauce. Store in the refrigerator, where the sauce will keep for many months.

HOT TIP

Tamarind Water

Use this acidic liquid in place of vinegar in hot sauces. Like vinegar, tamarind has been used as a preservative in condiments for centuries. Tamarind water adds a wonderful sweet-and-sour flavor to Asian- or South American–style sauces.

To make it, pour 1 cup boiling water over ¼ cup tamarind paste. Use a fork to mash up the paste, then let sit for 1 hour, continuing to stir and break up the mixture occasionally. Then, use the back of a wooden spoon to press the mixture through a fine sieve set over a bowl until you have pushed through all the pulp and liquid. It will be thicker than water or vinegar. Discard the seeds and fibers. Tamarind water will keep in the fridge in an airtight container for 1 to 2 weeks.

Quick Guide to Vinegar

There are many reasons why people add vinegar to fermented hot sauce. First, flavor! Choosing a naturally fermented vinegar with a complementary flavor brings out the chile's flavor. The acids also help balance that heat when it hits your mouth. Plus, preservation! Sugars added after fermentation, fruit or otherwise, will be more food for your hot sauce probiotics, with the result that fermentation continues and the flavors will change over time. Adding vinegar arrests fermentation and keeps any sweeteners or fruity additions stable. Do you have to add vinegar? Nope. Fermentation alone provides plenty of acidity, flavor, and preservation — just keep your ferment refrigerated for best results.

APPLE CIDER VINEGAR: Raw (unpasteurized) apple cider vinegar is a go-to choice. It has a fruity taste and is readily available. The pasteurized version has a similar flavor, though often it is a little more acidic and less fruity.

DISTILLED WHITE VINEGAR: Common in commercial hot sauces. It is strong, clear, clean, and cheap. If you are trying to immitate a hot sauce brand that you love, this vinegar may be the key. Industrially processed from grains, it isn't always gluten-free.

WHITE WINE VINEGAR: Made by introducing acetobacters into white wine. The quality varies greatly, as it is dependent on the quality of the wine used.

RED WINE VINEGAR: Also made from further fermenting wine, this time red wine, usually in oak barrels. Again the flavor is dependent on the quality of the wine, but it often has a smooth, lightly fruity acidity and sometimes wood aromas.

RICE VINEGAR: This vinegar is common in Asian-style sauces and has a mellow acidity and flavorful sweetness. It is a good choice for blending into ferments.

COCONUT VINEGAR: Like apple cider vinegar, coconut vinegar is often sold raw. It is tasty. Traditionally used in Southeast Asia, it has become widely available and is a good choice for diabetics and gluten-intolerant folks. It should be made with the sap from coconut trees; if you are looking for the health benefits, avoid the ones made from coconut water.

MALT VINEGAR: Malt vinegar starts out as a fermented barley ale that is further soured into this traditional English vinegar that is slightly malty and citrusy. It complements pickles, chutney, and hot sauces.

BALSAMIC VINEGAR (WHITE, DARK, OR THICK): Used since the Middle Ages, traditional balsamic is thick, syrupy, sweet, and expensive. It is made from white grape juice that is cooked and reduced, then fermented and aged for a minimum of 12 years. Commercial varieties are sometimes made from white wine vinegar with caramel color and thickeners added. Look for brands that clearly state that they are aged and have no added colors or thickeners.

MEET THE FERMENTISTA

Lisa Murphy, Sosu Sauces

OAKLAND, CALIFORNIA

Beware of conversations at a BBQ. You are sitting around the picnic table passing the ketchup and somebody remarks that all ketchup tastes the same. Before you know it, your friends are looking at you. "Hey, you like to cook. I bet you could make a better ketchup."

That challenge was the genesis of Sosu Sauces. (*Sosu* means "sauce" in Japanese.) Lisa Murphy, founder and chief sauce maker, was intrigued and went home to do some research. She learned that the word *ketchup* comes from her native country of China — *ke-tsiap* is a fermented, fish-based sauce. Lisa dove deep into the origins of the ubiquitous sauce, origins that involve sailors and trade routes and the fear of nightshades; ketchup wasn't even made with tomatoes until 1801.

Lisa knew she wanted to create complex flavors. During a 3-month-long visit to Southeast Asia (sign us up!), she was struck with the importance attributed to having all five flavors — sweet, salty, umami (savory), sour, and bitter — in the cuisines of Laos and Vietnam. She wanted to take the heavily sweet flavor of ketchup, add the spiciness of sriracha, and give it some umami. She found that fermentation was a wonderful way to layer the flavors without adding more (often unnecessary) ingredients.

Lisa had a coworker design and print a label for her creation. Her day job at the time was working at a software startup, which was conveniently located a few blocks from Rainbow Grocery in San Francisco. She took them two jars of her Srirachup, as well as her Classic Tomato Ketchup (a lovely orange condiment made with Golden Jubilee tomatoes). The buyer tasted them and ordered two cases. Sosu Sauces was born.

YIELD: 5 (10-ounce) bottles

TECHNIQUE: Basic Pepper Mash (page 30)

HEAT INDEX: 2–3

SOSU HOMEMADE FERMENTED SRIRACHA

- 5 pounds red chiles (jalapeños, Fresnos, and serranos all work)
- 8 ounces garlic
- 2.4 ounces sea salt
- 1–2 tablespoons fish sauce (optional)
- 10–15 tablespoons sugar (brown sugar, palm sugar, or cane sugar, depending on flavor profile you are going after)

MAKING THE MASH

1. Wash the chiles and trim off the green ends.
2. Combine the chiles, garlic, salt, and fish sauce, if using, in a food processor and process for 30 seconds to 1 minute, or until blended and broken down.
3. Pack the pepper mash into a jar and seal tight. (Remember to leave a couple of inches of headspace for expansion during active fermentation.)
4. Set the jar aside to ferment at room temperature, out of direct sunlight, for 10 to 15 days, or longer if you prefer a tangier flavor profile. The longer you let it ferment, the more acidic your sriracha will become. (A cupboard is a great place for fermentation!)

COOKING AND FINISHING

1. After fermentation, strain the skin and seeds out of the mash using a fine-mesh sieve.
2. Combine the strained sriracha with the sugar in a pot. Bring to a boil, let boil for 1 to 2 minutes, then remove from the heat and pour into bottles. The bottled sriracha will keep for up to 1 year at room temperature. Once you've opened a jar, refrigerate it to retain freshness. It will keep for 8 to 12 months in the refrigerator.

YIELD: About 1 pint

TECHNIQUE: Basic Pepper Mash (page 30)

HEAT INDEX: 1–2

COFFEE SAUCE

This is a smooth, warm, comforting sauce that's tasty on anything from scrambled eggs to a burrito. The mash is infused with coffee during fermentation, which creates a nice depth of flavor. We used fresh guajillo peppers, but any red, fruity pepper will do. Cherry bombs will give about the same heat; Fresnos will take it up a notch.

- 1 pound fresh chiles, stemmed and seeded
- 1 teaspoon salt
- 1 tablespoon freshly ground coffee beans, tied into a pouch made from a coffee filter

1. Process the chiles in a food processor to a salsa-like consistencey. Sprinkle in the salt. The chopped pepper will become juicy immediately.
2. Place the coffee pouch in the bottom of a pint jar. Pack the mash (covering the pouch) into the jar, pressing out any air pockets as you go. Leave about 1 inch of headspace. Screw the lid down tightly.
3. Set the jar aside to ferment, out of direct sunlight, for 14 to 21 days. For the first week or two, check daily to make sure that the mash is submerged in the brine (see Curing Notes, page 32). This isn't usually a problem with this ferment, as the coffee soaks up the brine that normally wants to separate.
4. Start tasting the ferment on day 14. It's ready when the flavors have mingled and taken on an acidic vinegar-like quality. Continue to ferment for more flavor and acidity.
5. Remove the coffee pouch, blend the sauce again if needed, and press it through a sieve to strain. Bottle and store in the fridge, where the sauce will keep for 12 months.

VARIATION: Mocha Sauce

Take your finished Coffee Sauce up a notch to the realm of Mexican hot chocolate. It's almost like liquid mole in a bottle — ready to dash on anything. Blend together the following ingredients:

- 1 cup Coffee Sauce
- 1 tablespoon raw cocoa powder
- ¼ teaspoon ground cinnamon
- ⅛ teaspoon ground cumin
- 1 tablespoon tart cherry molasses (page 109)

YIELD: About 1 pint

TECHNIQUE: Basic Pepper Mash (page 30)

HEAT INDEX: 4–5

VANILLA HABANERO MASH

We have taken this mash on the road to demos and classes. Among those hearty souls who love heat (beware: habaneros!) and are brave enough to try it in public, it has been very popular. The strong vanilla flavor provides an incredible surprise — right after the surprise, and right before the heat sinks in for a long burn, we usually hear, "I love it!"

- ¾ pound habaneros, stemmed and seeded
- 1 teaspoon salt
- 1 vanilla bean, cut into ¼- to ½-inch chunks

1. Combine the chiles and salt in a food processor and process into a mash.
2. Mix in the vanilla bean pieces and pack the mash into a pint jar, pressing out any air pockets as you go. Leave about 1 inch of headspace. Screw the lid down tightly.
3. Set the jar aside to ferment, out of direct sunlight, for 14 to 21 days. For the first week or two, check daily to make sure that the mash is submerged in the brine (see Curing Notes, page 32).
4. Start tasting the ferment on day 14. It's ready when the flavor is lightly acidic and the vanilla notes provide sweetness. Continue to ferment as needed.
5. Use as is, or blend to break down the vanilla beans (the mash will look flecked). Store the mash in the refrigerator, where it will keep for 12 months or more.

VANILLA-PEAR Habanero Sauces

For Vanilla-Pear Habanero Hot Sauce, blend ½ cup Vanilla Habanero Mash, ¼ cup white wine vinegar, and ⅓ cup pear syrup (page 109) until smooth. Bottle and store in the fridge, where the hot sauce will keep for 2 to 3 months.

For Vanilla-Pear Habanero Dessert Sauce, which is amazing on churros, ice cream, or "edgy" pancakes, blend ½ cup mash, ¼ cup white wine vinegar, and 1½ cups pear syrup. Store in the fridge and use within a week or two.

YIELD: About 1 pint

TECHNIQUE: Brine-Based Sauces and Pickles (page 34)

HEAT INDEX: 3–4

HABANERO CARROT SAUCE

This sauce is from Mary Alionis of Whistling Duck Farm in southern Oregon. When we stopped selling our ferments in the local retail markets, Mary — with our recipes and our crocks — took over where we left off. This is Mary's own habanero sauce, and it is mighty fine. The carrots make it reasonable in terms of heat, unless, of course, you choose to use more habaneros. We find that yellow carrots give this ferment a great color, but feel free to use any type of carrot.

- ½ pound yellow carrots, finely sliced
- 1 medium onion, finely sliced
- 3–6 habaneros, seeded and sliced thinly
- 3 cloves garlic, finely sliced
- Juice of 1 lime
- ½–1 cup brine (2 cups unchlorinated water with 1½ tablespoons salt)

1. Combine the carrots, onions, habaneros, and garlic in a bowl with the lime juice and mix well. Pack tightly into a jar to just under the shoulder.
2. Pour in enough brine to cover the vegetables completely. Screw the lid down tightly. (Reserve any leftover brine in the fridge. It will keep for 1 week; discard thereafter and make a new batch, if needed.)
3. Place the jar on a plate and set aside to ferment, out of direct sunlight, for 14 to 21 days. Burp the jar as needed to allow any built-up CO_2 to escape, and make sure the vegetables stay under the brine (see Curing Notes, page 32). If needed, top off with reserved brine solution to keep the vegetables covered.
4. As the vegetables ferment, the color of the carrots and peppers will stay vibrant, but the brine will become cloudy; this is when you can start to taste-test. The vegetables will taste nicely acidic when done.
5. After the fermentation period, purée your ferment, brine and all. If it is thicker than you'd like, you can add a little bit of salt water (¾ teaspoon salt to ½ cup water) until you have reached your desired sauce consistency. Adjust the salt to taste. Store the sauce in an appropriately sized jar or bottle in the refrigerator, where it will keep for 12 months.

VARIATION: Pineapple Habanero Sauce and Syrup

For Pineapple Habanero Sauce — a slightly sweeter, fruity hot sauce — add 3 tablespoons pineapple syrup (see below) when you blend the sauce. For Pineapple Habanero Syrup (a spicy dessert syrup — see Fried Bananas, page 246), add 1 to 2 tablespoons (or 1 teaspoon for mild) habanero sauce to 1 cup pineapple syrup.

Fruit Syrups

It was rather by accident that we discovered how well fruit juice reduction syrups work for crafting a delicious hot sauce. You will see fruit syrups in a few recipes in this book, but we encourage you to experiment. Use this ratio of juice, sugar, and lemon juice to reduce any fruit juice to a syrup that will complement your hot ferments:

- 1 quart pure fruit juice
- ½ cup evaporated cane sugar
- 1 tablespoon lemon juice

Use a wide saucepan with a large surface area to shorten the cooking time. Combine the juice, sugar, and lemon juice in the saucepan over medium-high heat. Stir until the sugar is dissolved. Bring the juice to a simmer, then reduce the heat to maintain a low simmer, stirring occasionally to check the consistency. It can take anywhere from 45 minutes to 1 hour or more to get a smooth syrup. When the juice is reduced to between 1½ and ¾ cups, it is ready.

Here are some variations on fruit syrup to get you going:

- We find **pineapple juice** makes great syrup for adding to hot sauces. See Pineapple Habanero Sauce, above.
- For a pure-fruit **pear syrup** with no added sugar, use pear juice (the thick, cloudy kind) and omit the cane sugar. Simmer the juice over very low heat to prevent the thick bubbles from splattering.
- For **pomegranate or tart cherry molasses**, use pure pomegranate or tart cherry juice, and add 1 extra tablespoon of sugar to the mixture if you're using cherry juice. Reduce the syrup to as little as ½ cup for a thick molasses.

YIELD: About 10 ounces

HEAT INDEX: 2–3

ALEPPO ZA'ATAR–POMEGRANATE SAUCE

This sauce is wonderful with Middle Eastern and Mediterranean cuisine. It has a rich, lingering heat, a nice tartness, and a smoky flavor. We tried four variations on the theme for this recipe, and this one beat out all the others. In the runner-up sauce, we infused the za'atar in the vinegar instead of blending it in the sauce, which created a smoother sauce, but it separated a bit on the plate. If you like a thinner, smoother sauce, use the same ingredients but bring the vinegar to a boil with the za'atar and allow to sit for 2 hours. Strain out the za'atar and blend the vinegar with the mash and molasses.

- 1 cup Basic Go-to Mash (page 92) made with fresh Aleppo peppers,* strained
- 2 teaspoons za'atar
- ¼ cup plus 1 tablespoon white wine vinegar
- 1½ tablespoons pomegranate molasses (page 109)

Combine the mash, za'atar, vinegar, and molasses in a blender and blend until smooth. Put in a hot sauce shaker bottle. This sauce will keep, refrigerated, for 6 months.

** Fresh Aleppo peppers are generally not available fresh for purchase in this country but are easy to grow in the garden. The seeds are readily available online. You may also substitute fresh Fresno peppers, or use the dried powdered Aleppo pepper in a red bell pepper mash (page 93).*

Make Your Own Za'atar Spice Blend

If you cannot find a za'atar spice blend, you can make your own. Combine the following:

- ¼ cup ground sumac berries
- 2 tablespoons dried marjoram
- 2 tablespoons dried oregano
- 2 tablespoons dried thyme
- 1 tablespoon toasted sesame seeds

JAMAICAN JERK SAUCE
ALEPPO ZA´ATAR – POMEGRANATE SAUCE
COOKED TOMATO HOT SAUCE
SWEET CHILE SAUCE
HABANERO CARROT SAUCE
PIRI PIRI SAUCE

YIELD: About 2 pints

HEAT INDEX: Depends on how much pepper paste you use

POMEGRANATE BARBECUE SAUCE

We knew we wanted to create a barbecue sauce for this book, as fermented peppers lend themselves so well to sauces. We also knew we wanted to share a unique sauce flavor, instead of simply replacing the chile flakes with pepper mash in a Kansas City–style sauce or Texas-style sauce — which, we might add, is a perfectly delicious thing to do. This sauce was inspired by one given to our dear friend Vicki by her friend Mitra. It is wonderfully sweet and fruity, and you can decide your heat level by how much pepper paste you add.

- 1 onion
- 1–2 tablespoons olive oil, for frying
- 6 cloves garlic, minced
- 3 cups tomato sauce
- 1½ cups pomegranate molasses (see page 109)
- ½ cup dark molasses
- ⅛ cup honey
- 1 tablespoon apple cider vinegar
- 1 tablespoon freshly ground coriander
- 1 tablespoon freshly ground cumin
- 1 tablespoon smoked paprika
- 1 teaspoon ground cinnamon
- ½ teaspoon freshly ground allspice
- ½ teaspoon ground dry ginger
- ¼ teaspoon freshly ground black pepper
- ¼ teaspoon ground dry turmeric
- 2–6 tablespoons Basic Go-To Mash (page 92), other fermented pepper paste, or Habanero Carrot sauce (page 107)

1. Chop the onion finely in a food processer or with a vegetable chopper — the smaller the better. Warm the olive oil in a saucepan over medium heat, add the onion, and sauté, stirring frequently until translucent.

2. Add the garlic and sauté for a minute longer, taking care that it doesn't burn or stick. Place the onion and garlic in a slow cooker and add the tomato sauce, pomegranate molasses, dark molasses, honey, vinegar, coriander, cumin, paprika, cinnamon, allspice, ginger, black pepper, and turmeric.

3. Set the slow cooker on low heat and allow to simmer for 3 to 4 hours. Check occasionally to make sure the sauce is not burning on the edges (stir and lower heat, if it is). When the sauce is reduced to the thick, almost syrupy consistency of a BBQ sauce, add the pepper paste and simmer for 20 to 30 more minutes.

YIELD: 1½ pints

TECHNIQUE: Pastes and Mustards (page 37)

HEAT INDEX: 4

JAMAICAN JERK SAUCE

Allspice is the star ingredient in Jamaican jerk seasoning, so often found in rubs, marinades, and sauces. Use the pure ferment as a rub, add some vinegar and use it as a marinade, or add a little more vinegar and some tamarind water and you have a delicious sauce.

- ½ cup Basic Go-To Mash (page 92) made with fresh habaneros
- ½ bunch scallions
- 5 cloves garlic
- 1½ tablespoons freshly ground allspice
- 1 tablespoon freshly ground black pepper
- 1 tablespoon dried thyme
- 1 teaspoon ground cinnamon
- 1 teaspoon freshly ground coriander seed
- 1 teaspoon freshly grated nutmeg
- ½ cup white wine vinegar
- 1 cup tamarind water (page 100)

1. Combine the habanero mash with the scallions, garlic, allspice, black pepper, thyme, cinnamon, coriander, and nutmeg in a food processor and process to a paste consistency.
2. Pack the paste carefully into a jar that is just the right size for your ferment, pressing out any air pockets as you go. Leave about 1 inch of headspace. There will be only a small amount of thick brine that may be hard to distinguish from the rest of the paste. Don't worry if it disappears between pressings.
3. Press a piece of plastic (or other cartouche) against the surface of the ferment, being careful not to trap any air beneath it. Screw the lid down tightly.
4. Set the jar in a corner of the kitchen to ferment, and watch for air pockets forming. If you see any, open the lid and press the paste back down. If the lid starts to bulge, simply open it for a moment to burp the ferment.
5. Allow to ferment for 7 to 14 days. Though the peppers are already fermented and the sauce can be used immediately, this extra curing time allows the other ingredients to ferment and the flavors to mingle. It is done when you can't wait any longer.
6. If you want a rub rather than a sauce, stop now. Place a clean small round of plastic or parchment paper directly on top of the paste. Tighten the lid, then store in the fridge, where the rub will keep for 6 to 12 months.

(continued on next page)

7. Otherwise, put the finished paste in a blender, add the vinegar, and blend until smooth. If you want a marinade rather than a sauce, stop now. Pour the marinade into a bottle and store in the refrigerator, where it will keep for a year or more.

8. For the sauce, add the tamarind water to the blender and blend until smooth. Bottle and store in the refrigerator, where it will keep for 2 to 6 months.

YIELD: ½ gallon

TECHNIQUE: Brine-Based Sauces and Pickles (page 34)

HEAT INDEX: Depends on the chile variety

COOKED TOMATO HOT SAUCE

One strategy that folks are using to ferment hot sauces — especially tomato-based sauces — is to ferment, then cook, then add live cultures and ferment again to bring back that "live" taste. Fermenting tomatoes is troublesome because they are a fruit with a high sugar content. The sugars in fruits tend to ferment better with yeasts (think wine) than bacteria, so when you try to lacto-ferment you often get something else entirely — like the flavor of something going bad. You can work around this problem, by using dried tomatoes (or tomato leaves, as in the Mock Tomato Salsa recipe, page 123) or by cooking the tomatoes first.

It may sound like a tedious process, but the result is a wonderfully complex hot sauce that goes on everything. Brian Lyman, cofounder of Cauldron Fermented Foods in Boston, shared this recipe for a very delicious, live, salsa-style hot sauce.

PART 1

- 1½ pounds chiles, stemmed (serrano and cherry peppers are a fantastic combination of flavor and spice)
- 1 red onion, coarsely chopped
- 3 heads garlic, cloves separated and peeled
- 1 quart brine (1 quart unchlorinated water with 3 tablespoons salt)

1. Combine the chiles, onion, and garlic in a fermenting vessel and cover with the brine.
2. Set the mixture aside to ferment for 4 to 6 weeks.
3. When fermentation is complete, strain the pepper mixture, reserving the brine.
4. Using a food processor or blender, blend the peppers until smooth. This may take some time, as they still have their seeds, and you may need to add some brine. The sauce should have a sriracha consistency — thinner than ketchup, but thicker than Tabasco. At this point you have a fine hot sauce, which you can use as is (or strained for a thinner sauce) or take onward to part 2 to add the cooked tomatoes.

(continued on next page)

COOKED TOMATO HOT SAUCE *continued*

PART 2

- 6 large tomatoes, roasted
- 1 cup brown sugar
- ½ cup fire cider (page 238) or apple cider vinegar
- Cayenne pepper (optional)

5. Add the roasted tomatoes to the blender with the pepper medley and blend until smooth.

6. Combine the blended pepper and tomato mixture, brown sugar, and fire cider in a saucepan. Add the cayenne if you want the sauce to be spicier. Bring to a simmer and let simmer for 45 minutes, stirring occasionally.

7. Remove the sauce from the heat and let cool. Add 2 cups of the reserved fermenting brine to the sauce and stir to combine.

8. Pour the sauce into jars, leaving 1 inch of headspace. Store in a cool place and age for at least 3 weeks. The sauce will continue to slowly ferment and may need to be burped, so keep an eye on it. After 3 weeks, transfer to the refrigerator, where the sauce will keep for about a year. Enjoy.

CH 6

SALSAS, RELISHES, AND CHUTNEYS . . . OH MY!

These condiments include those strong-flavored pickle-y sides that add bling to our meals. What are the differences among them all? Good question; it's a bit subjective and, ultimately, a matter of preference and semantics. Here are our interpretations.

While we understand that *salsa* simply means "sauce" and could embody a myriad of flavors and textures, our salsa recipes are meant to be starters to which you add fresh ingredients that keep the salsa crisp and light. Relishes are pickled chopped-vegetable mixtures flavored with peppers and herbs; they have lighter flavors than chutney and achar. Chutney is made from a wide variety of fruits, veggies, and spices — part of this has to do with the branch of the chutney family that was developed by the British colonists in India who married their sweet fruit jams with strongly spiced Indian pickles. Chutneys are sweet and sour and, for the most part, thick and pungent. Achars we define as the ferment that uses sun and oil. They are pungent and creamy-rich but not sweet.

ABOUT SALSA STARTERS

Fresh salsa adds a delightful, lighthearted element to a meal. With fermentation, you can preserve spicy vegetable and pepper combinations that stay alive and crisp and then use these combinations as starters throughout the winter to create fun, lively salsas just by adding a few fresh ingredients — avocados, tomatoes, mangos, black beans, sweet corn, or even crabmeat. (Do you see a theme here? These "fresh" ingredients are the ones that are not easily preserved through fermentation.)

We've upped the salt in these starters a bit, since you will be adding other ingredients before serving — we wanted to make them as convenient as possible. Each of these starters makes about a quart. If you are a gardener, feel free to adjust the quantities to preserve your harvest.

The starters will last about 12 months if stored in the refrigerator. However, once you add the fresh ingredients, the salsa will taste good for about a week, maybe two, before it will begin to take on some of the fizz and funk of fermentation.

MOCK TOMATO SALSA

YIELD: About 1 quart

TECHNIQUE: Kimchis, Relishes, and Salads (page 40)

HEAT INDEX: 3

BASIC PICO DE GALLO STARTER

This simple starter can be used for any kind of salsa fresca, from tomato to watermelon. It also works well stirred into avocados for guacamole. After fermentation, to make salsa, add ½ cup of the starter to 3 cups diced fresh tomatoes (or whatever fresh ingredients you dream up).

- 2 onions
- 1 poblano
- 10 jalapeños, or a combination of chiles
- 1 bunch cilantro
- 6–8 cloves garlic
- Zest and juice of 2 limes
- 1½ teaspoons salt
- ½ teaspoon freshly ground black pepper

1. Dice and mince the onions, poblano, jalapeños, cilantro, garlic, and lime zest by hand, or pulse in a food processor to achieve a chunky fresh-salsa consistency. Mix in the lime juice, salt, and pepper.
2. Pack the mixture into a jar, pressing out any air pockets as you go. Press a ziplock bag against the surface of the ferment, fill the bag with water, and zip it closed.
3. Place the jar in a corner of the kitchen to ferment. If you see air pockets, remove the bag, press the ferment back down with a clean utensil, rinse the bag, and replace.
4. Allow to ferment for 7 to 14 days. You will know it is ready when the colors have muted and the flavor has an acidic lemon-like or pickle-y flavor.
5. Place a clean small round of plastic or parchment paper directly on top of the paste. Screw on the lid, then store in the fridge, where this ferment will keep for up to 12 months.

VARIATION: Salsa Verde

YIELD: ½ GALLON HEAT INDEX: 1–2

Unlike ripe red tomatoes, tomatillos and green tomatoes ferment well and hold up during storage. For salsa verde, add 1 more teaspoon salt and 4 cups diced tomatillos, green tomatoes, or a combination of the two to the Basic Pico de Gallo Starter.

YIELD: About 1 quart

TECHNIQUE: Kimchis, Relishes, and Salads (page 40)

HEAT INDEX: 4

XNI PEC

Xni pec is pico de gallo's fiery cousin from the Yucatán. The word is Mayan and roughly translates to "dog nose" or "snout." Some speculate that this salsa's name derives from the fact that it is so hot it makes you pant like a dog, or it makes your nose run (and a dog's nose is always wet), but *pico de gallo* translates as "rooster's beak," so who knows? Xni pec is so hot in part because it doesn't rely on tomato to make up the bulk of the salsa. After fermentation, to make salsa, add one chopped tomato to 1 cup of the starter.

- 3 large red onions, minced
- 12–16 habaneros, seeded and minced
- 4 tablespoons chopped cilantro
- Zest and juice of 6 limes
- 1½ teaspoons salt

Follow the instructions for Basic Pico de Gallo Starter (page 121), subsituting the ingredients at left.

HOT-AND-SWEET SALSA STARTER

This starter is primarily intended to become a fruit salsa, but it also works beautifully with avocados, tomatoes, or tomatillos. After fermentation, to make salsa, add 1 cup of the starter to 2 cups diced fruit — any combination of mango, papaya, orange wedges, pineapple, star fruit, et cetera.

- 1 large onion, diced
- 1 cup diced jicama
- 10–12 large serrano chiles, seeded and minced
- ½ red bell pepper, minced
- 2 teaspoons grated fresh ginger
- 3 tablespoons chopped fresh mint
- ¼ teaspoon freshly ground allspice
- Zest and juice of 2 oranges

Follow the instructions for Basic Pico de Gallo Starter (page 121), subsituting the ingredients at left.

YIELD: About 1½ pints

TECHNIQUE: Kimchis, Relishes, and Salads (page 40)

HEAT INDEX: 2

MOCK TOMATO SALSA

A lot of people ferment tomato salsa and love it, but we find the flavor of fermented fresh tomatoes to be a bit too close to the flavor of something going bad. However, you can get the flavor notes of fresh tomatoes into your ferments by using the leaves.

The tomato leaf's most notable proponent is Paul Bertolli, who used the leaves to infuse a sauce during his tenure at Chez Panisse, Alice Waters's acclaimed restaurant. Most of us have heard that they are toxic, a rumor left over, perhaps, from when humans thought the tomato itself was toxic. In fact, a study done by the FDA concludes that all parts of the tomato contain varying amounts of the alkaloid tomatine. The leaves have only slightly more than an unripe green tomato, and an adult would have to eat a whole pound of leaves to get a toxic dose. Some studies show tomatine may actually have some benefits for our immune system, as well as cancer-inhibiting properties. The takeaway is that tomato leaves can be safely used as an herb (and there is so much we don't know).

The thick-walled peppers that we recommend for this ferment give it an incredibly thick texture, though the recipe will work with any peppers, hot or sweet.

- 1½ pounds fresh cascabel, cherry bomb, or pimento peppers, seeded and roughly chopped
- ½ onion, roughly chopped
- ¼ cup loosely packed cilantro
- 5 sprigs (about 2 tablespoons chopped) young tomato leaves
- 3 cloves garlic
- Juice of 1 lime
- 1 teaspoon salt

1. Combine the peppers, onion, cilantro, tomato leaves, garlic, and lime juice in a food processor and process to the consistency of a thick fresh salsa. Sprinkle in the salt; the paste will become moist right away.
2. Pack the mixture into a jar, pressing out any air pockets as you go. Press a ziplock bag against the surface of the ferment, fill the bag with water, and zip it closed.
3. Place the jar in a corner of the kitchen to ferment. If you see air pockets, remove the bag, press the ferment back down with a clean utensil, rinse the bag, and replace.
4. Allow to ferment for 7 days. You will know it is ready when the ferment has a pleasing pickle-y smell and flavor.
5. Place a clean small round of plastic or parchment paper directly on top of the paste. Screw on the lid, then store in the fridge, where this ferment will keep for 12 months.

ACHAR: SUN PICKLES FROM THE INDIAN SUBCONTINENT

Achars are very different from the brine-drenched ferments that most folks are familiar with. In fact, they sit in the sun, proudly fermenting in a fairly dry mix of spices, ground mustard, and mustard oil. How?

Let's start with the oxygen. Lactic-acid bacteria (our pickle makers) are facultative anaerobes, which means that they do not require oxygen. That doesn't mean that they cannot survive in oxygen, but an oxygen-free brine bath keeps the yeasts and molds and other party spoilers out. We also generally keep our ferments out of the sun to keep them from getting too warm too quickly. But in the case of achar, which hails from the Indian subcontinent, the sun is a tool.

CUCUMBER ACHAR

Often the vegetables are first partially sun-dried, as you will see in the case of the Cucumber Achar (page 126) and Daikon Achar (page 128). Then the other ingredients are added and the mixture is placed in the sun. The sun does what the brine does in briny ferments — makes the environment inhospitable to mold and yeasts, in this case by destroying them with UV light.

Achar fermentation works for any vegetable you can think of, from whole chiles to green beans and radishes. Traditionally these ferments are made with mustard oil, which has antifungal and antibacterial qualities (along with a whole list of health benefits). Mustard oil can be found online or at Indian markets, but olive oil makes a fine substitute.

YIELD: About 1 pint

TECHNIQUE: Kimchis, Relishes, and Salads (page 40)

HEAT INDEX: 3

RHUBARB ACHAR

This achar is inspired by Nepalese flavors but does not use the oil and sun method like the other achar recipes do. It gets its heat from three places — mustard seed, Szechuan pepper, and chiles. At the onset this pickled relish hits the tongue mildly, with tart notes of lime, but don't get used to it. The heat builds to a flavorful burn that lingers for a bit, thanks to the Szechuan pepper.

Rhubarb is one of the first spring vegetables, and fresh hot peppers are still an entire growing season away, so this recipe uses premade fermented pepper mash that you will always want to have on hand for just these times.

- ½ pound rhubarb (2–3 medium stalks), sliced microthin crosswise at an angle
- 4 cloves garlic, sliced thinly
- 1 tablespoon grated fresh turmeric
- ½ teaspoon salt
- 3 tablespoons Basic Go-To Mash (page 92)*
- 1 teaspoon black mustard seeds, toasted and ground
- 1 teaspoon Szechuan pepper, toasted and ground
- ½ teaspoon fennel seeds, toasted and ground
- ½ teaspoon fenugreek seeds, toasted and ground

1. Combine the rhubarb, garlic, and turmeric in a bowl. Sprinkle with the salt and massage it in to help release the juices. Add the pepper mash and mix well. Then add the mustard seeds, Szechuan pepper, fennel seeds, and fenugreek seeds. At this point you should have a moist mixture with a chutney-like consistency.
2. Pack the mixture into a jar, pressing out any air pockets as you go. Press a ziplock bag against the surface of the ferment, fill the bag with water, and zip it closed.
3. Place the jar in a corner of the kitchen to ferment. If you see air pockets, remove the bag, press the ferment back down with a clean utensil, rinse the bag, and replace.
4. Allow to ferment for 6 to 7 days. The colors of this ferment will mute and the brine will become cloudy. When it is ready, the ferment will smell pleasingly acidic and taste pickle-y, and it may have a bit of an effervescent zing. You can let it ferment longer for more sour and punch.
5. Screw on the lid and store in the refrigerator, where this ferment will keep for up to 6 months.

**If you don't have fermented pepper mash, you can substitute two or three fresh Fresno peppers or other red chiles, diced and tossed with a scant ¼ teaspoon of salt.*

YIELD: About 1½ quarts

HEAT INDEX: 3

CUCUMBER ACHAR (KAKRO KO ACHAR)

These Nepalese pickles have a very different flavor from what our Western tastes are used to, but don't let that let scare you off. Authentic kakro ko achar uses mustard oil, which has wonderful preservative qualities and flavor but is hard to find. Olive oil is a suitable substitute. The ground spices, sesame, and oil have an almost pesto-like consistency, a counterbalance to the cucumber's crunch. The cool cucumber counters the heat of the Szechuan pepper. This pickle hits your tongue as mild and creamy, and then, slowly, the heat starts on the top front of your tongue and makes its way back through your throat with a lingering tingle. The first bite is confusing, but everybody comes back for more.

For gardeners, the best thing about this recipe is that it makes great use of the large cucumbers that hide under leaves and escape your notice. The Nepalese know all about it and even have a special word for a pickle made from matured cucumbers — *khalpi*.

While the flavor of this achar is unique, we find it versatile, whether you put it on a burger, atop a winter stew, in a wrap, or in a spicy fermented side salad.

- 2 pounds cucumbers
- 2 tablespoons salt
- ¾ cup sesame seeds
- 2 tablespoons toasted coriander seeds
- 2 tablespoons ground Szechuan pepper
- 1½ tablespoons freshly ground black pepper
- 1 tablespoon toasted cumin seeds
- 2 tablespoons tamarind pulp, deseeded*
- 4 tablespoons fermented pepper mash of choice or 1–2 tablespoons dried pepper flakes
- 5 tablespoons olive oil

** Tamarind pulp comes in a block. The deseeded variety still has some seeds. The best way to use it is to soak the pulp in warm water for about 20 minutes and then press it through a sieve to make a paste.*

1. Cut the cucumbers lengthwise into quarters. Remove the seeds. Partially dehydrate the cucumbers by leaving them overnight in a dehydrator at 100°F or in the bright summer sun for 2 days. The outer skin will be dry, and they will have a somewhat rubbery consistency. Chop into ½-inch chunks and place in a bowl.
2. Combine the salt, sesame seeds, coriander, Szechuan pepper, black pepper, and cumin seeds in a blender or food processor with the tamarind paste and pepper mash and blend to a smooth consistency. Toss with the cucumber chunks until they are well coated.
3. Pack the mixture into a jar that is just the right size for your ferment. Pour the olive oil over the top of the mixture and screw the jar lid down tightly.

4. Place the jar in a sunny window to ferment for 3 to 5 days (or longer in the winter). The achar will taste pickle-y sour when it is ready.

5. Store in the refrigerator, where this ferment will keep for about 3 months.

YIELD: About 1 quart

HEAT INDEX: 3

DAIKON ACHAR

The second time we made daikon achar, we dehydrated the daikons too long — okay, we forgot about them. By the time we remembered, they were quite a bit drier than we were aiming for, but not being ones to waste food we proceeded.

After a week and a half of fermentation, we opened up the jar to taste. The flavor was amazing. Usually radishes lose their special brand of nose-wrinkling heat with fermentation. We think that because the daikons were so dehydrated, their pungency was concentrated and sealed inside. It was a great discovery. When we repeated the recipe we "over"dehydrated again. The combined heat of the radish, mustard seed, Szechuan pepper, and chile peppers confuses the senses in a delightful way.

- 3 purple daikon radishes (about 1½ pounds), or whatever type of daikon you have
- 10 habaneros, sliced, or 2 tablespoons fermented habanero mash
- 2 tablespoons brown mustard seeds, toasted and ground
- 2 teaspoons salt
- 1 teaspoon ground turmeric
- ½ teaspoon Szechuan pepper, toasted and ground
- 4 tablespoons olive oil

1. Remove the stem ends and cut the daikons lengthwise into quarters. Place them in a dehydrator at 100°F (38°C) for 6 to 8 hours or in the bright summer sun for a day or two. They should be dry on the outside and a bit rubbery and leathery.
2. Chop the daikon into bite-size chunks and place in a bowl. Add the habaneros, mustard seeds, salt, turmeric, and Szechuan pepper, and toss to coat the daikon. Add 2 tablespoons of the oil and toss again.
3. Pack the mixture into a jar that is just the right size for your ferment. Pour the remaining 2 tablespoons of oil over the top of the mixture and screw the jar lid down tightly.
4. Place the jar in a sunny window to ferment for 7 to 14 days. The achar will taste pickle-y sour when it is ready.
5. Store in the refrigerator, where this ferment will keep for about 6 months.

YIELD: About 1 quart

HEAT INDEX: 2

LEMON ACHAR

Preserved lemons are delicious, but this condiment takes them a step further — they are tart and spicy and just a bit creamy. This recipe is loosely based on a vinegar pickle recipe, Nimbu Ka Achar, by food writer Smita Chandra.

- 10 red Thai chiles, thinly sliced*
- 4 Meyer lemons, quartered, seeded, and thinly sliced
- 5 cloves garlic, thinly sliced
- 1 (1-inch) piece ginger, thinly sliced
- 1½ tablespoons grated fresh turmeric
- 1 teaspoon toasted brown mustard seeds
- ½ teaspoon toasted cumin seeds
- ½ teaspoon toasted fenugreek seeds
- 1 teaspoon salt
- Juice of 1 lemon
- 4 tablespoons olive oil

1. Combine the chiles, lemons, garlic, ginger, and turmeric in a large bowl. Add the toasted spices: mustard seeds, cumin seeds, and fenugreek seeds. Add the salt, lemon juice, and 2 tablespoons of the olive oil and mix well.
2. Pack the mixture into a jar that is just the right size for your ferment. Pour the remaining 2 tablespoons of olive oil over the top of the mixture and screw the jar lid down tightly.
3. Place the jar in a sunny window to ferment for 7 to 14 days. It will taste pickle-y sour when it is ready.
4. Store in the refrigerator, where this ferment will keep for about 12 months.

**Hint: Hold these tiny chiles by the stem and cut them with scissors right over the bowl.*

YIELD: About 1 pint

TECHNIQUE: Kimchis, Relishes, and Salads (page 40)

HEAT INDEX: 3–4

BULGARIAN CARROT PEPPER RELISH

For some reason we find the Bulgarian Carrot peppers to be hotter, or at least harder to eat, than habaneros. Maybe it is because we grow our own peppers, and our conditions lend themselves to crazy hot Bulgarians and reasonable habaneros. Maybe it is because the heat comes on so bracingly strong before you even knew you took a bite. In this relish, the eggplant tempers the pepper and gives you a chance to catch your breath between bites.

- 1 medium eggplant (about ¾ pound)
- 1 tablespoon plus ½ teaspoon salt
- 14–16 (or 8 ounces) Bulgarian Carrot peppers
- 1 cup packed basil leaves
- 5 cloves garlic

1. Dice the eggplant into ¼-inch cubes and place in a bowl. Toss the eggplant with 1 tablespoon of the salt, making sure all the eggplant is coated. Cover and set aside for 2 hours.
2. Remove the seeds from the peppers and dice them. This relish is better with consistently sized pepper pieces, so hand dicing is better than a food processor. However, you can use the food processor to pulse the basil leaves, garlic, and remaining ½ teaspoon salt until consistent and moist. The mixture does not need to be a fine paste. Combine the diced peppers with the basil mixture in a medium bowl, mix well, cover, and set aside until the eggplant is ready.
3. After 2 hours, drain the eggplant cubes by squeezing them in a clean dish towel or pressing them in a colander. Mix the eggplant into the pepper mixture.
4. Pack the mixture into a jar, pressing out any air pockets as you go. Press a ziplock bag against the surface of the ferment, fill the bag with water, and zip it closed.
5. Place the jar in a corner of the kitchen to ferment. If you see air pockets, remove the bag, press the ferment back down with a clean utensil, rinse the bag, and replace.
6. Allow to ferment for 5 to 10 days. You will know the relish is ready when the flavors have mingled and it smells pleasantly acidic. The colors of this ferment blend and mute together.
7. Screw on the lid and store in the refrigerator, where this ferment will keep for 6 to 8 months.

Cold War Pepper Smuggling?

Rumor has it that the dramatically hot Bulgarian Carrot peppers were rustled out from behind the Iron Curtain sometime in the 1980s. Despite being called Bulgarian, these peppers are said to hail from Hungary, where they are called *shipkas*.

YIELD: About 1 pint

TECHNIQUE: Kimchis, Relishes, and Salads (page 40)

HEAT INDEX: 1–2

ADZHIKA, A GEORGIAN PEPPER RELISH

This is a spicy pepper relish that varies a bit from region to region. Traditional adzhika is pickled with wine vinegar and usually canned, but it was easy to imagine a fermented version. This recipe is adapted from one in *The Georgian Feast* by Darra Goldstein. We were intrigued by the combination of cilantro, which feels like such an Asian herb, and dill, which seems quintessentially European. But the combination of dill with hot peppers — well, that rocked our world.

It can be difficult to find fresh dill weed when the peppers are on. We have made this relish with fresh and dried dill, and either way the results are quite pleasing.

- ½ pound cayenne, Fresno, or your favorite red chiles, seeded and coarsely chopped
- ½ red bell pepper, coarsely chopped
- 1 stalk celery, coarsely chopped
- 2 cloves garlic, minced
- 1 cup loosely packed fresh dill weed, coarsely chopped, or 3 tablespoons dried dill
- ¼ cup loosely packed fresh cilantro, coarsely chopped
- 1 teaspoon salt

1. Combine the chiles, bell pepper, celery, garlic, dill, and cilantro in a food processor and process to a thick relish or almost paste-like consistency. Sprinkle in the salt. The paste will become moist right away but will not look juicy.
2. Pack the mixture into a jar, pressing out any air pockets as you go. Press a ziplock bag against the surface of the ferment, fill the bag with water, and zip it closed.
3. Place the jar in a corner of the kitchen to ferment. If you see air pockets, remove the bag, press the ferment back down with a clean utensil, rinse the bag, and replace.
4. Allow to ferment for 7 days. The relish is ready when it has a pleasing pickle-y smell and flavor.
5. Place a clean small round of plastic or parchment paper directly on top of the paste. Screw on the lid and store in the fridge, where the relish will keep for up to 12 months.

ADZHIKA
THAI-INSPIRED GREEN
BEAN RELISH
CARIBBEAN SALSA
HOT CINNAMON QUINCE
FERMENT

YIELD: About 1 quart

TECHNIQUE: Kimchis, Relishes, and Salads (page 40)

HEAT INDEX: 3

THAI-INSPIRED GREEN BEAN RELISH

This green bean relish is hot and crunchy. Its heat comes on slowly, after you have tasted the other flavors, which makes it unique. Then it lingers with a full-body warming effect. If you want more burn, simply add more Thai peppers.

- 1 pound green beans
- 1 teaspoon salt
- 13 fresh or dried Thai dragon chiles (or Thai bird's eye chiles), chopped with seeds
- 1 medium shallot, diced
- 1 tablespoon chopped fresh Thai basil
- 2 stalks lemongrass, cut into 1-inch segments

1. First prepare the green beans. Your goal is small slices, and how you get there is really up to you. We use a mandoline and are able to achieve a consistent, thin, slightly diagonal crosswise slice. If you don't have a mandoline, you may julienne your beans or use the slicer blade on a food processor. However you do it, when the green beans are thinly sliced, sprinkle in the salt and mix well.
2. Add the chiles, shallot, and Thai basil, and massage the whole mixture together. This ferment will not look very juicy.
3. Line the bottom of a quart jar with the stalks of lemongrass, then pack the green bean mixture in tightly, pressing out any air pockets as you go.
4. Press a ziplock bag against the surface of the relish, fill the bag with water, and zip it closed.
5. Place the jar in a corner of the kitchen to cure. If you see air pockets, remove the bag, press the ferment back down with a clean utensil, rinse the bag, and replace.
6. Allow to ferment for 10 to 21 days. The relish is ready when you see the color of the green beans mute; you may also see a cloudiness develop in the brine. The ferment will have a pleasing acidic smell and taste pickle-y, and it may also have a bit of an effervescent zing. You can let it ferment longer for more sour and punch.
7. Screw on the lid and store in the fridge, where the relish will keep for up to 12 months.

YIELD: About 1 quart

TECHNIQUE: Kimchis, Relishes, and Salads (page 40)

HEAT INDEX: 2

HOT CINNAMON QUINCE FERMENT

Quince is an ancient fruit you may see in the produce section in fall, near the apples and pears. It looks like a badass pear — tougher, a little misshapen, and larger, with sunny, vibrant yellow skin that is often a bit blemished and sometimes slightly fuzzy. It doesn't have the curbside appeal of a pear or apple. If you have experienced quince, you will know that it is not to be eaten raw, but cooked it is delicious, and it turns out to be tasty when fermented as well. This ferment tastes a bit like a fruity Red Hots candy with some citrus notes.

- 2 pounds quince, cored and chopped
- Zest and juice of 1 lemon
- 1 tablespoon salt
- 2 teaspoons grated fresh ginger
- 1¼ teaspoons ground cinnamon
- 1 teaspoon chile flakes
- ½ teaspoon finely ground white pepper

1. Process the quince to pea-sized pieces in a food processor. Combine the quince with the lemon zest and juice, salt, ginger, cinnamon, chile flakes, and white pepper in a bowl and mix well.
2. Pack the mixture into a jar, pressing out any air pockets as you go. Press a ziplock bag against the surface of the ferment, fill the bag with water, and zip it closed.
3. Place the jar in a corner of the kitchen to ferment. If you see air pockets, remove the bag, press the ferment back down with a clean utensil, rinse the bag, and replace.
4. Allow to ferment for 14 to 21 days. It's ready when you notice a pleasing acidic smell and the flavor becomes acidic in a lemony way, with a strong cinnamon flavor throughout. No need to wait for the quince to soften — it won't. You can let it ferment longer for more sour and punch.
5. Screw on the lid and store in the fridge, where the ferment will keep for up to 12 months.

YIELD: About 1½ pints

TECHNIQUE: Pastes and Mustards (page 37)

HEAT INDEX: 2

CHOCOLATE–CRANBERRY MOLE

A new favorite! Straight out of the jar? Yes, please! On a sandwich?! In a wrap? On a dessert (page 248)? In a plane? On a train? Absolutely.

If you don't have dried unsweetened cherries, you can substitute an equal amount of additional dried cranberries.

- 4 cups (1 pound) fresh cranberries
- 1 cup dried cranberries
- ½ cup dried unsweetened cherries
- 5 tablespoons (2 ounces) pasilla chile powder
- 2¼ teaspoons cocoa powder
- ½ cup fresh orange juice
- ¾ teaspoon salt

1. Combine the fresh cranberries, dried cranberries, cherries, chile powder, and cocoa powder in a food processor. Add the orange juice and process the mixture to a paste consistency. Sprinkle in the salt.
2. Pack the paste into a jar that is just the right size for your ferment, pressing out any air pockets as you go. Leave about 1 inch of headspace.
3. Press a piece of plastic (or other cartouche) against the surface of the ferment, being careful not to trap any air beneath it. Screw the lid down tightly.
4. Set the jar in a corner of the kitchen to ferment, and watch for air pockets forming in the paste. If you see any, open the lid and press the paste back down. If the lid starts to bulge, simply open it for a moment to burp the ferment.
5. Allow to ferment for 7 to 14 days. You will know it is ready when the cranberries have a delightful lemony flavor and all the flavors have mingled together.
6. When it is ready, place a clean small round of plastic or parchment paper directly on top of the paste. Tighten the lid, then store in the fridge, where this ferment will keep for up to 12 months.

YIELD: 1 quart

TECHNIQUE: Kimchis, Relishes, and Salads (page 40)

HEAT INDEX: 2

SPICY ONION–MANGO FERMENT

If you find comfort in walking into an Indian restaurant and being greeted by the warm aromas of curry and garam marsala, this is your ferment. If you don't like the smell of fermenting cabbage, this is your ferment. Its deep, rich smell invites you to go ahead and have some — on a sandwich, with a meal, in some soup, or straight out of the jar.

And the color of this ferment is unusual: the red of the onions drops away, leaving you with a deep golden color.

- 7 Thai chiles, thinly sliced
- 2 medium red onions, thinly sliced
- 3 ounces dried mango, thinly sliced*
- 2 tablespoons whole mustard seed, toasted
- 1 tablespoon plus 1 teaspoon salt-free curry powder
- 1 tablespoon grated fresh ginger
- 3 teaspoons salt

** We find it easiest to slice dried mangos with kitchen shears.*

1. Combine the chiles, onions, mango, mustard seed, curry powder, and ginger in a bowl and mix well (wear gloves, unless you don't mind yellowish hands for a couple of days). Sprinkle in the salt and massage it into the mixture. It should become moist quickly.
2. Pack the mixture into a jar, pressing out any air pockets as you go. Press a ziplock bag against the surface of the ferment, fill the bag with water, and zip it closed.
3. Place the jar in a corner of the kitchen to ferment. If you see air pockets, remove the bag, press the ferment back down with a clean utensil, rinse the bag, and replace.
4. Allow to ferment for 14 days. The color will change as the red onion mutes and mixes with the deepening gold of the curry, but this ferment will not develop that obvious soured pickle smell. It smells more like cooked onion and curry. You will, however, taste the acidic notes when it's ready.
5. Screw on the lid and store in the fridge where this ferment will keep for 10 to 12 months.

YIELD: About 1½ pints

TECHNIQUE: Kimchis, Relishes, and Salads (page 40)

HEAT INDEX: 4–5

CARIBBEAN SALSA

The thing with habaneros is that the heat comes on late. You always have enough time to (1) taste the rest of the ingredients and (2) think you made it without pain and sweat. The other thing about habaneros is that they have an incredibly strong fruity quality. After sampling this salsa, every one of our tasters argued that there must be tomato in the ferment. Nope.

- ½ pound habaneros or other Caribbean chiles, such as Scotch Bonnets
- ½ large white onion, chopped
- 2 teaspoons minced dried thyme
- 1 teaspoon freshly ground allspice
- ½ teaspoon salt

1. Chop the habaneros and mix them in a bowl with the onion, thyme, and allspice. Sprinkle in the salt and keep mixing. The mixture should become moist quickly.
2. Pack the mixture into a jar, pressing out any air pockets as you go. Press a ziplock bag against the surface of the ferment, fill the bag with water, and zip it closed.
3. Place the jar in a corner of the kitchen to ferment. If you see air pockets, remove the bag, press the ferment back down with a clean utensil, rinse the bag, and replace.
4. Allow to ferment for 7 to 14 days. It is ready when you see the colors of the ferment mute; the brine may become cloudy as well. The ferment will have a pleasing acidic smell and taste pickle-y, and it may have a bit of an effervescent zing. You can let it ferment longer for more sour and punch.
5. Screw on the lid and store in the fridge, where the salsa will keep for up to 12 months.

VARIATION: Habanero Relish

YIELD: ABOUT 1½ PINTS HEAT INDEX: 4–5

Prepare this ferment in the same way as the Caribbean Salsa but be prepared for a decidedly different flavor. It is very herbal and very hot, with no tomato notes. The heat comes on late and continues to build for quite some time. We like to put it into a soup right before serving. It is also a nice addition to flavor a creamy cheese, such as our buttermilk cheese (page 201).

- 8–10 habaneros, or other Caribbean chiles, such as Scotch Bonnets
- 1 shallot, finely chopped
- 3 garlic cloves, minced
- 3 tablespoons minced fresh chives
- 1 generous tablespoon minced fresh thyme
- 2 tablespoons minced fresh parsley
- ¼ teaspoon fresh ground black pepper
- ¼ teaspoon grated fresh ginger
- 4 tablespoons fresh lime juice
- ½ teaspoon salt

YIELD: About 1 pint

TECHNIQUE: Kimchis, Relishes, and Salads (page 40)

HEAT INDEX: 2

KUMQUAT CHUTNEY

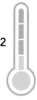

Why? Because kumquats are cute, and "kumquat chutney" is fun to say. This surprisingly watery ferment is somewhere between an anise marmalade and spicy preserved lemons. We like to mix it into soft cheeses or use the brine with some bits of the ferment in baking quick breads to give them moist texture and an acidic citrus flavor.

- 1 pound kumquats, thinly sliced
- 5 Thai dragon chiles, sliced into threads
- 2 tablespoons dried goldenberries
- ½ large red onion, finely diced
- 1 tablespoon grated fresh ginger
- ¾ teaspoon freshly ground star anise
- ½ teaspoon freshly ground white pepper
- ¼ teaspoon ground cloves
- ½–1 teaspoon salt

1. Combine the kumquats with the chiles, goldenberries, onion, ginger, star anise, white pepper, and cloves. Sprinkle in the salt. The mixture should become moist as soon as you start massaging everything together.
2. Pack the mixture into a jar, pressing out any air pockets as you go. Press a ziplock bag against the surface of the ferment, fill the bag with water, and zip it closed.
3. Place the jar in a corner of the kitchen to ferment. If you see air pockets, remove the bag, press the ferment back down with a clean utensil, rinse the bag, and replace.
4. Allow to ferment for 14 days. The chutney is ready when you see its colors mute; the brine may be become cloudy as well. The ferment will have a pleasing acidic smell and taste pickle-y, and it may have a bit of an effervescent zing.
5. Screw on the lid and store in the fridge for up to 6 months.

What Are Goldenberries?

Goldenberries hail from the mountains of Peru, where they have been cultivated since the time of the Incan empire. When fresh, a sand-colored papery husk surrounds this small golden fruit.

You can find goldenberry in dried form at many health food stores and, of course, on the Internet. Sometimes sold under the names Incan berry, Cape gooseberry, Pichuberry, Peruvian ground cherry, and husk cherry, it has its own unique flavor, which is a bit elusive. But it does taste orange — as in the color. It is tart and tangy but also sweet like a pineapple, and is a delightful addition to ferments — especially the fiery ones.

CH 7

FLAVOR PASTES

Cultures around the world have long used pastes as the starting flavor or the final touch in many meals. Think of curry paste in hot oil to get things started, or pesto dolloped on top of a pasta dish. In this chapter you will find our unique lacto-fermented riffs on many traditional pastes like red curry paste, harissa, and zhug. Others, like Habanero Basil Paste and Smoked Pineapple Pepper Paste, are our own one-of-a-kind recipes. All make wonderful additions to your fermented spice collection and add instant probiotic flavor to your meals.

YIELD: About ½ pint

TECHNIQUE: Basic Pepper Mash (page 30)

HEAT INDEX: 1 with cascabel, **3** with red jalapeños

SMOKED PINEAPPLE PEPPER PASTE

We like to make this paste with fresh cascabel or pimento peppers, which makes it mild and sweet. Change up the pepper to change up the heat: use cherry bombs or red jalapeños for a spicier version of the same paste. Everyone who smells this paste immediately says "pizza." It's like a Canadian bacon pineapple pizza sprinkled with chile flakes — so much so that the first thing we used it for was a pizza sauce. (Hint from a teenager: Sourdough toast, pepper paste, and melted mozzarella — instant pizza.)

- 1 pound fresh cascabel, cherry bomb, red jalapeño, pimento, or other thick-walled red peppers
- 1–2 teaspoons smoked salt*
- 2 ounces dried pineapple, diced
- 2 teaspoons yellow mustard seeds

**Most smoked salts are quite strong and pungent, but once in a while we find a milder one. Start with 1 teaspoon in this recipe and adjust slowly to taste.*

1. Process the peppers in a food processor. Sprinkle in the smoked salt. The chopped pepper will become juicy immediately. Add the dried pineapple and mustard seeds.

2. Pack the mash into a jar, pressing out any air pockets as you go. Leave about 1 inch of headspace. You should see some brine above the pepper pulp. Screw the lid down tightly.

3. Set the jar aside to ferment, out of direct sunlight, for 7 to 14 days, or up to 6 months. For the first week or two, check daily to make sure that the mash is submerged in the brine (see Curing Notes, page 32).

4. Start tasting the ferment any time after day 7. We prefer this pineapple mash at around 3 weeks. It's ready when it has an acidic vinegar-like quality.

5. Store this ferment in the refrigerator, where it will keep for a year or more.

VARIATION: Pineapple Turmeric Salsa

YIELD: ALMOST 1 PINT

During our testing trials we called this Pineapple #2. We were split — half of the tasters (friends and family) liked the sweet simplicity of the first recipe, while the rest of us preferred the savory, layered notes that the turmeric and pepper added. If you like pineapple, we encourage you to try both.

- 1 pound fresh pimento, cascabel, cherry bomb, or other thick-walled red peppers
- 2 ounces dried pineapple, diced
- ½ large onion, diced
- 1 teaspoon ground turmeric
- 1 teaspoon freshly ground black pepper
- 1 teaspoon grated fresh ginger
- ½–1 teaspoon salt

Follow the instructions for Smoked Pineapple Pepper Paste.

Turmeric + Black Pepper = a perfect blend for flavor and health

Curcumin is turmeric's superpower — a powerful anti-inflammatory. However, our body's ability to absorb it into our bloodstream is poor. Fortunately, the bioavailability of curcumin is greatly enhanced by the simple addition of piperine — the alkaloid responsible for black (and green) pepper's heat.

YIELD: About ½ gallon

TECHNIQUE: Pastes and Mustards (page 37)

HEAT INDEX: 3–4

TRADITIONAL GOCHUJANG

Gochujang is a rich, velvety, deep red Korean hot pepper paste, a wonderful mix of sweet, hot, sour, and salty. It has been called the Korean miso and is dolloped on just about anything. Making it in the traditional style is a commitment, however, so we also include a "quick" version (see page 148). We experimented quite a bit and based this recipe on one by Emily Kim in her book *Maangchi's Real Korean Cooking: Authentic Dishes for the Home Cook*. Perhaps our biggest adjustment to all the traditional recipes that we tried was to significantly reduce the salt — though the final flavor of this paste still has the important saltiness along with the rich, sweet heat. That said, if you love salt, feel free to double the amount in this recipe — you'll find it brings out different elements of gochujang's heat.

This ferment sits in a sunny place, probably for much of the same reasons an achar ferments in the sun (see page 124). We believe it was traditionally left open to the sun in order to allow a dried skin to form on top, which probably helped seal it.

- 8 cups water, at a tepid 100°F (38°C)
- 2 cups barley malt powder*
- 5 cups sweet rice flour (also called glutinous rice flour)
- 6 cups Korean hot pepper powder (*gochujangyong gochugaru*)
- 1 cup fermented soy flour**
- 3 cups brown rice syrup
- ¾–1 cup salt

*Malt *is the key word here; it means that the barley has gone through a soaking and drying process that converts the starches into sugars. It can be found in Asian markets under the Korean name* yeotgireum.
**Fermented soy flour can be found in Asian markets under the Korean name* meju garu. *We had trouble finding it locally, so we used Bob's Red Mill organic soy flour, which worked well.*

1. Combine the tepid water and barley malt in a saucepan, whisking to blend. Then whisk in the rice flour. Allow to sit for 2 hours.

2. Set the saucepan on your stovetop over medium-low heat and cook until reduced by a third, about 1 hour. Stir regularly to prevent sticking.

3. Let the mixture cool completely, and then stir in the hot pepper powder, fermented soy flour, rice syrup, and salt. Stir until thoroughly mixed. The mixture will be shiny and creamy.

4. Transfer to a gallon jar, a onggi pot, or your favorite fermenting vessel. Cover; for a more traditional method, cover with cheesecloth secured with a rubber band, followed by the lid.

5. Set in a sunny spot to ferment for 3 months. Emily Kim recommends removing the lid on sunny days to allow some sunlight to shine through the cheesecloth onto the ferment. In midsummer or in a hot climate, move it to a cooler location in the afternoons. We live in Oregon and have many days with very little sunshine in the wintertime. We have found fermenting this paste in a sealed Weck jar in a window to be our most successful method.

6. After fermentation, transfer the paste to the refrigerator, where it will keep indefinitely. In Korea this paste is not refrigerated.

VARIATION: Gluten-Free Gochujang

Replace the barley malt with an extra cup of rice flour and an extra cup of hot pepper powder.

YIELD: About 1 pint

TECHNIQUE: Pastes and Mustards (page 37)

HEAT INDEX: 3–4

"I-DON'T-WANT-TO-WAIT-3-MONTHS"
QUICK GOCHUJANG

We wanted to find a way to make a gochujang-like flavor paste without the long-term extra-credit fermenting project and too many difficult-to-procure ingredients. This paste is quite complex and delicious, despite being a cheater's gochujang.

- 3 tablespoons rice flour
- 3 tablespoons salt
- 2 cups water
- 1¼–1¾ cups Korean hot pepper powder (*gochujangyong gochugaru*)
- 2–3 tablespoons brown rice syrup

1. Whisk the rice flour and salt into the water. Slowly add the hot pepper powder and mix until you have a smooth, even consistency.
2. Pack the paste into a jar that is just the right size for your ferment, pressing out any air pockets as you go. Leave about 3 inches of headspace. We allow extra room for this one, because in our experience this ferment creates a lot of effervescent action. Since the paste is thick, if it bubbles up out of the jar, you suffer more of a loss than if it were just a little brine overflowing. Screw down the lid tightly.
3. Allow to ferment for 14 days. This paste may float, leaving the brine below. This can be remedied one of two ways: Open the lid slightly to burp the jar, reseal, and shake the jar to redistribute the contents. Or open the jar, stir with a clean utensil, and reseal.
4. Start tasting the ferment on day 14 (though we like to let it go an extra week). It's ready when the flavors have mingled and have taken on an acidic vinegar-like quality.
5. Stir in the brown rice syrup to taste. Allow to ferment for a few more days.
6. When it's ready, transfer the paste to the refrigerator, where it will keep for up to a year.

Mortar and Pestle 101

Thai pastes (like the Red Curry Paste on page 151) are traditionally ground together with a mortar and pestle. We mention this because there is a texture difference: the fibers of lemongrass and roots don't break down as well in a food processor, though the flavor will still be delicious. We realize that most people do not have the time or inclination to go full-on old-world style, but if you have a long Saturday afternoon to enjoy releasing the flavors of your ingredients, give it a try.

Grinding a paste with a mortar and pestle instead of a food processor takes a long time and some finesse. Start by slicing up your larger ingredients (chiles, shallots, and so on). Once that is done, you are ready to pound.

Depending on your pounding prowess and technique, choose either the counter or the floor as your work surface. To avoid damaging your work surface, place a folded towel under your mortar and pestle.

The word is *pound*, but the pestle doesn't come down with a lot of force; it is more of a little lift and then a pound-grind motion. Hold the pestle at a 45-degree angle and pound slowly in a clockwise or counterclockwise motion around the base of the mortar. You want sufficient force to break up the ingredients but not so much that your ingredients fly all over the place. With a little practice, you'll find your groove.

We have found that grinding the paste in little batches makes it easier to keep everything in the bowl of the mortar. Start with the dry ingredients, and add the wetter fresh ones as you go. Pound each ingredient thoroughly before adding the next one. Scrape down the sides with a spoon as needed to achieve a consistent texture. When the mixture resembles a paste, you can scrape it out with a spoon and put it into a bowl while you do the next batch.

HARISSA
FERMENTED GREEN CHILI BASE
ZHUG
RED CURRY PASTE

YIELD: About ¾ pint

TECHNIQUE: Pastes and Mustards (page 37)

HEAT INDEX: 3

RED CURRY PASTE

Traditional Thai red curry paste is not generally considered a fermented food, though after it is made, it is stored airtight for about 2 weeks. It's one of our favorite flavorings, and we thought it would be fun to see what happened if we made a lacto-fermented version of it. At first we weren't sure we liked it, but as time and fermentation continued, the flavors blended and created a pleasingly complex red curry flavor.

In this recipe we use dried chiles, so after seeding them we let them soak in a bit of warm water for about half an hour to rehydrate. You can keep the spicy soaking liquid to add to a soup or a cocktail later. If you have fresh chiles, then simply omit the soaking (sorry, no spicy cocktail later).

- 9–10 dried small red Thai chiles, seeded, soaked, drained, and diced
- 8 medium cloves garlic
- ⅓ cup loosely packed chopped cilantro (the leaves and, if possible, root)
- 4 tablespoons chopped shallot (about 1 medium shallot)
- 3 tablespoons chopped fresh lemongrass
- 2 tablespoons grated fresh galangal root
- 2 teaspoons kaffir lime* juice
- 1½ teaspoons kaffir lime zest (take care not to zest the bitter pith)
- 1½ teaspoons salt

**Kaffir limes are also called makrut limes. If they are not available, you can substitute regular limes.*

1. Combine the chiles, garlic, cilantro, shallot, lemongrass, galangal, and lime juice and zest in a food processor and process to a paste consistency. Sprinkle in the salt. It will become juicy immediately.
2. Pack the paste into a jar that is just the right size for your ferment, pressing out any air pockets as you go. Leave about 1 inch of headspace. The thick brine will be hard to distinguish from the rest of the paste.
3. Press a piece of plastic (or other cartouche) against the surface of the ferment, being careful not to trap any air beneath it. Screw the lid down tightly.
4. Set the jar in a corner of the kitchen to ferment, and watch for air pockets forming in the paste. If you see any, open the lid and press the paste back down. If the lid starts to bulge, simply open it for a moment to burp the ferment.
5. This ferment takes a little longer to reach acidity, usually about 14 days. It can be a little more difficult than, say, with a traditional pickle to distinguish the acidic flavors as they develop and know when the paste is ready. We like to use a pH strip to be sure; the final pH should be 4.3 or lower.
6. When it is ready, place a clean small round of plastic or parchment paper directly on top of the paste. Tighten the lid, then store in the fridge, where this ferment will keep for 8 to 12 months.

YIELD: A little less than 1 pint

TECHNIQUE: Pastes and Mustards (page 37)

HEAT INDEX: 4

THAI DRAGON MINT–CILANTRO PASTE

The mint lures you in. After that first bite, you think, *this isn't so hot*, as the cooling quality of mint gives your mouth that feeling of a cool breeze. Then, *wham!* — the heat lands on your tongue like stepping barefoot into hot sand. Ouch. It hurts so good. In this recipe we use green Thai dragon chiles, partly because as gardeners we don't want to wait out the long ripening period, and partly because the green pepper hasn't turned sweet yet and still has a nice vegetal flavor that pairs well with the herbs. If you don't have access to fresh green Thai chiles, use serranos (not as hot) or dried red Thai chiles; you will still get a wonderful juxtaposition of flavors. And, as always, feel free to add more chiles for a higher heat.

- 12–15 green Thai dragon chiles
- 3 bunches cilantro (about ½ pound)
- 3 bunches mint (about ½ pound)
- 1 teaspoon salt

1. Combine the chiles, cilantro, and mint in a food processor and process to a paste consistency. Sprinkle in the salt. The paste will become moist right away and will look juicier than some pastes.
2. Pack the paste into a jar that is just the right size for your ferment, pressing out any air pockets as you go. Leave about 1 inch of headspace.
3. Press a piece of plastic (or other cartouche) against the surface of the ferment, being careful not to trap any air beneath it. Screw the lid down tightly.
4. Set the jar in a corner of the kitchen to ferment, and watch for air pockets forming in the paste. If you see any, open the lid and press the paste back down. If the lid starts to bulge, simply open it for a moment to burp the ferment.
5. Allow to ferment for about 7 days. You will know it is ready when the verdant green mixture becomes a dull olive color and the brine layer on top is a cloudy green. It will smell of minty cilantro, with a pickled edge. The flavors will have mingled.
6. When it is ready, place a clean small round of plastic or parchment paper directly on top of the paste. Tighten the lid, then store in the fridge, where it will keep for up to 8 months.

TRADITIONAL GOCHUJANG
HABANERO BASIL PASTE
THAI DRAGON MINT-CILANTRO PASTE

YIELD: About ¾ pint

TECHNIQUE: Pastes and Mustards (page 37)

HEAT INDEX: 2

HARISSA

The sixteenth-century arrival of the chile pepper in the North African area known as Maghreb was a game changer in the local cuisine. While harissa is generally thought to have originated in Tunisia, it is part of the broader Maghreb cuisine and varies slightly from region to region.

This fermented paste is deep crimson, so rich it feels almost opulent. It has a bold chile flavor to match, yet it does not scorch the palate. A milder condiment, it should still please fiery folk because of its robust flavor. Traditionally, harissa is not fermented but preserved with an olive oil seal that is replaced each time the paste is used.

- 8 dried ancho chiles, seeded
- 2 dried Anaheim (New Mexico) chiles, seeded
- 5 cloves garlic, chopped
- 1 red bell pepper, seeded and chopped
- 1 red bell pepper, roasted
- 2 teaspoons caraway seed, freshly ground
- 2 teaspoons coriander seed, freshly ground
- 1 teaspoon cumin seed, freshly ground

1. Combine the ancho chiles, Anaheim chiles, garlic, fresh red pepper, roasted red pepper, caraway seed, coriander seed, and cumin in a food processor and process to a paste consistency. The mixture will become moist right away but will not look juicy.
2. Pack the paste into a jar that is just the right size for your ferment, pressing out any air pockets as you go. Leave about 1 inch of headspace. The thick brine will be hard to distinguish from the rest of the paste.
3. Press a piece of plastic (or other cartouche) against the surface of the ferment, being careful not to trap any air beneath it. Screw the lid down tightly.
4. Set the jar in a corner of the kitchen to ferment, and watch for air pockets forming in the paste. If you see any, open the lid and press the paste back down. If the lid starts to bulge, simply open it for a moment to burp the ferment.
5. Allow to ferment for 14 to 21 days. When it's ready, the harissa will have a pleasing, subtle acidic smell. It will taste more developed and acidic than it did when fresh.
6. When it is ready, remove the cartouche and place a clean small round of plastic or parchment paper directly on top of the paste. Tighten the lid, then store in the fridge, where this ferment will keep for 10 to 12 months.

YIELD: About 1 pint

TECHNIQUE: Pastes and Mustards (page 37)

HEAT INDEX: 3

ZHUG (SKHUG)

This is our fermented version of a classic Yemeni chile paste. This paste has a rich flavor, as the cilantro and garlic do not get drowned out by the heat. Zhug traveled from Yemen to Israel and is a common sight on Israeli food carts, where you might spoon it onto shwarma or falafel sandwiches. It is wonderful in hummus, and we have used it for flavoring many spreads and salads. We recommend it on the table as a condiment for almost any type of dish.

- 12 large serrano peppers (about ½ pound), stemmed and seeded
- 2 bunches cilantro
- ½ bunch parsley
- 12 cloves garlic
- 1 teaspoon freshly ground black pepper
- 1 teaspoon coriander seeds, toasted and ground
- 1 teaspoon cumin seeds, toasted and ground
- ¼ teaspoon ground cardamom
- 2 tablespoons fresh lemon juice
- 1 teaspoon salt

1. Combine the serranos, cilantro, parsley, garlic, black pepper, coriander seed, cumin seed, cardamom, and lemon juice in a food processor and process to a paste consistency. Sprinkle in the salt. The paste will become moist right away and will look juicier than some pastes.
2. Pack the paste into a jar that is just the right size for your ferment, pressing out any air pockets as you go. Leave about 1 inch of headspace.
3. Press a piece of plastic (or other cartouche) against the surface of the ferment, being careful not to trap any air beneath it. Screw the lid down tightly.
4. Set the jar in a corner of the kitchen to ferment, and watch for air pockets forming in the paste. If you see any, open the lid and press the paste back down. If the lid starts to bulge, simply open it for a moment to burp the ferment.
5. Allow to ferment for at least 5 to 7 days. (We have allowed zhug to ferment for 3 weeks, and it was delicious.) You will know it is ready when the verdant green mixture becomes a dull olive color and the brine layer on top is a cloudy green. It will smell of cilantro and salsa, with a pickled edge. The flavors will have mingled and taken on a strong garlicky pickled-cilantro heat.
6. When it is ready, place a clean small round of plastic or parchment paper directly on top of the paste. Tighten the lid, then store in the fridge, where it will keep for up to 8 months.

YIELD: 2–2½ quarts

TECHNIQUE: Basic Pepper Mash (page 30)

HEAT INDEX: 1–2

FERMENTED GREEN CHILI BASE

This recipe uses the three most common peppers in Southwestern cooking, and it's wonderfully convenient to have on hand whenever you make chili; the flavorful chile peppers, veggies, and spices are already prepared and ready to dump into the pot. The batch size seems large, but you will use at least 1 to 2 cups per meal. For about 45 minutes of work, you'll have six to eight future pots of chili.

We wanted this recipe to be perfect for a family meal — a hint of heat to add some excitement to the dish but not so much that children or non-heat lovers would feel smoked out. That said, for more heat feel free to increase the jalapeños and reduce the green chiles and ancho peppers.

- 8 ancho chiles, stemmed and seeded
- 8 green chiles, stemmed and seeded
- 8 jalapeños, stemmed and seeded
- 8 large cloves garlic
- 2 large onions, roughly chopped
- 2 tablespoons whole coriander seed, roasted and crushed
- 2 tablespoons whole cumin seed, roasted and crushed
- 1 generous tablespoon salt

1. Combine the anchos, green chiles, jalapeños, garlic, onions, coriander seed, and cumin seed in a food processor and process until roughly chopped. Sprinkle in the salt. The chopped pepper will become juicy immediately.
2. Pack the mash into jars, pressing out any air pockets as you go. Leave about 1 inch of headspace. You should see some brine above the pepper pulp. Screw the lids down tightly.
3. Set the jars aside to ferment, out of direct sunlight, for 10 to 14 days or as long as 3 months. For the first week or two, check daily to make sure that the mash is submerged (see Curing Notes, page 32).
4. Start tasting the ferment on day 10. It's ready when it has an acidic vinegar-like quality.
5. Store this ferment in the refrigerator, where it will keep for 12 months.

YIELD: ½ pint

TECHNIQUE: Pastes and Mustards (page 37)

HEAT INDEX: 4

HABANERO BASIL PASTE

You don't usually see the kind of heat that habaneros deliver paired with basil — but it works. This is a fun way to surprise yourself and others with an unexpected combination. We like this paste best as the base for spreads, like Cacao Nib Habanero Pesto or Pumpkin Seed Spread, both on page 224.

- 2 ounces fresh basil (3–4 bundles of leaves)
- 4 habaneros
- 3 cloves garlic
- ½ teaspoon salt

1. Combine the basil, habaneros, and garlic in a food processor and process to a paste consistency. Sprinkle in the salt. Since the cell walls of the ingredients are already broken down, the paste will become moist right away.
2. Pack the paste into a jar that is just the right size for your ferment, pressing out any air pockets as you go. Leave about 1 inch of headspace.
3. Press a piece of plastic (or other cartouche) against the surface of the ferment, being careful not to trap any air beneath it. Screw the lid down tightly.
4. Set the jar in a corner of the kitchen to ferment, and watch for air pockets forming in the paste. If you see any, open the lid and press the paste back down. If the lid starts to bulge, simply open it for a moment to burp the ferment.
5. Allow to ferment for 7 to 10 days. You will know it is ready when the verdant green mixture becomes a dark olive color. The flavors will have mingled, with the basil followed by pickle-y heat.
6. Place a clean small round of plastic or parchment paper directly on top of the paste. Tighten the lid, then store in the fridge, where this ferment will keep for up to 8 months.

YIELD: About 1 pint

TECHNIQUE: Pastes and Mustards (page 37)

HEAT INDEX: 3–4

REMPAH

Rempah literally means "spice," and it is a cornerstone of Nyonya cuisine (a cross of the Chinese and Malay traditions) found in the regions of Penang, Malacca, Indonesia (where it's called *bumbu*), and Singapore. Rempah starts in a mortar and pestle with chiles, shallots, and garlic. This trinity is ground together and used as is, or it may be further adorned by the cook. Additions could include but are not limited to galangal, fresh turmeric, lemongrass, shrimp paste (*belacha* or *trassi*), coriander, and candlenut.

We use this rempah recipe as a starting place for fried rice (*nasi goreng*) or fried noodles (*bami goreng*). After heating the frying oil, we add a few tablespoons of rempah before adding the vegetables. It can also be a base for a quick sambal (see the next recipe).

- 1 pound shallots
- 15–20 dried long Thai peppers
- 10–15 fresh Thai bird's eye chiles
- 10 cloves garlic
- 1 teaspoon salt

1. Combine the shallots, long peppers, bird's eye chiles, garlic, and salt in a food processor or mortar and pestle and process to a paste consistency. It will become moist right away.
2. Pack the paste into a jar that is just the right size for your ferment, pressing out any air pockets as you go. The shallots in this paste can cause it to be more active than many of the other pastes, so give it a little more room to expand — about 3 inches of headspace.
3. Press a piece of plastic (or other cartouche) against the surface of the ferment, being careful not to trap any air beneath it. Screw the lid down tightly.
4. Put the rempah in a corner of the kitchen to ferment, and check daily for air pockets forming in the paste. If you see any, open the lid and press the paste back down. If the lid starts to bulge, simply open it for a moment to burp the ferment.
5. Allow to ferment for 14 to 21 days. You will know it is ready when it has a nice acidic flavor and the harsh, pungent flavor of raw garlic and shallots has become smooth.
6. When it is ready, place a clean small round of plastic or parchment paper directly on top of the paste. Tighten the lid, then store in the fridge, where this ferment will keep for 8 to 12 months.

YIELD: About ½ pint

TECHNIQUE: Pastes and Mustards (page 37)

HEAT INDEX: 4–5

SAMBAL

Sambal (*sambal oelek*) in its simplest form is just a pungent pepper mash — salt and tiny hot peppers, seeds and all. There are many variations on the theme of sambal throughout Southeast Asia, though it is usually very hot — a blazing fire that will blow your mind and mouth and send your senses packing. This recipe takes its cue from Indonesian-style sambals. In Indonesia, sambal is as integral to a meal as kimchi is in Korea. We have come across two sayings that illustrate the importance of this fiery condiment: one says that a meal without sambal is not a meal at all, and another says that even an ugly girl will find a husband if she can make a good sambal.

- 20–25 fresh chiles, the hottest you can find (about ½ cup when processed to paste)
- 10 cloves garlic
- 5 candlenuts or macadamia nuts
- 1 teaspoon grated fresh galangal
- Scant ½ teaspoon salt
- 1 tablespoon tamarind water (page 100)
- 1–2 teaspoons palm sugar (optional)

1. Combine the chiles, garlic, nuts, galangal, salt, and tamarind water in a food processor (or a mortar and pestle) and process to a paste consistency. The mixture will become moist right away.
2. Pack the paste into a jar that is just the right size for your ferment, pressing out any air pockets as you go. Leave about 1 inch of headspace.
3. Press a piece of plastic (or other cartouche) against the surface of the ferment, being careful not to trap any air beneath it. Screw the lid down tightly.
4. Set the jar in a corner of the kitchen to ferment, and watch for air pockets forming in the paste. If you see any, open the lid and press the paste back down. If the lid starts to bulge, simply open it for a moment to burp the ferment.
5. Allow to ferment for 14 to 21 days. You will know it is ready when it has a nice acidic flavor and the harsh, pungent flavor of raw garlic has become smooth.
6. After the fermentation period, stir in sugar to taste, if desired.
7. Place a clean small round of plastic or parchment paper directly on top of the paste. Tighten the lid, then store in the fridge, where this ferment will keep for 8 to 12 months.

Quick Sambal

Since rempah is a base for many sauces, you can use fermented rempah (page 159) as the base for a quick fermented sambal. Simply process 10 fresh hot chiles into a paste, add a few teaspoons of the rempah and, if you like, 1 tablespoon of shrimp paste (available at Asian markets), and mix until you have an even paste.

Rempah and Sambal: The Hea(r)t and Soul of Southeast Asian Cuisine

Southeast Asia boasts cuisines of multifaceted and delicious flavors. While there are distinct regional styles, there is also a lot of sharing and mixing that has taken place throughout the centuries. Many of the regional cuisines rely on chile pastes ground with a mortar and pestle. These pastes may be the first thing tossed in hot oil to begin a dish (generally a curry or stir-fry), or the last thing dolloped on top of the bowl for a garnish.

Rempah and sambal are not traditionally fermented. They are made fresh to be consumed immediately or within the week. Both are often made in massive quantities (as in all hands on deck peeling mountains of shallots and garlic) in preparation for multiday feasts and celebrations like weddings. Then again, they come from a region of the world that has fresh ingredients available year-round. But why not ferment them and store them in your refrigerator so that you can add instant live flavor to your meals at any time of year, no matter where you are?

CH 8

KIMCHIS AND FERMENTED SALADS

Kimchi is the name for any vegetable that is lacto-fermented in Korea's rich pickling tradition. That said, kimchi is more than just a word for pickle. It is a great source of national pride, and it varies from season to season, region to region, and family to family. For the purposes of this book, recipes that are inspired by that delicious trio — ginger, garlic, and chile — are called kimchi. Many traditional types of kimchi undergo a process of overnight brining to salt the leafy greens and begin fermentation. You will see this method in our Nettle Kimchi (page 168).

The taste of fermented salads is different from the decidedly Asian flavor of kimchi, but we've put them together as light and juicy ferments with bigger pieces of vegetables. With many of them, you'll feel like you could serve yourself more than just a condiment-sized dollop.

YIELD: About 1 quart

TECHNIQUE: Kimchis, Relishes, and Salads (page 40)

HEAT INDEX: 3

TURMERIC GOLDEN BEET SALAD

The heat level here depends entirely on the fresh pepper that you use — we have made this with mild pimento peppers, and the salad was mild and easygoing. You will notice in this recipe that we soak the fenugreek for a few minutes. This will soften the seed and its bitterness and bring out the sweeter maple syrup notes.

- 2 large golden beets, sliced microthin on a mandoline-type slicer
- 5–6 Fresno, jalapeño, or other chiles, sliced
- 1 teaspoon black peppercorns
- 1 teaspoon ground turmeric or 2 teaspoons finely grated fresh turmeric
- ½ teaspoon fenugreek seeds, soaked in just-boiled water for 5 minutes
- ¼ teaspoon ground cardamom
- 1 scant tablespoon salt

1. Combine the beets, chiles, black peppercorns, turmeric, fenugreek seeds, and cardamom in a bowl and mix well. Sprinkle in the salt. The mixture should become moist as soon as you start massaging everything together.
2. Pack the mixture into a jar, pressing out any air pockets as you go. Press a ziplock bag against the surface of the ferment, fill the bag with water, and zip it closed.
3. Place the ferment in a corner of the kitchen to cure. If you see air pockets, remove the bag, press the ferment back down with a clean utensil, rinse the bag, and replace.
4. Allow to ferment for 10 to 21 days. The colors of the ferment will mute, and the brine will become cloudy. The ferment is ready when it smells pleasingly acidic and tastes pickle-y, and it may have a bit of an effervescent zing. You can let it ferment longer for more sour and punch.
5. Screw on the lid and store in the refrigerator, where this ferment will keep for 10 to 12 months.

VARIATION: Sweet, Sour, and Spicy Beet Salad

The following ingredients yield a sweeter, gingery take on this salad.

- 2 large golden beets, sliced thinly
- 5–6 Fresno, jalapeño, or other chiles, chopped finely
- 2 tablespoons goldenberries
- 1 tablespoon dried cranberries
- 1–2 tablespoons sliced candied ginger
- Zest and juice of 1 lemon
- 1 teaspoon salt

Use the same method as for Turmeric Golden Beet Salad.

SPICY CARROT AND LIME SALAD
SWEET, SOUR, AND SPICY BEET SALAD
GREEN BEAN KIMCHI
NETTLE KIMCHI
TURMERIC GOLDEN BEET SALAD
BAECHU KIMCHI

YIELD: ½ gallon

TECHNIQUE: Kimchis, Relishes, and Salads (page 40)

HEAT INDEX: 4

BAECHU KIMCHI

We couldn't make a book of fiery ferments without including a burning kimchi. This is a style of cabbage kimchi that is made with a thick rice and pepper paste.

Traditional kimchis often use fish sauce, fermented shrimp, anchovies, or other seafood to give them not only flavor but a dose of amino acids. We experimented with a number of bases for the paste and loved this one: a broth made with Japanese bonito shavings. It gives this kimchi a slight smoky flavor. Plan to soak the cabbage overnight before you begin.

SOAKING BRINE

- ½ cup salt
- 2 quarts unchlorinated water

1. In a crock or large bowl, mix the salt and water for the brine and stir to dissolve. Rinse the cabbage halves in cold water, then immerse in the brine solution. Use a plate as a weight to keep the cabbage submerged. Set aside at room temperature for 6 to 8 hours.
2. Using a colander set over a large bowl, drain the cabbage and reserve the liquid. Chop the cabbage crosswise into pieces ½ to 1 inch wide and put them in a large bowl. (Or, if you are feeling traditional, keep the halves whole. You will then mix the other veggies with the pepper paste and smear this in and around every leaf before stuffing into a fermentation vessel.)
3. Bring 2 cups of water to a boil in a saucepan. Drop in the bonito flakes and soak according to package instructions.
4. Meanwhile, add the carrot, scallions, turnip, garlic, and ginger to the cabbage bowl and toss to combine.
5. When the bonito broth is ready, strain out the flakes and then return the broth to the saucepan. Whisk in the rice flour and bring to a boil, whisking occasionally as it thickens. When the texture is like smooth gravy, remove the pan from the heat and stir in the gochugaru and chile flakes. Let cool, then add the broth to the bowl of veggies and cabbage.

KIMCHI

- 1 head napa cabbage (about 3 pounds), cut in half lengthwise
- 1 (.176-ounce) package shaved tuna bonito flakes (available at Asian markets)*
- 1 carrot, grated
- 1 bunch scallions, cut into ½-inch pieces
- ½ medium to large turnip or daikon, grated
- 1 head garlic, cloves peeled and grated
- 2 tablespoons grated fresh ginger
- 2½ tablespoons sweet rice flour (also called glutinous rice flour)
- ¾ cup gochugaru (Korean red pepper flakes)
- 1 teaspoon chile flakes

**For a vegan version, replace the bonito broth with 4 tablespoons coconut aminos mixed with ¾ cup water.*

6. Pack the kimchi into a mason jar, leaving about 1 inch of headspace. Add enough reserved brine to completely cover the veggies and discard the remainder. Screw the lid down tightly.

7. Set the jar aside to ferment, out of direct sunlight, for 7 to 14 days. Check daily to make sure there aren't CO_2 bubbles developing and that the vegetables are submerged; simply press down as needed. Burp the jar once a day or more if the lid is bulging.

8. Start taste-testing the kimchi on day 7. You will know it is ready when the flavors have mingled and the pungency is pleasantly fused with acidic tones. However, this ferment benefits from some cool curing time: move it to the refrigerator and let it sit another week to allow the flavors to continue to develop.

9. Store in the refrigerator, where the kimchi will keep for 8 to 12 months.

YIELD: About 1 pint

TECHNIQUE: Kimchis, Relishes, and Salads (page 40)

HEAT INDEX: 2

NETTLE KIMCHI

This recipe requires a little advanced thinking, as the nettles should be soaked overnight. Remember to use gloves when working with the nettles; they can still sting even after sitting in salt water for 10 hours. Nettles and green onions grow in the early spring. Garlic greens appear at about the same time; if you happen to have some, add them to the mixture.

SOAKING BRINE

- ¼ cup salt
- 1 quart unchlorinated water

KIMCHI

- About ½ pound spring nettles, the top two or three bracts of leaves, still attached to the stems
- 4 green onions, sliced crosswise into ½-inch pieces
- 1 tablespoon minced fresh ginger
- 3–4 cloves garlic
- 1–2 tablespoons chile flakes or gochugaru flakes

1. In a crock or large bowl, mix the salt and water for the brine and stir to dissolve. Rinse the nettles in cold water, then immerse in the brine solution. Use a plate as a weight to keep the nettles submerged. Set aside at room temperature for 6 to 8 hours.
2. Using a colander set over a large bowl, drain the nettles and reserve the liquid.
3. Combine the the green onions, ginger, garlic, and chile flakes in a separate bowl, blending thoroughly.
4. Take all the nettles in a clump, roll it up, and cut crosswise into 1- to 2-inch pieces. Place the nettles in a large bowl and add the green onion mixture, massaging them together.
5. Pack the kimchi into a mason jar, leaving about 1 inch of headspace. Add enough reserved brine to completely cover the veggies. Screw the lid down tightly.
6. Set the jar aside to ferment, out of direct sunlight, for 10 to 14 days. Check daily to make sure there aren't CO_2 bubbles developing and that the vegetables are submerged; simply press down as needed. Burp the jar once a day or more if the lid is bulging.
7. Start taste-testing the kimchi on day 10. You will know it is ready when the flavors have mingled and the pungency is pleasantly fused with acidic tones. During fermentation, the green of the nettle leaf turns a translucent brown-khaki-green color.
8. Store in the refrigerator, where the kimchi will keep for 8 to 12 months.

YIELD: About 1½ quarts

TECHNIQUE: Kimchis, Relishes, and Salads (page 40)

HEAT INDEX: 3–4

GREEN BEAN KIMCHI

For this kimchi we use fresh peppers, because green beans and fresh red peppers are often in season at the same time of year and we wanted the juicy peppers to provide the brine. The result is a tangy ferment with a distinctive lemon flavor, despite the fact that no lemon was harmed in the making of this recipe. Use a thick-walled hot pepper such as red jalapeño or cherry bomb, or, if you are a gardener and you planned ahead, the fresh gochu pepper. The gochu has a milder heat than the red jalapeño, so plan accordingly.

- 1 pound green beans, cut into ½- to 1-inch pieces
- 1 bunch scallions, cut into ½-inch pieces
- 5 cloves garlic, minced
- 2 tablespoons grated fresh ginger
- 2 teaspoons good-quality fermented fish sauce (or shoyu sauce for a vegan kimchi)
- 1 pound fresh gochu peppers, or other thick-walled hot red peppers
- 1½ teaspoons salt

1. Combine the green beans and scallions in a large bowl. Add the garlic, ginger, and fish sauce. Mix and set aside while you prepare the peppers.
2. For a hotter ferment, leave the seeds in the peppers. Process them with the salt to a mash-like consistency in a food processor. Add the pepper mash to the green bean mixture and massage everything together with your hands. Remember to wear gloves.
3. Pack the kimchi into a jar, pressing out any air pockets as you go. Press a ziplock bag against the surface of the ferment, fill the bag with water, and zip it closed.
4. Place the jar in a corner of the kitchen to ferment. If you see air pockets, remove the bag, press the ferment back down with a clean utensil, rinse the bag, and replace.
5. Ferment for 10 to 12 days. You will know the kimchi is ready when the flavors have mingled and the pungency is pleasantly fused with acidic tones. During fermentation, the red of the pepper will become more orange and the green beans will turn a dull yellowish green.
6. Screw on the lid and store in the refrigerator, where the kimchi will keep for 8 to 12 months.

YIELD: 1 quart

TECHNIQUE: Kimchis, Relishes, and Salads (page 40)

HEAT INDEX: 1

SUMMER SQUASH KIMCHI

This recipe uses a little more salt than the other kimchis because zucchini and other summer squashes are so much softer. The added salt helps these vegetables retain some character. Notice we didn't say crunch — while this kimchi is not crunchy, the texture is pleasant and the taste is complex. We omitted the usual ginger and substituted turmeric for a unique twist of flavor. The mild heat comes from mild gochugaru flakes and black pepper, but you can easily increase the heat with hotter flakes or add chile pepper flakes or cayenne.

- 1 pound zucchini or other summer squash, diced
- 8 cloves garlic, minced
- 4–5 tablespoons gochugaru (Korean red pepper flakes)
- 1 tablespoon grated fresh ginger
- 2¼–2½ teaspoons salt
- 1 teaspoon freshly ground black pepper
- ¼ teaspoon ground turmeric

1. Combine the squash in a bowl with the garlic, gochugaru, ginger, salt, black pepper, and turmeric. Toss everything together. There will be brine immediately.
2. Pack the mixture into a jar, pressing out any air pockets as you go. Press a ziplock bag against the surface of the ferment, fill the bag with water, and zip it closed.
3. Place the jar in a corner of the kitchen to ferment. If you see air pockets, remove the bag, press the ferment back down with a clean utensil, rinse the bag, and replace.
4. This ferment is finished quickly. Start taste-testing the kimchi on day 3 in warmer weather, or day 5 or 6 if the weather is mild. You will know it is ready when the colors change, showing a nice orange from the gochugaru and a duller, cooked look to the squash. You can let this ferment go a little longer for more acidity, but often you don't need to, and the squash can get softer if it ferments longer.
5. Screw on the lid and store in the refrigerator, where the kimchi will keep for up to 3 months.

YIELD: 1 pint

TECHNIQUE: Kimchis, Relishes, and Salads (page 40)

HEAT INDEX: 2

RHUBARB KIMCHI

Rhubarb has long been relegated to sweet desserts, and that's still a mighty fine place for it; however, this spring stalk should not be typecast. This kimchi will forever change rhubarb's reputation.

Rhubarb is an early spring crop, and peppers are not. Therefore, it is nice if you have pepper paste from the previous fall to spice up this condiment. If not, use chile flakes or gochugaru and it will still be delicious. Either way, you can always make this recipe spicier with the addition of more pepper.

- ½ pound rhubarb (2-3 medium stalks), thinly sliced
- 3 scallions, thinly sliced, or about ½ cup thinly sliced spring onions
- 1 teaspoon salt
- 3 large cloves garlic, finely grated
- 2 tablespoons fermented pepper paste, or 1 tablespoon chile flakes or gochugaru flakes
- 1 tablespoon finely grated fresh ginger
- 1 tablespoon slivered candied ginger
- ½ teaspoon dulse flakes

1. Combine the rhubarb and scallions in bowl, sprinkle in the salt, and toss. Add the garlic, pepper paste, fresh ginger, candied ginger, and dulse flakes, and massage together. You will have a chunky but juicy mixture.
2. Pack the mixture into a jar, pressing out any air pockets as you go. Press a ziplock bag against the surface of the ferment, fill the bag with water, and zip it closed.
3. Place the jar in a corner of the kitchen to ferment. If you see air pockets, remove the bag, press the ferment back down with a clean utensil, rinse the bag, and replace.
4. Allow to ferment for 5 to 7 days. You will know it is ready when the colors have muted, the flavors have mingled, and the pungency is pleasantly fused with acidic tones. Ferment longer if needed to develop more acidity.
5. Screw on the lid and store in the refrigerator, where the kimchi will keep for up to 6 months.

YIELD: 1 quart

TECHNIQUE: Kimchis, Relishes, and Salads (page 40)

HEAT INDEX: 3

WINTER SQUASH & KOHLRABI KIMCHI

This ferment has a complex texture and flavor. The kohlrabi will retain a bit of crunch, while the shiitakes soften. Those shiitakes also dominate the flavor a bit, so if you are not a mushroom fan, be forewarned.

SOAKING BRINE

- ½ teaspoon salt
- 1 cup unchlorinated water

KIMCHI

- 10 dried shiitake mushrooms
- 2 pounds butternut squash
- 1 pound kohlrabi, thinly sliced
- 10 cloves garlic, minced
- 5 tablespoons gochugaru (Korean red pepper flakes)
- 2 tablespoons finely grated ginger
- 2 tablespoons salt
- 2 tablespoons sweet rice flour (also called glutinous rice flour)

1. In a small bowl, mix the salt and water for the brine and stir to dissolve. Immerse the mushrooms in the brine.
2. Prepare the squash by peeling, halving, and removing the seeds. Halve again so that you have quarters, and slice thinly.
3. Combine the squash and kohlrabi in a bowl. Slice the soaked mushrooms and add them, followed by the garlic, gochugaru, ginger, salt, and sweet rice flour. Toss everything together, gently massaging to preserve the mushroom slices.
4. Pack the mixture into a jar, pressing out any air pockets as you go. Press a ziplock bag against the surface of the ferment, fill the bag with water, and zip it closed.
5. Place the kimchi in a corner of the kitchen to ferment. If you see air pockets, remove the bag, press the ferment back down with a clean utensil, rinse the bag, and replace.
6. This ferment is finished quickly, so check it daily. Start taste-testing the kimchi on day 3 in warmer weather, or on day 5 or 6 if the weather is mild. You will know it is ready when the colors change, showing a nice orange from the gochugaru and a duller look to the squash (especially next to the bright red pepper). You can let this ferment go a little longer for more acidity, but often you don't need to, and the squash can get softer if it ferments longer.
7. Screw on the lid and store in the refrigerator, where the kimchi will keep for 3 months.

YIELD: About 1 quart

TECHNIQUE: Kimchis, Relishes, and Salads (page 40)

HEAT INDEX: 3

FERMENTED NOPAL SALAD

Nopal is the Mexican name for prickly pear cactus pads. When the pads are diced and prepared for eating, they are called *nopalitos*. Nopalitos are often served at breakfast with eggs.

If you're familiar with nopalitos, then you won't be surprised by the mucilaginous texture of this salad. If you're not, then be aware that the texture, similar to that of okra, can be a challenge for some. This ferment is absolutely delicious, though, with a pleasing tart flavor that works well with the Mexican oregano and chile.

- 1 pound cactus pads, thinly sliced
- 1 small onion, sliced
- 1 teaspoon ground Mexican oregano
- 1 teaspoon smoked paprika
- Juice of 1 lemon
- 1 generous teaspoon smoked salt
- 2 habaneros, sliced into long, thin threads

1. Combine the cactus, onion, oregano, paprika, and lemon juice, and mix well. Sprinkle the smoked salt into the mixture and massage until moist. Add the habaneros and mix again.
2. Pack the mixture into a jar, pressing out any air pockets as you go. Press a ziplock bag against the surface of the ferment, fill the bag with water, and zip it closed.
3. Place the jar in a corner of the kitchen to ferment. If you see air pockets, remove the bag, press the ferment back down with a clean utensil, rinse the bag, and replace.
4. Allow to ferment for 1 month. The colors of the ferment will mute, and you'll see a slight cloudiness develop in the brine. When it's ready, the ferment will have a pleasing acidic smell and taste pickle-y, and it may also have a bit of an effervescent zing. You can let it ferment longer for more sour and punch.
5. Screw on the lid and store in the refrigerator, where the ferment will keep for up to 3 months.

The Oreganos

Mexican oregano is native to Mexico, not the Mediterranean, where all the other oreganos come from. The savory Greek oregano, the milder Italian variety, and the stronger Turkish oregano are all members of the mint family. Mexican oregano is a member of the verbena family. The differences are subtle, yet it adds a different mood to a dish: a little more floral and citrusy, perhaps a bit stronger. It is often finely ground to the consistency of cinnamon. You can substitute ground marjoram for a similar flavor, or regular oregano.

YIELD: About 1 quart

TECHNIQUE: Kimchis, Relishes, and Salads (page 40)

HEAT INDEX: 3

SPICY CARROT AND LIME SALAD

This has become one of our favorite ferments. Crunchy, with a bright flavor, it is easy to make and easy to eat. It is perfect as a small side salad to accompany many dishes. We make it with Fresno peppers, as they provide a nice heat and the red strips are striking against the bright carrots. That said, you can use any pepper, depending on availability and the heat level you are trying to achieve. Want more burn? Choose habaneros, Thai chiles, or jalapeños (red or green). Pimento or cherry bell peppers will mellow out the heat.

- 1¾ pounds carrots, sliced as thinly as possible on a grater or mandoline (peeling is optional)
- 3–4 Fresno or other red peppers, thinly sliced, or 1 tablespoon dried chile flakes
- Zest and juice of 2 limes
- 1 (1- to 2-inch) piece fresh ginger, thinly sliced
- 2 teaspoons salt

1. Combine the carrots, peppers, lime zest and juice, and ginger in a bowl. Add the salt and massage it into the mixture.
2. Pack the mixture into a jar, pressing out any air pockets as you go. Press a ziplock bag against the surface of the ferment, fill the bag with water, and zip it closed.
3. Place the jar in a corner of the kitchen to ferment. If you see air pockets, remove the bag, press the ferment back down with a clean utensil, rinse the bag, and replace.
4. Allow to ferment for 7 to 10 days. The carrots tend to stay bright, so look for a slight cloudiness to develop in the brine. When it is ready, it will have a pleasing acidic smell and taste pickle-y, and it may also have a bit of an effervescent zing. You can let it ferment longer for more sour and punch.
5. Store in the refrigerator, where this fermented salad will keep for up to 12 months.

YIELD: About 1 quart

TECHNIQUE: Kimchis, Relishes, and Salads (page 40)

HEAT INDEX: 4

MANGO–PLANTAIN HABANERO FERMENT

Raw plantains don't show up on the menu much but are very good for feeding our microbiota (see Your Hungry Microbiome, page 221). Fermentation and hot island flavors seemed like the perfect way to serve up plantains in a new way. When you first taste this ferment, the mango and plantain are front and center, but after a few seconds they give way to the habaneros, which provide the finish.

- 2 small green plantains, peeled and diced
- 5 habaneros, sliced lengthwise in very thin strips
- 2–3 tablespoons very thinly sliced dried mango
- 6 whole allspice berries
- Zest and juice of 1 lime
- 1 teaspoon salt

1. Combine the plantains, habaneros, mango, allspice berries, and lime zest and juice in a bowl. Add the salt and massage it into the mixture.
2. Pack the mixture into a jar, pressing out any air pockets as you go. Press a ziplock bag against the surface of the ferment, fill the bag with water, and zip it closed.
3. Place the jar in a corner of the kitchen to ferment. If you see air pockets, remove the bag, press the ferment back down with a clean utensil, rinse the bag, and replace.
4. Allow to ferment for 14 to 21 days. You will know it is ready when it has a nice sour taste. The plantains will stay starchy but very palatable.
5. Screw on the lid and store in the refrigerator, where this ferment will keep for 6 months or more.

CH 9

HOT PICKLES

Peppers brine-pickle well: after all, Peter Piper was lucky enough to pick a peck of (already?) pickled peppers. The only problem is that lacto-fermented brine-pickled peppers don't tend to stay crisp and crunchy — the flesh softens. And some, like classic green chiles and Bulgarian Carrot peppers, have a skin that is just too tough after fermentation. A few, however, stay firmer and have excellent texture and taste, most notably the jalapeño, cherry bomb, and sweet piquanté (Peppadew). Just know you are not going to get the same crispness you'll find in commercial vinegar-based pickles. We offer some of our favorite hot pickle recipes here, as well as a universal recipe with suggestions and ideas to help you make your own custom hot pickles.

UNIVERSAL RECIPE FOR LACTO-FERMENTED PICKLED PEPPERS

SUGGESTED PEPPERS FOR PICKLING

- Red or green jalapeño
- Cherry bomb
- Sweet piquanté (Peppadew)
- Pimento
- Hungarian wax pepper
- Banana pepper
- Serrano
- Thai chile

STEP 1: CHOOSE YOUR PEPPER. You may use any combination of peppers. For example, jalapeño rings with a few slices of habanero are delicious. Add some dried cayenne or other dried chile varieties if you want a more multifaceted flavor profile.

STEP 2: PREP THE PEPPERS. This is where you decide whether you want your pickles to be whole or sliced. If you want whole peppers, most of the time it is best to remove the stems (tiny Thai chiles are the exception). You can leave the seeds or remove them — this is truly a matter of personal preference. Most peppers are nice sliced in rounds or thin strips; we don't recommend diced or square chunks.

NOTE: *If you are pickling whole peppers and you want to leave the stem end intact, you will need to make a small slit in the side wall of the pepper to allow the brine to enter the pepper.*

HOT TIP

Tannic Leaves Promote Crunch

Using tannin-rich grape leaves to top your pickle ferment will help keep everything tucked under the brine and also add tannins into the mix. Tannins help pickles keep their crunch. Other tannic leaf choices include horseradish leaves, oak leaves, sour cherry leaves, and currant leaves.

PICKLING SPICES

- Garlic cloves
- Onion wedges
- Wedge of horseradish root
- Dried hot chiles
- Peppercorns (any color)
- Long pepper pods
- Whole Szechuan pods
- Dill flower heads, seed heads, or seeds
- Coriander seeds
- Mustard seeds
- Fennel seeds
- Bay leaves
- Cumin seeds
- Allspice seeds
- Cinnamon sticks
- Ginger slices
- Oregano sprigs
- Rosemary sprigs
- Thyme sprigs

STEP 3: CHOOSE YOUR PICKLING SPICES. Pickled hot peppers have a lot of flavor, and you can pickle them in the brine just as they are. That said, the addition of whole herbs and spices will infuse your brine and peppers with superb rich flavors. The list of pickling spices (left) is a great place to start, but by no means are these the only possibilities. Dream up your own ideal pickle combinations! Or turn to our Five Pickling Spice Recipes (page 184) for some of our favorite mixes.

Place pickling spices in the bottom of your crock or jar, where they'll be weighted down by your peppers; this will help keep the lighter seeds from floating to the top of the brine.

STEP 4: MAKE A BRINE. Review the tips for successful brine making on page 36. We always use ½ cup of salt per gallon of unchlorinated water for our brine, as we don't mind the peppers having a softer texture. However, you can use up to ¾ cup of salt if you want a firmer finished product. The salt hardens the pectin in the cell walls, slowing fermentation and helping retain crispness.

Mix your brine well. Some unrefined salts contain a few trace minerals, which will leave a little sediment on the bottom. This will not affect the pickling process, but if you find it unappealing, use a clearer unrefined sea salt.

STEP 5: PACK YOUR JAR OR CROCK. Pack the peppers in tightly to just under the shoulder of the jar or crock, following the technique for Brine-Based Sauces and Pickles (page 34).

STEP 6: WAIT. Your peppers will be fermented in about 7 to 8 days (sooner in hot weather). You will know they are done when the brine is cloudy and the pickles have that acidic, pleasing (but funky) pickle-y smell. Eat them now, or continue to ferment until you achieve the funk and flavor you desire.

UNIVERSAL RECIPE FOR LACTO-FERMENTED HOT PICKLED VEGGIES

Choose any single vegetable (see the list below for possibilities) or combination of vegetables that inspires you — or that your garden throws your way. Cut your veggies into pieces and tuck them into a jar or crock with plenty of dried chile pods, peppercorns, ginger, and other spices (see Five Pickling Spice Recipes, page 184).

Review the tips for successful brine making on page 36. Then follow the technique for Brine-Based Sauces and Pickles (page 34). For most vegetables, use a brine ratio of ½ cup salt per 1 gallon unchlorinated water. For cucumbers, however, use ¾ cup salt. Cucumbers just want to get soft — they have a collection of enzymes ready and waiting to break them down. Many of these enzymes are hanging out in the blossom end, so use a small brush or the edge of a spoon to scrape off any trace of leftover blossom that may still be on the end of the cucumber. Some people just cut the whole end off, but we like our pickles whole, without any cuts in the skin.

YOU CAN PICKLE IT!

- Asparagus
- Carrots
- Cauliflower florets
- Celeriac
- Celery sticks
- Chard stems
- Cucumbers
- Garlic cloves
- Green beans
- Green tomatoes
- Kohlrabi
- Okra
- Radishes — all varieties
- Rutabaga
- Sweet corn on the cob, cut crosswise into 3-inch segments
- Turnips

FAVORITE VEGETABLE MEDLEYS

HOT DILLY BEANS: green beans, rounds or strips of jalapeño, generous garlic

EDGY VEGGIES: cauliflower florets, onion slices, jalapeño slices, carrot slices, garlic

RADISH AND CARROT: carrot sticks, radish rounds or sticks, the bulb ends of scallions

COLD-SEASON ROOT PICKLES: a combination of your favorite roots — kohlrabi, rutabaga, turnips, et cetera — with plenty of hot spices to heat you up

FERMENTATION TIMES

How long do you have to wait until you can savor your pickle-y creation? There isn't a set time for most vegetables. Denser veggies, particularly root veggies, tend to have more leeway in regard to fermentation time than, say, asparagus or cucumbers. Depending on the air temperature, they can take a week (when it's warm) or three weeks (when it's cool); it's more a matter of observation. Look for cloudy brine, sediment, and that characteristic acidic smell of pickles. The brine will taste acidic instead of just salty. On green vegetables, such as okra, watch for their vibrant green to turn dull. Ferment until the flavor is as acidic as you like, and then refrigerate. The exception is cucumbers. We find that cucumbers are done in six days, and we don't believe there is any reason to take this veggie through a longer ferment, as they just get softer.

Is Cloudy Brine Okay?

It's not only okay — it's perfect! Cloudy brine, created by lactic-acid bacteria, is a sign that the fermentation process is working. In fact, seeing the brine change from clear to cloudy is one of the ways to know that the ferment is getting close to finished. All brine-pickled vegetables get cloudy, and when they clear up (usually while sitting in the fridge), they develop a layer of sediment at the bottom (like a snow globe) or on top of the veggies. We have not noticed different veggies getting more or less cloudy, though sometimes the brine gets a hue — for example, purple carrots give the brine a pink color.

FIVE PICKLING SPICE RECIPES

"Pickling spice" is not one spice but a combination blended by the pickle maker to get the desired effect. Our universal recipe for lacto-fermenting hot peppers (page 180) lists some of the common ingredients used in pickling spice mixtures. Here we share a few combinations that we find work well. Each of these mixes makes enough pickling spice for 1 gallon of pickles, or four 1-quart jars. For best flavor, toast the spices before using (see Getting the Most from Your Spices, page 55).

SPICY DILLY PICKLE MIX

- 8 dried whole cayenne peppers
- 3–4 heads fresh dill or 3 tablespoons dill seed
- 2 tablespoons black peppercorns
- 1 tablespoon coriander seeds
- 1 tablespoon mustard seeds

TRADITIONAL ENGLISH-STYLE SPICY MIX

- 8–10 dried Thai bird's eye chiles or 6–8 dried whole cayenne peppers
- 3 tablespoons whole allspice berries
- 2 tablespoons black peppercorns
- 2 tablespoons dried ginger root pieces (not ground)
- 1½ tablespoons mustard seeds
- 1 tablespoon coriander seeds
- 1 teaspoon mace pieces (not ground)

FRENCH-STYLE SPICY MIX

- 3–4 dried whole cayenne peppers
- 5 bay leaves, broken up
- 2 teaspoons whole cloves
- 2 teaspoons dried thyme
- 2 teaspoons white peppercorns
- 1 teaspoon coriander seeds
- 1 teaspoon dried marjoram
- 1 sprig fresh rosemary or 1 teaspoon dried

CURRY-STYLE SPICY MIX

This mix has curry leaves in it. They are optional, but if you have a little curry leaf plant (*Murraya koenigii*) growing in a pot on your balcony, put a stem in a pickle blend. This plant has nothing in common with curry powder, but it adds a flavor to curries that brings them to the next level. It is used in Indian and Himalayan cuisine, where this small shrublike herb is native. We use it in this mix to add another layer to the complexity of flavors in this spicy blend.

- 8 cardamom pods
- 8 whole cloves
- 8 fresh or dried sprigs or leaves of the curry leaf plant, optional
- 4–8 dried cayenne pepper pods or other dried spicy chile
- 1 cinnamon stick, broken up
- 4 tablespoons coriander seeds
- 2 tablespoons cumin seeds
- 1 tablespoon black peppercorns
- 1 tablespoon fennel seeds
- 1 tablespoon mustard seeds
- 1 teaspoon fenugreek seeds
- 1 teaspoon ground turmeric

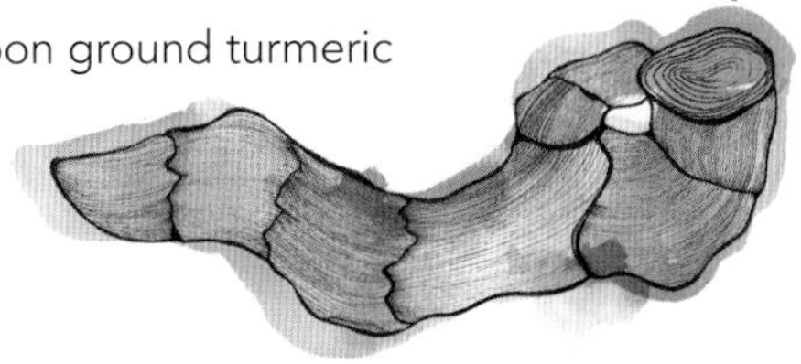

THE SPICE ROUTE

This early European–style mix comes from Bartolomeo Scappi, Italian Renaissance "celebrity" chef, who recommended this blend in his 1570 cookbook *Opera dell'Arte del Cucinare*. He didn't specifically intend it to be a pickling mix, as he also included brown sugar, but it has all the makings of a B.C. (Before Chiles) spice mix.

- 8 cinnamon sticks, slightly broken up
- 2 tablespoons whole cloves
- 1 tablespoon dried ginger root pieces (not ground)
- 1 tablespoon cracked nutmeg (break the whole seed into pieces)
- 2 teaspoons grains of paradise
- 2 teaspoons saffron threads

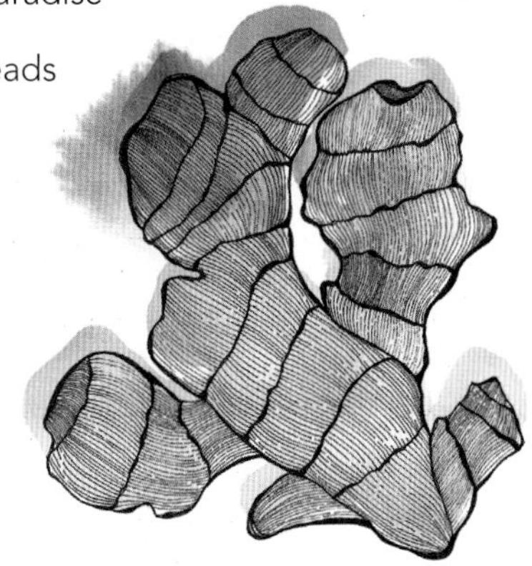

SWEET PIQUANT
PICKLED PEPPERS
CARROT-STUFFED
HOT PEPPERS
DRIED ALEPPO
PEPPER PICKLES
KIMCHI-STUFFED
JALAPEÑOS
BRINED MIXED-MEDIA MAS
(BEFORE BLENDING)

YIELD: About 1½ quarts

TECHNIQUE: Brine-Based Sauces and Pickles (page 34)

HEAT INDEX: 3

CARROT–STUFFED HOT PEPPERS

This recipe is good with a number of different kinds of peppers, but for us, green jalapeños top the list. These stuffed peppers just feel like they belong aside a taco.

- 2–3 medium carrots, julienned
- 6–8 cloves garlic, grated
- 3 tablespoons crumbled dried oregano
- 1 teaspoon cumin seed, freshly ground
- 2 pounds medium-sized hot peppers (red or green jalapeños, Fresnos, Hungarian wax, or round peppers like cherry bomb)
- 2 tablespoons whole coriander seeds
- 1 tablespoon whole mustard seeds
- 1–2 quarts brine (2 quarts unchlorinated water with 4 tablespoons salt)

1. Combine the carrots in a bowl with the garlic, oregano, and cumin.
2. Use a jalapeño corer to remove the stems and seeds from the peppers. Stuff the whole peppers with the carrot mixture. Combine the coriander and mustard seeds in the bottom of a jar, and pack the peppers tightly in, wedging them under the shoulder so they'll stay submerged in the brine.
3. Pour in enough brine to cover the peppers completely. If the peppers float up above the brine, use a grape leaf or other weight to keep them submerged. Screw down the lid tightly. (Leftover brine will keep in the fridge for 1 week; discard thereafter and make a new batch, if needed.)
4. Place the jar on a plate and set aside to ferment for 7 to 14 days. Burp the jar as needed to allow any built-up CO_2 to escape, and make sure the vegetables stay under the brine (see Curing Notes, page 32). If needed, top off with reserved brine solution to keep the vegetables covered.
5. You will start to see changes in about 5 days. As the peppers ferment, the brine will get cloudy; this is when you can start to taste-test your pickles. If they're not sour enough, allow to ferment longer while continuing to monitor the brine level.
6. When they're ready, transfer the pickles to the refrigerator; they will keep for 6 to 10 months.

YIELD: About 1½ quarts

TECHNIQUE: Brine-Based Sauces and Pickles (page 34)

HEAT INDEX: 3

KIMCHI-STUFFED JALAPEÑOS

These pickles are hot little kimchi packages. Red jalapeños make a visual statement — pretty in the jar and striking on the plate. The flavor is what we think a pepper kimchi would taste like. After all, you are doubling up — think chile pepper on chile pepper.

- 2 pounds red or green jalapeños (or other medium-size peppers, such as Fresnos or Hungarian wax peppers)
- 1–2 cups fermented kimchi
- 1–2 quarts brine (2 quarts unchlorinated water with 4 tablespoons salt)

Follow the instructions for Carrot-Stuffed Hot Peppers (page 187), using the kimchi to stuff the peppers instead.

HOT TIP

A Handy Tool

Use a jalapeño corer to deseed any thick-walled, cherry-shaped peppers (and keep some of the capsaicin off your fingers!).

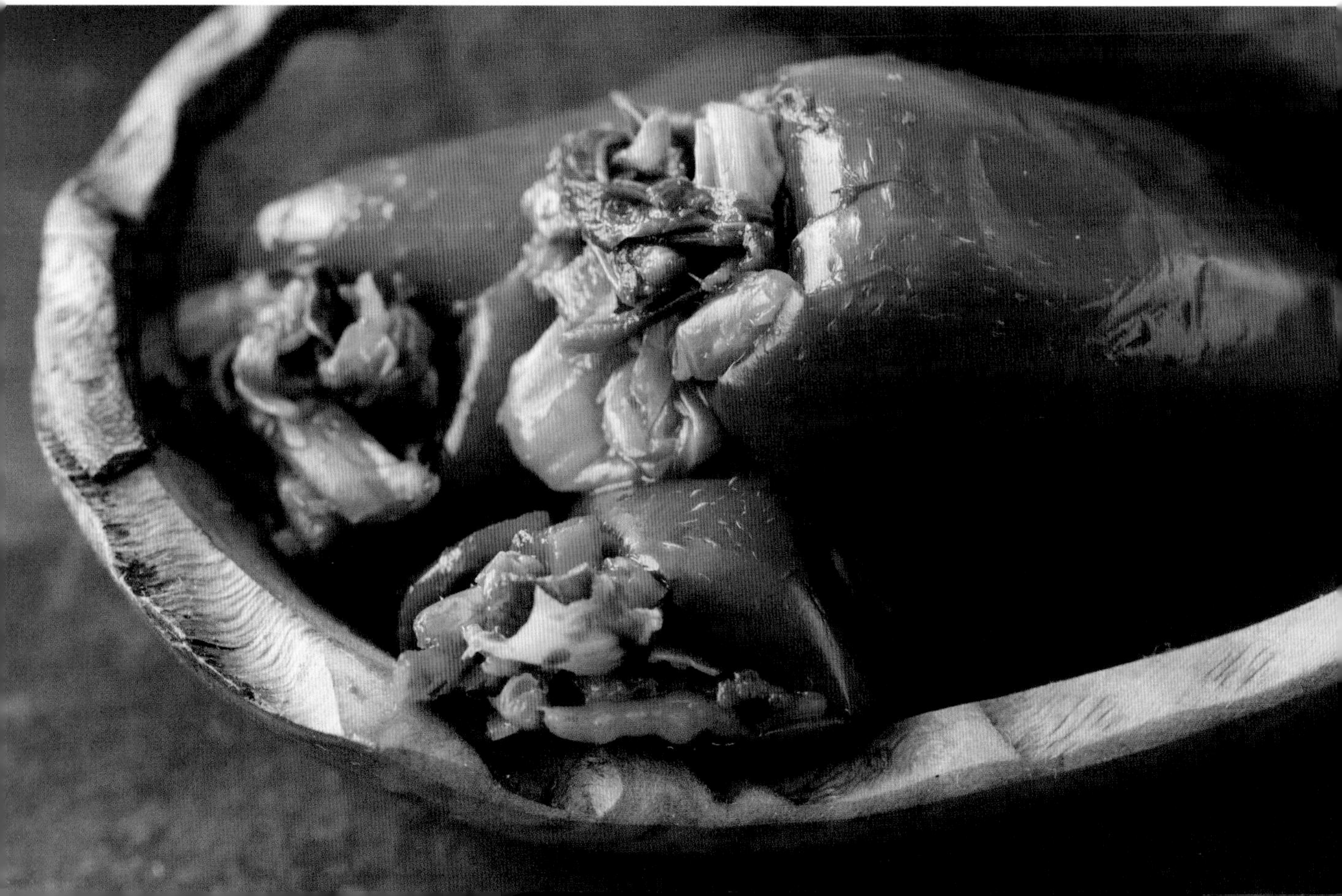

YIELD: 1 pint

TECHNIQUE: Brine-Based Sauces and Pickles (page 34)

HEAT INDEX: 4

DRIED PEPPER PICKLES

Because so many chile varieties are available in dried form, we wanted to find fun ways to ferment them. We are not sure that we can describe this ferment as either a pickle or a relish — it stands in its own category. We found them to be hotter than pickles made with the fresh version of the same pepper, likely due to the concentration of flavor from dehydration. The texture is similar to water-soaked sun-dried tomatoes, and we like to use these bright pickles to garnish hummus and small plates.

Use dried chile strips or pods that have their stems and seeds removed. Chipotle, Aleppo, habanero, Fresno, and other varieties with thinner skins and meaty walls work well. (Dried Aleppo with pomegranate brine is out of this world.)

- 3–4 ounces dried chiles, enough to stuff into a pint jar
- 1½–2 cups light unsweetened fruit juice (pomegranate or cranberry works well)
- 2–3 teaspoons salt

1. Cut or break the dried chiles into bite-size pieces (or not; you can also pickle them whole and simply slice them thinly before serving).
2. Place the peppers in a pint jar. Mix the fruit juice with the salt and pour it over the peppers, submerging them completely. If the peppers try to float up above the brine, use a grape leaf or some type of weight to keep everything under the brine. Screw the lid down tightly.
3. Place the jar on a plate and set aside to ferment for 10 to 21 days. Burp the jar as needed to allow any built-up CO_2 to escape, and make sure the vegetables stay under the brine.
4. Start to taste-test the pickles after 10 days. When they're ready, the peppers will be hot, sweet, and slightly acidic. They will have a soft fruit-leather consistency, since they started as dried peppers. You will not see the same color changes as you might with fresh vegetables.
5. When they're ready, transfer the pickles to the refrigerator, where they will keep for up to 6 months. After 6 months they begin to soften too much to use whole on the plate, but they are still excellent to add to dishes for flavor. We like to mince them for sauces or tabouli-style salads or put a few in the blender with a spread to spice it up.

MEET THE MAKERS

Dominique Fevry and Sylvain Gilliand, PICKLIZ

LONDON

Pikliz (pronounced *pik-leez*), a spicy vinegar-steeped chopped pickle, is a traditional Haitian condiment that you'll find on the table at almost every meal in most Haitian households. It was no different in Dominique Fevry's home in Montreal. Her mother cooked Haitian food because she wanted her children to understand their roots. She would pull the whole family together to make big batches of *pikliz*, and during the hours of meticulously chopping the ingredients, the family would tell stories.

Dominique learned early on that cooking is all about love. As a young girl, she noticed that even when her mother was upset with something that was happening in the family, she still put a beautiful meal on the table. When Dominique asked about it, her mother said simply, "This is how I show my love."

So it is no surprise that when Dominique and Sylvain began to date and she wanted to do something special for him, she cooked a five-course Haitian meal. Sylvain loved Dominique's *pikliz* and searched Paris (where they were living) and then London (where they moved) for this magical Haitian condiment. He couldn't find anything similar. When he approached Dominique with the idea of producing these pickles for sale, she said no. She explained that she had made the pickles from the heart and she was not a businesswoman. Sylvain persisted, and one day Dominique said yes (she admits it could have been a little too much wine). And so their company, PICKLIZ, was born.

PICKLIZ pickles are made by hand — no food processors. Dominique concedes that as the business grows, they may come to a point where a different decision has to be made, but she is adamant that the flavor, texture, mouthfeel, and finish all come from the care put into hand-cutting the ingredients. Part of that honesty in flavor comes from her desire to regard the vegetables in the same way they do in Haiti, where fresh ingredients are of the utmost importance and vegetables are harvested often only a few hours before they are eaten. The one ingredient that Dominique just cannot duplicate for her PICKLIZ are the limes. Haitian limes have a terroir all their own (to borrow a word from wine).

As soon as we tasted PICKLIZ's *pikliz*, we knew we had to include it in the book, even though it isn't strictly a lacto-fermented pickle. That said, because we experiment relentlessly, we had to try letting the lactobacilli do the work; see page 192 for our variation.

YIELD: About 1 quart

HEAT INDEX: 4

PIKLIZ (BY PICKLIZ)

This Haitian recipe can be described as hot pickled peppers or slaw and is made with the very hot Scotch Bonnet pepper. It is a wonderful accompaniment for your fish, eggs, soup, meat, cheese, avocado . . . only your imagination can stop you. In Haiti, it is traditionally served with fried meat like pork or goat, and fried plantains.

There are several recipes for pikliz, and each household has their own tricks. Here is one basic recipe, easy to make at home. If you really do not have time to spare and would like to have some pikliz quickly, you can chop the ingredients in a food processor, although the result will not be as great as cutting the vegetables by hand or using a mandoline.

- 2 cups shredded green cabbage
- 3–6 Scotch Bonnet peppers (or habaneros), seeded and very thinly sliced
- 1 medium bell pepper, seeded and thinly sliced
- 1 carrot, grated
- 1 onion, thinly sliced
- 1 scallion, thinly sliced (optional)
- Pinch of sea salt
- 8–10 whole black peppercorns
- 3 whole cloves
- Pinch of thyme
- 3 cups white vinegar
- Juice of ½ lime

1. Combine the cabbage, Scotch Bonnets, bell pepper, carrot, onion, scallion (if using), salt to taste, peppercorns, cloves, and thyme in a bowl. Mix well.
2. Pack the vegetables into a large jar. Mix the vinegar and lime juice and pour them over the vegetables, until the vegetables are completely submerged in liquid.
3. Screw the lid down tightly and set in the refrigerator to cure for at least 5 days before opening.
4. Store the pikliz in the refrigerator, where it will keep for 3 months.

YIELD: About 2 quarts

TECHNIQUE: Kimchis, Relishes, and Salads (page 40)

HEAT INDEX: 4

LACTO-FERMENTED PIKLIZ

This is our fermented version of the Haitian-style pikliz recipe provided by Dominique Fevry and Sylvain Gilliand of PICKLIZ (see the profile on page 190).

- 1 small head green cabbage (about 2 pounds), shredded
- 3–6 Scotch Bonnet peppers (or habaneros), seeded and very thinly sliced
- 1 medium bell pepper, seeded and thinly sliced
- 1 carrot, grated
- 1 onion, thinly sliced
- 1 scallion, thinly sliced
- 3 whole cloves
- ½ teaspoon freshly ground black pepper
- ½ teaspoon thyme
- Juice of ½ lime
- 1 tablespoon salt

1. Combine the cabbage, Scotch Bonnets, bell pepper, carrot, onion, scallion, cloves, black pepper, thyme, and lime juice in a large bowl and mix well. Sprinkle in the salt. Massage the mixture until a brine has formed.
2. Pack the mixture into a jar, pressing out any air pockets as you go. Press a ziplock bag against the surface of the ferment, fill the bag with water, and zip it closed.
3. Place the jar in a corner of the kitchen to ferment. If you see air pockets, remove the bag, press the ferment back down with a clean utensil, rinse the bag, and replace.
4. Allow to ferment for 10 to 21 days. The colors of the ferment will mute, and the brine will become cloudy. When it is ready, the ferment will smell pleasingly acidic and taste pickle-y, and it may have a bit of an effervescent zing. You can let it ferment longer for more sour and punch.
5. When it is ready, screw on the lid and store in the refrigerator, where this pikliz will keep for 10 to 12 months.

YIELD: 1½ quarts

TECHNIQUE: Brine-Based Sauces and Pickles (page 34)

HEAT INDEX: 2–3

STUFFED PICKLED CHERRY BOMB PEPPERS

These pickles are beautiful to look at and fun to eat. They are ready in a few weeks, but we have allowed them to ferment for 6 months and found them quite tasty. You can dial down the smoky flavor, if you want, by choosing an unsmoked salt for the brine.

- 2–3 pounds cherry bomb peppers
- ¾ pound shallots, diced
- 3 cloves garlic, minced
- 5 dried tomato halves, chopped
- 1 tablespoon dried oregano
- ½ teaspoon smoked salt
- 1–2 quarts brine (2 quarts unchlorinated water with 4 tablespoons salt)

1. Use a jalapeño corer to remove the stems and seeds from the peppers. Make the stuffing by mixing together the shallots, garlic, dried tomatoes, oregano, and smoked salt. Stuff the cherry bomb peppers.
2. Pack the peppers tightly into a jar, wedging them under the shoulder so they'll stay submerged in the brine.
3. Pour in enough brine to cover the peppers completely. If the peppers try to float up above the brine, use a grape leaf or some type of weight to keep everything under the brine. Screw the lid down tightly. (Reserve any leftover brine in the fridge. It will keep for 1 week; discard thereafter and make a new batch, if needed.)
4. Place the jar on a plate and set aside to ferment for 7 to 14 days. Burp the jar as needed to allow any built-up CO_2 to escape, and make sure the vegetables stay under the brine (see Curing Notes, page 32). If needed, top off with reserved brine solution to keep the vegetables covered.
5. You will start to see changes in about 5 days. As the peppers ferment, the brine will get cloudy and the other vegetables will dull; this is when you can start to taste-test your pickles. If they're not sour enough, allow to ferment longer while continuing to monitor the brine level.
6. When they're ready, transfer the pickles to the refrigerator, where they will keep for 6 to 10 months.

Part 3
On the Plate

We are inspired simply by what tastes good. We know when something works because it is more than the sum of its parts — it is comfort and nourishment for the mind, body, and soul. We subscribe to no specific diet or philosophy but simply follow our passion for whole, real foods.

We love flavor, spice, heat, and ferments, so we hope this section not only helps you put tasty dishes on your table but gives you a glimpse into the versatility (oh yes, there are desserts), convenience, and fun that come with cooking with fiery ferments. In a way, you are getting a peek at the eclectic meals that deck our table at home, from warm loaves of bread to savory soups. We use gluten and we don't. Sometimes we use sustainably grown meats, dairy, and eggs, and sometimes we eat vegan meals. Some recipes follow the GAPS protocol and are gut healing, like our Simple Creamy Squash Soup (page 223), while some are just about yummy comfort, like our spicy twist on breakfast toast (page 198).

We hope you will find some delicious flavors that inspire you, and that you'll add your own twists of flavor to make them favorites in your family.

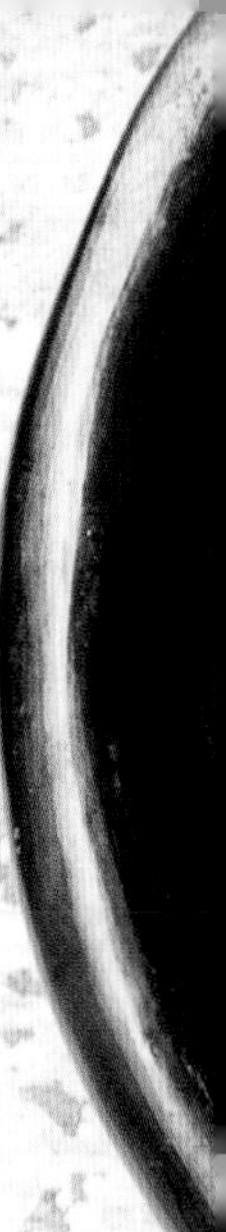
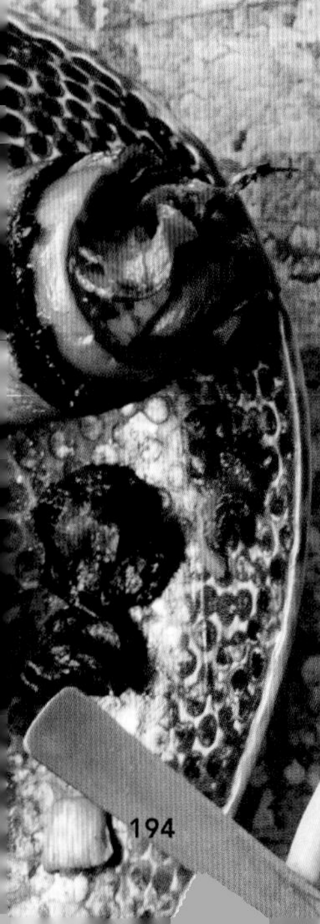

CH 10

BLAZING PLATES

Small plates are in style these days, and we often see tables adorned with many little dishes instead of a few large ones. This fun, social way of eating also seems to blur the lines between breakfast, lunch, and dinner, so we have put together an assortment of dishes and meals that can be easily mixed and matched. For example, some spicy breakfast sausage (page 204) or Cheesy Quinoa (page 202) can go as easily with an egg as they can with some Quelites (page 219) and Spicy Lemon Paneer (page 226) for a tapas-style lunch or dinner.

We also see the need for grab-and-go lunches increasing with our busy lifestyles, but we want our foods to be whole and nourishing, too. Many of these recipes are perfect for when you're on the move. Toss some healthy probiotic Apricot-Cranberry Pepper Crunch Bars (page 216) into your lunch, breathe new life into your sandwich with Cacao Nib Habanero Pesto (page 224), and make converts at the next tailgater with Fermented Jalapeño Poppers (page 214). We invite you to explore and enjoy and be inspired to create your own spicy favorites.

ADVENTURES IN TOAST

Toast can be as simple as white bread and marmalade, but we want to share some ideas that propel toast to a whole new status — complete (read: healthy), filling, and delicious. To this end, we introduce the three most important rules for good toast. Use this guide as a stepping-stone to your own amazing toast adventures.

RULES FOR GOOD TOAST

1. **ALL TOAST STARTS WITH GREAT BREAD.** Choose anything from a crusty levain sourdough to a heavy dark pumpernickel, a raw seed bread, or a tasty gluten-free option.

2. **ADD A FAT/PROTEIN.** This is the soul of toast, or at least the smooth, warm inner heart, rich and nourishing. Butter, creamy cheeses, nut butters, coconut butter . . . but don't stop there. This is a fantastic place to add those strong spicy ferments, either mixed into your creamy fat for flavor or spread right on top.

3. **ADD SOMETHING FRESH.** This can be anything from greens or fresh fruit to a ferment (Dried Pepper Pickles, page 189, using Aleppo peppers in a pomegranate brine — oh my!). We often pair cucumber with a hot ferment on toast to temper the heat.

The Art of Toast

Here are some delectable combinations to get you started:

- Toasted sourdough, Piri Piri Sauce (page 98), cucumber slices
- Toasted pumpernickel, Horseradish Anchovy Butter (page 200), slices of hard-boiled egg, cucumber slices
- Toasted whole grain, nut butter mixed with fermented Sweet Chile Sauce (page 100), sautéed kale
- Toasted crusty bread, hard-boiled eggs mashed with aioli, dollop of Pikliz (page 191)
- Toasted rye (light or dark), Adzhika Anchovy Butter (page 200), spinach and/or dandelion greens
- Toasted seed bread, avocado smashed with Zhug (page 156), pomegranate seeds sprinkled on top
- Toasted sourdough, Simple Buttermilk Cheese (page 201) mixed with Kumquat Chutney (page 140), thin slices of pear or radish
- Toasted gluten-free coconut-based bread, Red Curry Anchovy Butter (page 200), apple slices and/or shredded napa cabbage

SOURDOUGH, PIRI PIRI, CUCUMBER

SEED BREAD, AVOCADO MASHED WITH ZHUG, POMEGRANATE SEEDS

GLUTEN-FREE BREAD, RED CURRY ANCHOVY BUTTER, APPLE SLICES, NAPA CABBAGE

PUMPERNICKEL, HARD BOILED EGGS MASHED WITH AIOLI AND PIKLIZ

SOURDOUGH, SIMPLE BUTTERMILK CHEESE, KUMQUAT CHUTNEY, RADISHES

YIELD: ½ cup

SPICED ANCHOVY BUTTER

This simple spread is beyond easy, keeps well in the refrigerator, and is an excellent vehicle for many of the ferments in this book. A powerhouse of tasty fat, it is a great as a spread on toast but also much more. Put it in your baked or mashed potatoes, melt it over roasted root veggies or cauliflower, or drop a dollop into a bowl of soup right before serving.

Not an anchovy fan? We hear you. It took us a long time to work anchovies, sardines, and other small fish into our diet. These fish are low on the food chain and healthy sources of good fats and protein. A little goes a long way, so spring for a good brand, packed in oil, in a glass jar (you'll avoid an overly salty, metallic taste). If you still don't think anchovies are for you, or if you are a vegetarian, just add a ferment to plain salted butter or raw coconut butter.

- 8 tablespoons (1 stick) unsalted butter, at room temperature
- 1 tablespoon finely chopped oil-packed anchovies
- 2 tablespoons ferment of your choice (see the suggestions below)

1. Place the butter in a bowl and smash it with a fork.
2. Add the chopped anchovies and mix until evenly distributed.
3. Add the ferment, to taste. Pastes work the best; if you're using a watery ferment, drain the brine and chop it before adding.

Suggested Butter Blends

- **ADZHIKA** (page 131): Use 2 tablespoons or more. This mild ferment has a fresh dill flavor that marries beautifully with anchovy.
- **HORSERADISH FERMENT** (page 80): Use 2 to 3 tablespoons. Brown bread, salty fish, horseradish — it works! Mild and sublime.
- **RED CURRY PASTE** (page 151): Use 2 tablespoons for a mellow butter; we like 3 to 4 tablespoons. This flavor powerhouse is not for the faint of heart (maybe brunch, not breakfast).
- **LONG PEPPER CURRY PASTE** (page 86): Use 2 tablespoons. Add to any recipe for a warm flavor and a touch of curry.

YIELD: About 2 cups

SIMPLE BUTTERMILK CHEESE

(NO CULTURES REQUIRED)

This cheese (adapted from a recipe by Norene Gilletz in her book *MealLeaniYumm!*) is beautifully simple, even if you have never made cheese. The buttermilk is already fermented and acidified, so you are just separating the curds and whey. Similar to what some call farmer's cheese, *quark*, or *tvarog*, it is deliciously creamy and mild and a little less sour than a *leban* (yogurt cheese).

The best part about this cheese is that it is great for highlighting your spicy ferments. Try mixing in a few tablespoons of Adzhika (page 131) or Zhug (page 156) for a mild savory cheese, or chop in a few tablespoons of Kumquat Chutney (page 140) for a spicy citrus flavor, or step up the heat by stirring in a little Vanilla-Pear Habanero Hot Sauce (page 106). Spread it on your toast, use it to stuff your pickled peppers (page 180), or enjoy it by the spoonful.

- 2 quarts cultured buttermilk

1. Preheat the oven to 375°F (190°C).
2. Pour the buttermilk into a large, ovenproof glass or ceramic (not metal) casserole dish with a cover. Heat in the oven for 15 to 20 minutes, until it separates into curds and whey.
3. Line a colander with cheesecloth and place it over a bowl. Carefully pour the curds and whey into the colander. Tie the ends of the cheesecloth together and hang it over a bowl, allowing it to drain for several hours. For a firmer cheese, squeeze out most of the liquid. (Save the whey for use in baking or soup stock.)
4. Place the drained curd in a bowl. Use immediately or store in the refrigerator in an airtight container. It will keep for about 1 week.

YIELD: 4 servings

CHEESY QUINOA

The inspiration behind this recipe was green chile cheese grits, with quinoa substituted for the grits. Serve it with eggs, or have a bowl of this protein-rich dish and forget the eggs altogether. The Fermented Green Chili Base we use here adds wonderful flavor to the dish but is not at all hot. For some heat, shake on your favorite hot sauce.

- 1 cup raw quinoa, rinsed and dried on a paper towel*
- 1 cup water
- 2 tablespoons butter
- 4 ounces cheddar cheese, grated
- 2 tablespoons heavy cream or kefir
- 5–6 tablespoons Fermented Green Chili Base (page 157)

1. Combine the quinoa in a pot with the water and butter. Cover the pot, bring to a boil, then reduce the heat and simmer until the quinoa has absorbed all the water and become fluffy, about 15 to 20 minutes.
2. Remove from the heat and stir in the cheese, cream, and green chili base.

**Quinoa seeds are coated with saponins, which can leave the quinoa tasting bitter. Rinse the seeds by putting them in a sieve and running cool water over them. Though other grains benefit from a good soak, soaking quinoa is not recommended, as the saponins can leach into the seed.*

SAUSAGE

When it comes to flavoring ground meat, mixing in the ferment and spices ahead of time to let it marinate makes all the difference. Here are some ideas to get you started, but we encourage you to play with your own ferments and flavors to make one-of-a-kind, preservative-free tasty sausage.

The process is the same for each of these sausages. The night before you plan to cook the sausage, mix in the ferment along with the herbs and spices. Refrigerate in an airtight container. Cook as you would any fresh sausage.

BREAKFAST SAUSAGE

- 1 pound ground pork
- 3 tablespoons (or more) fermented pepper mash of choice
- 2 large cloves garlic, grated on a microplane grater
- 1½ teaspoons freshly ground white or black pepper
- 1 teaspoon fennel seed, freshly ground
- 1 teaspoon finely chopped fresh sage or ½ teaspoon dried
- 1 teaspoon salt
- ¼ teaspoon ground cloves

CHICKEN SAUSAGE

This sausage is wonderful as meatballs. We shape it into small balls and drop them in chicken stock that has been brought to a boil. Pour the broth and meatballs over a bowl of udon or rice noodles, top with a spicy fermented salad or kimchi, and you have a wonderful meal. (See Build Your Own Bowls, page 208.)

- 1 pound ground chicken
- 2–3 tablespoons Green Peppercorn Paste (page 84)
- ¼ teaspoon salt

GREEN PEPPERCORN PASTE

CHORIZO

- 1 pound ground pork
- 4 tablespoons fermented pepper mash of choice
- 1½ teaspoons smoked paprika
- 1 teaspoon freshly ground coriander seed
- ½ teaspoon finely ground Mexican oregano

SPICY BEEF OR LAMB SAUSAGE (OR FILLING)

While not a traditional breakfast sausage, this beef or lamb sausage formed into small patties is a nice change from your typical pork sausage. Sautéed with onions this mixture makes a good stuffing for anything from empanadas (page 213) to burritos. You can use it for beef chili, too, and if you do, be sure to add the Fermented Green Chili Base (page 157) at the end of the cook time.

- 1 pound ground beef or lamb
- 4 tablespoons (or more) fermented pepper mash of choice
- 3 large cloves garlic, minced

FERMENTED PEPPER MASH

YIELD: 1 serving

HOT AND FRUITY SMOOTHIE

It goes in a glass, not on a plate, but this full-meal smoothie has it all: it's fruity, hearty, and probiotic, it has fiber, it tastes great, and, best of all, it will give you a shot of capsaicin to wake you up. We find it convenient to bake the sweet potato in advance and keep it in the fridge, mashed and ready to go. For a smooth texture, make sure to finely chop the ginger pickle to help break down its fibers.

- 1 cup cooked sweet potato
- 1 apple, cored and chopped
- 1 orange, peeled and sectioned
- ¼ cup fresh cranberries
- 1 teaspoon finely chopped Fermented Ginger Pickles (page 78) or Ginger Paste variation
- ½ cup liquid (almond milk, hazelnut milk, or water)
- ¼–½ teaspoon Habanero Carrot Sauce (page 107)
- Maple syrup (optional)

Combine the sweet potato, apple, orange, cranberriers, and ginger pickle in a blender. Add the liquid, habanero sauce, and maple syrup (if using). Blend until smooth and thick.

HOT TIP

Spice Up Your Smoothies with Ginger

We add a teaspoon of fermented ginger to just about every smoothie we make. Not only does it add a wonderful spicy note, it's also an excellent digestive herb and, in this case, offers a little probiotic punch.

HOT MOCHA SMOOTHIE

This smoothie is rich and creamy and plenty warming. For a little more burn in your morning, substitute 1 (or more) teaspoons of Vanilla-Pear Habanero Hot Sauce (page 106) for the Coffee Sauce.

- 2 bananas, frozen or fresh
- 4 tablespoons almond butter
- 2 tablespoons coconut oil
- 2 teaspoons cocoa powder
- 1 cup almond milk
- 3–4 teaspoons Coffee Sauce (page 104)

Combine the bananas, almond butter, coconut oil, and cocoa powder in a blender. Add the almond milk and Coffee Sauce and blend until smooth and thick.

BUILD YOUR OWN BOWLS

As the week wears on and planned meals give way to more creative ways to use what's lurking in the fridge, one strategy to keep everyone in our household happy and fed is to put out bowls of rice, noodles, or even baked potatoes and a lot of condiments to "decorate." But there is also something exciting about composing a meal in a bowl. What flavors are you going for? How heavy or light do you want the meal to be? How many people are eating? If you are preparing bowls for the family, you can load everyone's bowl with the substrate, say rice noodles in a broth, and then lay out the table with ferments and fresh veggies as garnishes to be selected individually. Use the guide below to choose your own adventure!

CHOOSE A SUBSTRATE:

- Udon noodles
- Buckwheat noodles
- Rice noodles
- Brown rice
- Scented rice, such as Thai jasmine or basmati
- Quinoa
- Cauliflower Rice (page 210)
- Yellow Coconut Rice (page 211)

CHOOSE A BROTH:

- Bone broth
- Chicken broth
- Vegetable broth
- Miso

CHOOSE A FERMENT (OR TWO):

- Anything goes

CHOOSE A PROTEIN:

- Egg
- Tempeh (see Hot Crispy Tempeh Strips, page 212)
- Tofu
- Avocado
- Crispy nuts (page 217)
- Bacon
- Beef
- Pork
- Chicken
- Fish

CHOOSE FRESH VEGGIES:

- Grated carrots
- Micro greens
- Chopped fresh herbs
- Cucumber slices
- Whatever you have

YIELD: 2–3 servings

CAULIFLOWER RICE

This "rice" is a nice way to eat more veggies. Use it as a base for a build-your-own-bowl meal (page 208).

- 1 head cauliflower
- 1–2 cups broth (a light broth like chicken or vegetable works best)

1. Cut the cauliflower in half, then cut out the core and discard it. Snap off the florets and add them to the bowl of a food processor. Don't overfill the bowl, or it might be hard to get an even chop.
2. Pulse a few times until the cauliflower is chopped to the consistency of rice.
3. Heat the broth in a saucepan and add the cauliflower. Cook until heated but not mushy. Drain in a strainer and serve like rice.

YIELD: 4–6 servings

YELLOW COCONUT RICE (*NASI KUNING*)

As a young girl in Indonesia, one of my favorite things to eat (besides fried bananas) was the bright yellow coconut rice made for special occasions. There was something special about the texture and scent, and who doesn't like bright yellow? Helen Bartels, a star cook in our family, taught me (from her mother's recipe) that traditionally made *nasi kuning* takes time and care and a double steaming: the rice is steamed until half-cooked, then soaked in coconut milk and cooked the rest of the way. This quick version is tasty and healthy and a wonderful base for a spicy ferment.

Making the coconut milk is the heart of the dish. Using canned coconut milk does not produce the same texture or flavor. Start it about half an hour before you intend to cook the rice.

- 2 cups dried grated coconut
- 3¼ cups boiling water
- ½ teaspoon ground turmeric
- 2–3 strips lemon peel (zest only)
- 2 cups long-grain white, basmati, or jasmine rice

1. Place the coconut in a bowl and pour the boiling water over it. Add the turmeric and lemon peel. Mix. Let soak for 30 minutes.
2. Using a strainer or a cheesecloth-lined colander, drain the coconut liquid into a bowl, squeezing the coconut to release all the liquid. (You can save the leftover coconut meat for baked goods or smoothies.)
3. Combine the rice with all the coconut milk you've just made. Cover, bring to a boil, then reduce the heat to low and let steam until the rice has absorbed all the coconut milk and is fluffy, about 20 minutes. (Alternatively, you can cook the rice in the coconut milk in a rice cooker, using the amounts specified for your cooker. You can use any leftover milk in a smoothie.)

YIELD: 4 servings

HOT CRISPY TEMPEH STRIPS

These strips are tasty and easy. They are a wonderful protein accompaniment for a bowl of rice or noodles. Tempeh has its own nutty flavor, but it takes on other flavors well. Use any fermented flavor paste or hot sauce as a marinade. For a Southwestern flavor, try the Fermented Green Chili Base (page 157); for an Indonesian taste, soak the tempeh in rempah (page 159) with a bit of salt water. The tempeh strips should be crispy on all sides — we pan-fry them, but deep-fry if you prefer.

- 3–4 tablespoons fermented paste
- ½ cup fermentation brine (or ½ cup water with ¼ teaspoon salt)
- 1 (8-ounce) package tempeh, cut into ⅛- to ¼-inch slices (thinner slices will be crispier)
- ½–1 cup coconut oil

1. Mix the fermented paste and brine in a shallow bowl. Add the tempeh strips and let marinate for an hour or more.
2. Remove the tempeh from marinade and place it on a paper towel to soak up extra moisture.
3. Heat the oil over high heat until it is very hot but not smoking. The oil should be about ¼ inch deep across the pan.
4. Carefully place the tempeh strips in the hot oil and fry on each side until crispy — about 2 minutes per side. Drain on paper towels or a baking rack. Serve immediately.

Don't Toss It!

ZERO WASTE TIP #1: After the tempeh has marinated, the leftover ferment and water is still fine to eat. Use it to make a dip or spread for the tempeh or for toast: mix it with a bit of sour cream or about ½ cup of peanut butter and 1 tablespoon of brown rice syrup or honey.

ZERO WASTE TIP #2: Why throw out good coconut oil with the dishwater? The frying tempeh soaks up most of it, but often there is a nice layer of fat seasoned with bits of pepper flakes in the pan. Slice some onions or shallots and brown them in the oil to garnish your meal, or toss in some greens to braise as a side dish.

YIELD: About a dozen

EMPANADAS

Our son Kelton married a pastry chef, Nicole, who has come down with a kimchi addiction. This is their recipe, arising from the realization that a deep-fried hand pie is the perfect vehicle for all kinds of spicy ferments. Here are two filling options, one with kimchi and one with rhubarb achar. We encourage you to experiment with your own, and remember to make extra — the cold leftovers are great for an on-the-go lunch.

DOUGH

- ¼ teaspoon salt
- 1 cup water
- 5 tablespoons butter, melted
- 1⅓ cups flour
- 1¼ cups cornstarch
- 1 egg
- 1 tablespoon milk
- About 1 cup vegetable oil or shortening, for frying

KIMCHI FILLING

- 1½–2 cups Baechu Kimchi (page 166)
- 8–10 ounces cheese of your choice, grated

RHUBARB ACHAR FILLING

- 1 cup Rhubarb Achar (page 125)
- 1 pound fresh mozzarella or burrata balls, sliced thinly

1. Prepare the dough: Add the salt to the water and stir to dissolve. In a mixer, combine the butter, flour, and cornstarch. Add the salty water and mix until a dough forms. Let stand for 30 minutes.
2. Combine the egg and milk in a bowl and whisk until combined. Set aside.
3. Roll out the dough to about ⅛ inch thickness. Cut into 5-inch circles using a plate or other guide.
4. Place a few spoonfuls of filling in the center of each dough circle. Paint the edges of the dough circles with the beaten egg mixture, then fold into half circles, gently pressing out any air around the filling. Use a fork to press the edges together.
5. Heat the oil in a deep pan to 350°F (177°C). When you drop in a small bit of "test" dough, it should sizzle immediately. Fry the empanadas, turning once, for a few minutes on each side, until golden brown. You can also use a deep fryer.

YIELD: 10 poppers

FERMENTED JALAPEÑO POPPERS

A fun twist on a popular finger food! Once fermented, the stuffed peppers are a little delicate, so it takes some extra care to put these poppers together, but it's very doable and worth it. If you would like to use a hard cheese instead of cream cheese, choose an aged one like Kasseri that doesn't run when it melts.

- 10 Carrot-Stuffed Hot Peppers (page 187)
- 4 ounces cream cheese
- 10 strips bacon (or 5 strips, cut lengthwise, if the bacon is very thick)

1. Preheat the oven to 400°F (200°C).
2. Slit each pepper lengthwise along one side to open it slightly. Leaving the carrot stuffing in place, add about 1 teaspoon of cream cheese.
3. Wrap the stuffed pepper tightly with a strip of bacon.
4. Place the poppers on a baking sheet (or a wire rack set on a baking sheet), with the slit side up and the bacon ends tucked underneath. Bake for 20 to 25 minutes, or until the bacon has reached your desired crispness. Serve hot.

YIELD: About a dozen bars

APRICOT–CRANBERRY PEPPER CRUNCH BARS

The tart-sweet combination of apricots and cranberries goes well with hot sauce, so for this one we called up one of our favorites in this book, the fiery Vanilla Habanero Mash (page 106). If you want something less hot, just pick a paste with a lower heat level. Almonds and a host of seeds provide the crunch.

- 1 cup crispy almonds (see Crispy Nuts, opposite)
- 1/3 cup raw pumpkin seeds
- 1/3 cup raw sunflower seeds
- 1/3 cup raw quinoa, rinsed and dried on paper towel
- 2/3 cup dried apricots
- 1/3 cup dried cranberries
- 2 tablespoons brown rice syrup
- 3/4 teaspoon salt
- 2 tablespoons Vanilla Habanero Mash or your favorite fermented pepper mash

1. Preheat the oven to 200°F (90°C).
2. Oil your favorite cast-iron skillet and line it with parchment paper.
3. Combine the almonds, pumpkin seeds, sunflower seeds, and quinoa in a food processor. Pulse a few times, until the almonds are broken up and the mixture starts to bind together. Empty into a medium bowl.
4. Process the apricots, cranberries, brown rice syrup, salt, and pepper paste in the food processor until smooth. You may need to scrape down the sides of the bowl between pulses. Add to the almond mixture and mix well.
5. Transfer the mixture into the prepared skillet. Press it into place to evenly cover the bottom of the skillet. There are a couple of methods for this: you can wet your fingers with water or coconut oil and press by hand, or you can cover the mixture with a sheet of parchment paper and press it with something flat, like the bottom of a measuring cup or jar.
6. Bake for 25 to 30 minutes, until firm. Let cool, then cut into squares. You will have at least a few corners and trimmings left over, which are, of course, best consumed immediately to keep everything tidy.

Crispy Nuts

Crispy nuts will be familiar to readers of Sally Fallon's book *Nourishing Traditions*. Soaking nuts in salt water increases their digestibility, and for some folks this makes the difference between getting a bellyache or not. We use soaked nuts in all our recipes and have gotten into the habit of putting them in a bowl of salt water right out of the grocery bag and popping them in the dehydrator the next morning.

The process is the same for whatever nut you choose (and you can do seeds, too).

- 4 cups raw, unsalted nuts
- 2 teaspoons salt
- Enough water to completely submerge the nuts

STEP 1: Soak the nuts in the salted water for 12 hours, stirring occasionally if convenient. (For soft nuts like cashews and pine nuts, a 3-hour soak is long enough.)

STEP 2: Spread the nuts out on a dehydrator tray.

STEP 3: Dehydrate at 103°F or less for 12 to 14 hours.

STEP 4: Check the nuts after 10 to 12 hours. If they are dry, they will be hard to the touch and lightly crispy; if not, the mouthfeel will be soft and pithy and you should continue dehydrating for another couple of hours. Make sure your nuts are fully dry, as they could become moldy when stored.

STEP 5: Store in an airtight container. They'll keep fresh for several weeks.

YIELD: About 1 pound

BUTTERY PEPPER PECANS

Addictive. Crazy buttery, salty, spicy addictive. We tested this recipe more than was necessary because they are just so good.

- 6 tablespoons unsalted butter
- 2 teaspoons Vanilla Habanero Mash (page 106) or your favorite fermented pepper mash
- ¾ teaspoon salt
- ½ teaspoon freshly ground white pepper
- ½ teaspoon garlic powder
- 4 cups crispy pecans (see Crispy Nuts, page 217)

1. Preheat the oven to 300°F (150°C).
2. Melt the butter in a small saucepan. Remove from the heat and add the pepper mash, salt, pepper, and garlic powder, and whisk until combined.
3. Toss the pecans with the melted butter mixture. Spread out evenly in a large cast-iron skillet.
4. Bake for 30 to 35 minutes, until the pecans are nicely browned, stirring occasionally to prevent burning. Let cool, then store in an airtight container.

YIELD: 4 servings

QUELITES (MEXICAN GREENS)

Quelites is the Mexican word for wild greens — most commonly lamb's-quarter or its relatives. This recipe calls for lamb's-quarter or spinach, which makes a good substitute. If you're using lamb's-quarter, be sure to remove the tough stems before chopping the leaves. As for the mash, jalapeño or Fresno is nice; use less if using chile pequin or another fiery pepper.

- 1–2 tablespoons olive oil
- ½ medium onion, thinly sliced
- 1 pound lamb's-quarters or spinach, chopped
- 2 tablespoons fermented pepper mash of choice
- Salt

1. Heat the olive oil in a saucepan over medium-high heat. Add the onion and sauté until translucent and beginning to caramelize around the edges, about 5 to 10 minutes.
2. Turn down the heat and add the chopped greens. Cook for 1 minute, tossing to evenly coat and wilt the greens. Turn off the heat before they are completely wilted, as they will continue to cook in the latent heat of the pan.
3. Add the pepper paste to the pan and toss until the greens are evenly coated. Season with salt to taste. Serve immediately.

YIELD: 4 servings as a small plate, or 2 as a full meal

BLACK BEAN SALAD
WITH MANGO-PLANTAIN HABANERO FERMENT

A plantain ferment gives this dish its pizazz. It makes a fun dip to serve with corn chips, if you are after a quick finger food. We also like to serve it on a bed of hot fried plantains. (Look for plantains that are turning from green to slightly dark; they have the beginnings of that warm banana sweetness in their flavor, which pairs delightfully with the cool, spicy black bean salad.)

- 2 cups cooked black beans
- 1 avocado, diced
- 1 fresh tomato, diced
- ½ cup Mango-Plantain Habanero Ferment (page 177)

Combine the beans, avocado, tomato, and habanero ferment. Toss lightly so as not to mush the avocado.

Your Hungry Microbiome

We now know our body's microbiome is a teeming ecosystem. The healthier and happier our microbiota are, the healthier and happier we are. Eating fermented foods is one way to keep up a strong and healthy microbiome. Turns out, to keep your biota fit and full of energy, you need to feed them a good meal regularly too.

You may have seen (and been confused by) the word *prebiotic*. Looks like *probiotic*, sounds like *probiotic*, but it's not. A prebiotic is a nondigestible (by us) food component that promotes the growth and health of beneficial organisms. An example is resistant starch, found in foods such as potatoes, rice, and plantains — but only when they are cold. What? We know you don't want your potatoes cold, but stick with us. When this coil-shaped starch is heated, it melts into a blob, but as it cools it slowly recoils, becoming once again resistant to digestion. And why, you ask, is this a good thing?

When resistant starch lands in the large intestine, it meets a group of bacteria waiting for dinner. As they break it down, they release small carbohydrate molecules (waste) that neighboring bacteria consume. They then secrete even smaller waste molecules called short-chain fatty acids. The most important of these fatty acids are butyrates, which are happily absorbed by the colon's lining, encouraging blood flow, keeping tissues healthy, and providing an energy source for your body.

YIELD: 4–5 cups

SPICY CAPONATA

This is a twist on the classic sweet-and-sour Sicilian side dish. It also makes a great dip or sandwich spread.

- 2 eggplants (about 2 pounds total), chopped into ½-inch cubes
- 2 tablespoons salt
- 1 cup olive oil
- 1 fennel bulb, diced
- 1 red onion, diced
- 3 cloves garlic, thinly sliced
- 1 cup diced tomatoes, fresh or canned
- ⅓ cup red wine vinegar
- ¼ cup dried cranberries
- 2 tablespoons coconut sugar or brown sugar
- ¼ cup fermented pepper mash, preferably made with Fresno, Aleppo, or red jalapeño

1. Toss the diced eggplant with the salt. Place in a colander set over a bowl; let rest for at least 3 hours and up to overnight. When it's done draining, wrap the eggplant in cheesecloth or a clean kitchen towel and squeeze out any excess liquid.
2. Heat ½ cup of the olive oil in a large heavy skillet over high heat. Add the eggplant and fennel and cook, stirring as needed, until the eggplant is golden brown and the fennel is soft, about 20 minutes. Transfer to plate lined with paper towels to drain.
3. Heat the remaining ½ cup olive oil in the same skillet over medium heat. Add the onion and garlic and cook, stirring occasionally, until translucent, about 5 to 10 minutes. Add the tomatoes and cook for 5 minutes. Stir in the eggplant mixture, along with the vinegar, cranberries, and sugar. Continue to cook until everything is heated through and glazed with sauce.
4. Remove from the heat, let cool for a few minutes, and stir in the pepper mash.

YIELD: 4–6 servings

SIMPLE CREAMY SQUASH SOUP

This soup is ridiculously simple (once you have peeled the squash), has a wonderful rich flavor, and is a great base for a lot of fiery ferments, from Long Pepper Curry Paste (page 86) to Harissa (page 155). The recipe calls for whey, which you can get by making cheese at home, like our buttermilk cheese (page 201) or paneer (page 226). If you don't have any whey, just substitute a rich vegetable stock, broth made with parmesan rind, or chicken stock. If you like, you can rinse and save the squash seeds, toss them with a teaspoon of pepper paste and a pinch of salt, and bake them — they make a perfect soup topping. We especially enjoy this soup with a dollop of Pumpkin Seed Spread (page 224).

- 1 kabocha squash (2½–3 pounds)
- 2–3 tablespoons olive oil
- 1 large yellow onion, diced
- 4–5 cups whey or chicken stock
- fermented pepper mash of choice

1. Peel the squash, cut it in half, and remove the seeds. Dice the squash into ½-inch pieces.
2. Warm the oil in a saucepan over medium heat. Add the squash and onion and sauté until they have begun to soften and brown, about 8 to 10 minutes.
3. Add the whey to the pan and bring to a boil, then reduce the heat and let simmer until the squash is soft, about 30 minutes.
4. Remove from the heat. Let cool slightly, and purée to a creamy consistency.
5. Add a generous dollop of spicy ferment to the whole soup, or allow each person to top their serving with their favorite choice.

YIELD: About 1 cup

PUMPKIN SEED SPREAD

This spread works with many of the paste-type ferments, but the herb-based ones are our favorites, with Habanero Basil Paste (page 158) and Thai Dragon Mint-Cilantro Paste (page 152) topping the list. While a great spread, it is also nice to dollop on top of soups. It lasts in the refrigerator for at least 2 weeks, so it is nice to make ahead and use in lunches or snacks throughout the week.

- ½ cup crispy pumpkin seeds (see Crispy Nuts, page 217)
- 3 cloves garlic
- 3–4 tablespoons olive oil
- 1 tablespoon fermented pepper paste of choice
- 1 teaspoon fresh lemon juice

Combine the pumpkin seeds, garlic, 3 tablespoons of the olive oil, pepper paste, and lemon juice in a food processor and process until smooth. Add more olive oil as needed to reach the desired consistency.

CACAO NIB HABANERO PESTO

This recipe was influenced by a recipe by Alice Medrich, one of our country's foremost experts on chocolate (not a bad job), for a "nibby pesto." We knew we wanted to combine the Habanero Basil Paste with cacao nibs to make a pesto spread — it's that chocolate and chile thing. We started with olive oil, pumpkin seeds, nibs, and the paste. But there was something missing. A search turned up Alice's recipe with salty dry olives — bingo!

This pesto is tasty on top of crusty sourdough toast, and even better on crusty sourdough toast with cream cheese.

- ½ cup crispy pumpkin seeds, (See Crispy Nuts page 217)
- 3 tablespoons cacao nibs
- 6 dry, salty niçoise olives
- 4–5 tablespoons olive oil
- 1 tablespoon Habanero Basil Paste (page 158)

Combine the pumpkin seeds, cacao nibs, olives, 4 tablespoons of the olive oil, and the basil paste in a food processor and process until smooth. Add more olive oil as needed to reach the desired consistency.

SPICY CHERRY–CHOCOLATE BALLS

We combined a couple of our favorite trail bar recipes with pepper paste to give these little protein-packed energy balls a spicy, probiotic twist.

- 1½ cups mixed nuts (almonds, walnuts, and pecans are good choices)
- ½ cup dried cherries (or your favorite dried fruit)
- ½ cup pumpkin seeds
- 2 tablespoons chia seeds
- 2 tablespoons flax seeds, ground
- 2 tablespoons hulled hemp seeds
- 1 cup medjool dates, pitted and chopped coarsely
- 2 tablespoons cocoa powder
- 1 tablespoon cacao nibs
- 2 tablespoons fermented pepper mash of choice
- 1 tablespoon coconut oil

1. Combine the nuts, dried cherries, pumpkin seeds, chia seeds, flax seeds, and hemp seeds in a food processor and pulse repeatedly until they have a breadcrumb-like consistently.
2. Add the dates, cocoa powder, cacao nibs, pepper mash, and coconut oil, and process until the mixture balls together.
3. Roll the mixture by hand into balls. Store in an airtight container in the refrigerator, where they will keep for 2 weeks or so.

YIELD: About 10 ounces

PANEER: REGULAR AND BRINE-FLAVORED

Paneer is a quick, nonmelting cheese from the farming region of northern India, where it is a protein staple. We totally understand how an unripened cheese — easy and quick to make — can become an important food. There were about ten years when our kids were milking goats and cows, and we'd often make paneer just to reduce the volume of milk in the fridge. Our pig happily took care of the whey. This cheese is versatile. Cut it into squares and fry it to make crispy little snacks for a South Asian mixed plate, or add it to rich, spicy sauces.

Usually the milk is turned to curds and whey by adding lemon juice. However, we decided to see what would happen if we acidified the milk with a flavorful vegetable brine instead. We've used jalapeño pickle brine and kimchi brine — the flavor is distinctive and delightful. The whey is amazing as stock for a creamy soup (see Simple Creamy Squash Soup, page 223).

- ½ gallon whole milk (not ultra-pasteurized)
- ¼ cup lemon juice or a scant ¾ cup fermented brine

NOTE: *Sometimes the curds don't separate immediately. It may be that the temperature isn't quite warm enough. Keep the pot on the heat and continue to warm slowly. You may need to add more acid to encourage curd separation, but proceed cautiously, as too much acid will cause the curds to be small, like ricotta, and the cheese won't set as well.*

1. Put the milk in a heavy-bottomed, nonreactive pot. Heat slowly, stirring occasionally, to the point just before a boil (around 190°F [88°C]).
2. Add the lemon juice (or brine) and stir gently. Remove from the heat. You will see the curds begin to separate. Stir a few more times. Allow the curds to sit for a few minutes. The longer you let them sit, the firmer the cheese will be, but too long and the cheese will be rubbery. You will be able to see the curds tighten.
3. Line a colander with cheesecloth and place it over a large bowl or pot. Gently pour in the curds and whey and let drain for a minute or two. When most of the whey is drained, pull the corners of the cheesecloth together, lift it out with the curds, and place the whole thing on a cutting board. Fold the sides of the cheesecloth over the top of the curds, and place the pot of whey on top to press out any residual liquid. Let it sit for about 1½ hours.
4. Cut the cheese into chunks. Store it in an airtight container in the refrigerator and use within the next 5 days.

VARIATION: Spicy Lemon Paneer

When the curds are drained but not yet pressed, add 3 tablespoons chopped Lemon Achar (129). Stir in gently so that the achar is evenly distributed. Then continue with the pressing instructions.

YIELD: 4 servings

CALDO VERDE
WITH PIRI PIRI SAUCE

We wanted this soup to be hearty and hot for a cold winter day. It is based on the Portuguese kale soup of the same name, but this version is more like a spicy stew. For a vegan version, simply omit the sausage and use vegetable broth.

- 2–3 tablespoons olive oil
- 6 cloves garlic, chopped
- 1 small yellow onion (or a half a large one), diced
- ½ pound chorizo (page 205), linguiça, or other hot sausage, sliced
- 5–6 medium red potatoes (about 1½ pounds), diced
- 3–4 cups rich beef or vegetable broth
- 1½ bunches lacinato or other kale, sliced crosswise very thinly
- 4 tablespoons Piri Piri Sauce (page 98)
- Salt

1. Warm 2 tablespoons of the olive oil in a pot over medium-low heat. Add the garlic and sauté until brown, less than a minute. Add the onion and sauté until translucent, about 5 to 10 minutes. Add the sausage and cook, stirring regularly, for 5 minutes. Then add the potatoes and cook for 5 minutes, stirring regularly to coat them in the oil. Add a little more oil if needed to prevent sticking.
2. Add the broth and bring to a simmer. Cover and let simmer until the potatoes are soft, about 30 minutes. Add the kale and simmer, covered, for another 5 to 10 minutes, or longer if you want your kale softer.
3. Remove from the heat and stir in the Piri Piri Sauce. Season to taste with salt (with the salt in the broth and the hot sauce you may not need to add much, if any).

YIELD: 4 servings

FRA DIAVOLO SAUCE

This is our take on the spicy Italian sauce traditionally served over pasta or with fish. It's easy and crazy good, and it works with a number of different ferments.

The Habanero Basil Paste is a devilish brother indeed — the hottest choice — and the basil is delicious in this sauce. If you choose the Piri Piri Sauce, it will bring out the fruity notes. If you don't have those sauces but have a little plain pepper mash, this sauce will still shine. We like a nice burn, but feel free to choose your own heat level by adding more or less hot ferment.

- 3–5 tablespoons olive oil
- 8 large cloves garlic, finely chopped
- 1 small red onion, roughly chopped
- 1 bay leaf
- ½ generous teaspoon thyme
- 1 (15-ounce) can tomato sauce
- 1 (15-ounce) can black olives, drained and sliced
- 1 (15-ounce) can green olives, drained and sliced
- 2 tablespoons capers
- 1–2 tablespoons Habanero Basil Paste (page 158), 2–3 tablespoons Piri Piri Sauce (page 98), or 2–4 tablespoons Basic Go-To Mash (page 92)

1. Warm 3 tablespoons of the olive oil in a saucepan over medium-low heat. Add the garlic and sauté slowly until brown, about 1 to 2 minutes.
2. Combine the onion in a food processor or blender with 1 tablespoon of the olive oil. Blend until the mixture is a smooth paste.
3. Add the onion paste to the browned garlic, along with the bay leaf and thyme. Sauté gently until the onion is soft, about 5 to 10 minutes. If the mixture begins to stick, add a little more olive oil.
4. When the onion is soft, add the tomato sauce and bring to a simmer. Add the olives to the sauce and simmer for about 15 minutes. Remove the pan from the heat, stir in the capers and the pepper ferment, and serve hot.

Just Go with It

Here is where I, Kirsten, admit that I have never tasted an authentic fra diavolo sauce. But in writing a spicy cookbook, who can resist a recipe that means "brother devil"? Sometimes, I imagine, my family thinks I am chaos in the kitchen. Many times, as I am cooking something, I cannot answer the question "What are we having?" until I am ready to serve it. I don't always know why I do what I do, and this fra diavolo sauce definitely was an amalgamation of a lot of things — an olive-laden sauce (not spicy) I once ate in Geneva, and a technique I learned in an Indian cooking class. And capers, well, they reminded me of fish.

I was testing this particular recipe again and getting ready to put it to paper when I remembered something I read in Elizabeth Gilbert's book *Big Magic*. She thinks there are ideas just hovering around out there trying to find someone who will let them in and say, *okay, let's go with that*, instead of turning them away. It was a big aha moment: the ideas that land in my kitchen come from far and wide, because the word has gotten out that I am just crazy enough to listen.

YIELD: 2 servings as a main dish, or 4 as an appetizer

MINT-CILANTRO CEVICHE

Our daughter-in-law Nicole grew up in Chile, so ceviche is an important meal to her. She also studied to be a chef at Ecole Culinaire Française in Santiago. Clearly, we had to ask her to help us come up with a ferment-inspired ceviche recipe (after all, ceviche is made by "cooking" fish with acidity). She made a few variations, and the mint-cilantro one turned out to be everyone's favorite.

- 1 pound fresh fish (we recommend sole)
- Salt and freshly ground black pepper
- Juice of 6–7 lemons, plus more as needed
- ½ green bell pepper, diced
- ½ red bell pepper, diced
- ½ red onion, diced
- 1 teaspoon minced fresh cilantro
- 1 teaspoon minced fresh parsley
- 1 tablespoon olive oil
- 2 tablespoons Thai Dragon Mint-Cilantro Paste (page 152)
- 1 teaspoon Basic Go-To Mash (page 92) or your favorite mash
- 2 avocados, halved, pitted, and cubed

1. Cut the fish into ½-inch squares and place in a bowl. Sprinkle with salt and pepper. Pour the lemon juice over the fish. Then add the green and red bell peppers, onion, cilantro, and parsley. Drizzle the olive oil over everything, then add the mint-cilantro paste and pepper mash and stir everything together gently. Check the juice level; if it doesn't completely cover the fish, add more.
2. Cover the bowl and set in the refrigerator to "cook" or "pickle" for 15 to 20 minutes. (After 30 minutes it will still be good, but the acid will start breaking down the fish.)
3. Stir in the avocado right before serving.

VARIATION: Kimchi Ceviche

Though the Mint-Cilantro Ceviche became our favorite, when we asked for Nicole's help, her first thought was "kimchi ceviche." So here it is: follow the instructions for Mint-Cilantro Ceviche but omit the mint-cilantro paste, parsley, and cilantro, and add ½ cup chopped kimchi.

Choosing Your Fish

While tilapia is one of our favorite white fish for many recipes, we haven't found the flavor to be appealing in ceviche. We use sole and have been happy with the results. We also recommend the Monterey Bay Aquarium Seafood Watch website for keeping track of which fish to eat and which to avoid due to various concerns ranging from heavy metals to overfishing.

YIELD: 4 servings as a side, or 2 as a main course

CHICKPEA PANCAKES

Who doesn't like breakfast for dinner now and then? These savory dinner pancakes give you that pancake comfort with a twist — and there's no rule saying you can't have them for breakfast too. We developed this recipe for pumpkin and squash ferments, and specifically our Winter Squash & Kohlrabi Kimchi, but feel free to use any type of ferment. Serve with a dollop of plain yogurt or kefir cheese and a fresh salad.

- 1 egg
- ½ cup water
- 3–4 tablespoons sunflower oil or other good-quality frying oil
- ¾ cup chickpea (garbanzo bean) flour
- ¼ teaspoon baking powder
- 1 cup Winter Squash & Kohlrabi Kimchi (page 172)

1. Whisk together the egg, water, 1 tablespoon of the oil, chickpea flour, and baking powder in a bowl. Set aside for a few minutes to allow the flour to hydrate. Meanwhile, roughly chop the kimchi, then add it to the batter. Stir gently.

2. Heat 1½ to 2 tablespoons of the oil in a skillet over medium heat. When hot, dollop a few tablespoons of batter onto the pan. This batter is thick, so you will have to gently spread it out with a spoon; you're aiming for ¼-inch thickness. If the batter seems too thick to spread, add a little more water.

3. Cook until the bottom is nicely browned, about 3 to 4 minutes. Flip carefully and cook until browned and cooked through, another 2 minutes. Transfer to a covered plate, or keep warm in the oven while you're working through the rest of the batter.

YIELD: 4 hearty servings

WHITE CHILI

This chili requires very little time to prepare and a few hours to simmer — though you will need to start soaking the beans the day before. Because the fermented chili base is added after the chili has been taken off the stove, it has a bright, fresh flavor. You can adjust the amount of chili base you add to adjust the heat to your liking. The basic green chili base has a medium heat that we think makes comfortable chili for most palates. For more of a fire-engine flavor, garnish individual bowls with Habanero Carrot Sauce (page 107) or your favorite fermented hot sauce.

- 2 cups dry cannellini beans
- 2 tablespoons salt
- 4 quarts water
- 1 tablespoon whey (optional)
- 1 tablespoon sunflower oil or other good-quality oil
- 4 skin-on, bone-in chicken thighs
- 1 large onion, diced
- 2 quarts unsalted chicken broth or water
- 1 cup Fermented Green Chili Base (page 157)

1. Place the dry beans in a bowl. Dissolve the salt in the water and stir in the whey, if using. Pour the water over the beans and let soak at room temperature for 24 hours. Then drain the beans and rinse well.

2. Heat the oil in a Dutch oven or pot over medium-high heat. Place the chicken thighs, skin side down, in the oil and sear until browned, 8 to 12 minutes. Turn to sear the other side, another 10 minutes. Remove the chicken from the pot and set aside.

3. Add the onion to the pot and sauté until caramelized, about 10 minutes. Add the beans and stir quickly to coat in the oil. Add the broth and return the chicken to the pot. Bring to a boil, skimming any foam off the beans if necessary. Then reduce the heat and simmer (or place in a slow cooker on high heat) until beans are tender, about 3 hours.

4. Remove the chicken thighs with a slotted spoon and allow them to cool. Remove the bones and skin and return the chicken meat to the chili. Stir in the fermented chili base and serve hot.

YIELD: 4–6 servings

LEMON ACHAR ROAST CHICKEN
WITH CARROTS

This roast chicken is quick and uncomplicated, but the flavor is anything but. Feel free to play around with other fiery ferments to season this roast. Use the leftover carcass to make a chicken stock or soup the next day.

- 5 tablespoons Lemon Achar (page 129)
- 1 whole chicken (4½ to 5 pounds)
- 1 teaspoon freshly ground grains of paradise (or ¾ teaspoon freshly ground black pepper plus ¼ teaspoon ground cardamom)
- 1 teaspoon salt
- 2–3 tablespoons sunflower oil
- 6 carrots, sliced into 1-inch chunks
- 4 large cloves garlic, smashed
- 1 large shallot, sliced

1. Preheat the oven to 425°F (220°C).
2. Chop 2 tablespoons of the achar and use it to coat the cavity of the chicken. Then coat the entire outside of the chicken with the grains of paradise and salt.
3. Heat the oil in a deep, ovenproof lidded skillet or Dutch oven over medium-high heat. Carefully place the chicken, breast down, in the skillet and brown until golden, about 10 minutes. Carefully rotate the chicken, trying not to rip the skin, and brown the other side another 10 minutes or so. When both sides are brown, transfer the chicken to a plate and set aside.
4. Toss the carrots, garlic, and shallot into the skillet and sauté until lightly browned, 5 to 10 minutes. Add the remaining 3 tablespoons achar. Toss to distribute, then put the chicken on top of the vegetable mixture, breast facing up.
5. Place the lid on the skillet or Dutch oven and transfer to the oven. Roast for 50 minutes to 1 hour, or until cooked through. Check for doneness by cutting at the thigh joint and seeing the juices run clear, or use a meat thermometer — it should read 165°F (74°C) when inserted into the thickest part of a thigh.
6. Remove from the oven and allow to sit, uncovered, for 10 minutes before serving. Serve the chicken and vegetables with generous ladlefuls of the pan juices.

CH 11

SPIRITED SIPS AND RACY DESSERTS

Drinking seems to be the new eating these days. Brine, once thought of as a waste product, is hip. Health-promoting smoothies, shrubs, and tonics are everywhere. Drinks are perfect vehicles for featuring the flavor and kick of your favorite fiery ferment. And the nonalcoholic versions, at least, carry a solid dose of probiotic goodness. (The probiotic bacteria, as a general rule, will not survive an alcohol bath.) Several of the recipes that follow were created by Kirsten's sister (and family mixologist) Ursula Raymond. We provided the spicy stuff, and she did the heavy lifting.

Incorporating fiery ferments into desserts is another fun way to show off your culinary creativity. Sauces and syrups lend themselves beautifully to desserts. Ginger, cinnamon, fiery chiles, coffee, vanilla — the possibilities are endlessly tantalizing.

YIELD: 1½–2 quarts

FIRE CIDER

How could we not include fire cider, a folk remedy to cure what ails you, popularized by herbalist Rosemary Gladstar? This is a shrub with attitude (no sugar and spice and everything nice) — pungent, fiery, and sour. Okay, you can mix it with plenty of honey. It is a remedy for colds, sinus congestion, circulation, and digestion. The roots and herbs are steeped in vinegar for a month or more, which draws out the healthy components. Folks drink it straight up, put it in cocktails, and cook with it. Here is our take.

- 1–2 heads garlic, cloves separated and minced
- 1 onion, diced
- ¾ cup finely diced horseradish root
- 1 (6-inch) piece fresh ginger, diced
- 1 (6-inch) piece fresh turmeric root, diced
- 1 lemon, cut crosswise and sliced
- 6 tablespoons fermented pepper mash of choice (or less if you're using habanero mash)
- 2–3 tablespoons peppercorns
- 1½–2 quarts unfiltered, raw apple cider vinegar

1. Combine the garlic, onion, horseradish, ginger, turmeric, lemon, pepper mash, and peppercorns in a 2-quart jar. Pour in enough vinegar to fill the jar. Stir. Screw on the lid; use a plastic lid or, if you're using a metal lid, place a piece of parchment paper between the lid and the vinegar to avoid corrosion.
2. Set the jar aside to steep for 4 to 6 weeks. Shake or stir the contents when you think of it.
3. Strain the vinegar into a clean jar or bottle. Store in the refrigerator, where the cider will keep for up to 12 months.

YIELD: 1½–2 quarts

SPICY PINEAPPLE KVASS

Kvass is one of our favorite fermented drinks. And it's easy: we make it; we drink it; we make more. The health benefits of this tonic are innumerable — it aids digestion, alkalizes blood, and is probiotic, good for the liver and kidneys, full of good enzymes, minerals, and vitamins . . . really, why go on?

This kvass is light, carefree, and spicy like an early summer day. We usually use golden beets for this kvass, as their flavor is a bit lighter than that of their red counterparts.

- 2 pounds beets, chopped into ½-inch chunks
- 1 (2-inch) piece fresh ginger, sliced
- 1 (1-inch) piece fresh turmeric root, sliced
- 5 dried pineapple rings, cut into ½-inch segments
- 5 Thai volcano or other small hot chiles
- 2 tablespoons goji berries
- 1 tablespoon whole peppercorns
- 2 quarts brine (2 quarts unchlorinated water with 1 teaspoon salt)

1. Combine the beets, ginger, turmeric, dried pineapple, chiles, goji berries, and peppercorns in a half-gallon jar or a 2-liter bail-top jar. Fill the jar with brine, leaving at least 2 inches of headspace. Screw the lid down tightly.
2. Set aside to ferment for 5 to 21 days. Burp the jar every few days to allow any built-up CO_2 to escape. This is extremely important, especially if you are using a bail-style jar. (The only real glass explosion we have had in 15 years of fermenting was with a beverage.)
3. Taste the kvass beginning on day 5, and continue to ferment until it develops a nicely acidic bubbly flavor. We find that, more than with other ferments, this one varies quite a bit in terms of fermentation time. In the winter, our kvass tends to take a few weeks. In the summer, we get a better flavor by moving the ferment into the fridge at day 5 or 6 to ferment slowly for another week or two.
4. When it's ready, transfer the kvass to the refrigerator. We prefer not to strain until serving. In the refrigerator, the kvass will keep its effervescence for a few weeks. As a "flatter" tonic, it will keep for 6 months.

YIELD: 1½–2 quarts

HORSERADISH BEET KVASS

Kvass originated in Russia, so we came up with two recipes aimed to warm you like a good vodka — well, at least they will warm your mouth.

This kvass is amazing: dense, earthy, and warm like the inside of a log cabin in the woods. For us, this is a go-to winter kvass partly because of its mood and partly because of that sinus-clearing horseradish heat. Remember not to add the horseradish until the kvass has developed some acidity; otherwise, you'll lose the heat.

- 2 pounds red beets, chopped into ½-inch chunks
- 2 quarts brine (2 quarts unchlorinated water with 1 teaspoon salt)
- 1 cup diced horseradish root

1. Put the beet cubes in a half-gallon jar or a 2-liter bail-top jar. Fill the jar with brine, leaving at least 2 inches of headspace. Screw the lid down tightly.
2. Set aside to ferment for 5 to 21 days. Burp the jar every few days to allow any built-up CO_2 to escape. This is extremely important, especially if you are using a bail-top jar. (The only real glass explosion we have had in 15 years of fermenting was with a beverage.)
3. Taste the kvass beginning on day 5. When the kvass begins to taste acidic, prepare the horseradish and add it to the jar. Continue to ferment another 5 to 14 days, or until it develops a nicely acidic bubbly flavor. We find that, more than with other ferments, this one varies quite a bit in terms of fermentation time. In the winter, our kvass tends to take a few weeks. In the summer, we get a better flavor by moving the ferment into the fridge at day 5 or 6 to ferment slowly for another week or two.
4. When it's ready, transfer the kvass to the refrigerator. We prefer not to strain until serving. In the refrigerator, the kvass will keep its effervescence for a few weeks. As a "flatter" tonic, it will keep for 6 months.

HOT TIP

Once or Twice?

When you finish drinking a batch of kvass, the ingredients can be used for one more batch — just refill with more salt water and repeat. The second batch will be a little weaker in punch and effervescence, but still quite tasty and healthy.

HOT BOURBON CIDER SPRITZ

A perfect blend of our fermenting passions — fermented vegetables and cider! We like to use a sauce made with Fresno peppers, but feel free to experiment with your favorite creation.

- 3 ounces dry hard cider
- 2 ounces sweet cider
- ½ ounce rye whiskey
- 2 teaspoons strained Basic Go-To Mash (page 92)
- Splash of club soda

Fill a rocks glass with ice. Add the hard cider, sweet cider, whiskey, and strained mash. Top off with a splash of club soda. Stir gently and serve.

THE SEBASTIAN

This is Ursula's take on the popular Moscow Mule, introduced by the Cock 'n' Bull restaurant in the 1940s to promote its ginger beer and a Russian vodka named Smirnoff. Though it was originally served in a copper mug, Ursula chose a mason jar because of the wall of jars we have in our commercial kitchen. And the name? Well, it comes from the rescued wild donkey that Christopher and the kids brought home for Kirsten's fortieth birthday surprise. His name was Sebastian, and while not a mule, he certainly thought of himself as more than a burro.

As is the case for the Hot Bourbon Cider Spritz, we prefer to use a mash made with Fresno peppers for this drink. Strain the seeds and skin out of the mash with a fine mesh strainer before using.

- 2 ounces vodka
- ½ teaspoon strained Basic Go-To Mash (page 92)
- Juice of ½ lime
- 1 bottle ginger beer

Fill a mason jar with ice and pour the vodka over it. Then splash in the strained mash and lime juice. Add the ginger beer and stir gently.

YIELD: 1 serving

AJÍ MARGARITA

This time Ursula riffs on one of the most requested drinks at the bar, the classic margarita. Leave commercial sweet-and-sour mixes behind, and add Vanilla Habanero Mash to take it to a different place entirely. Enjoy.

- ½–1 teaspoon Vanilla Habanero Mash (page 106)
- ½ ounce freshly squeezed orange juice
- Juice of 1 lemon
- Juice of 1 lime
- 1 ounce simple syrup
- 1½ ounces tequila
- 1½ ounces triple sec or Grand Marnier
- Water

Fill a pint glass with ice and add Vanilla Habanero Mash to your heat preference. Add the orange, lemon, and lime juices and the simple syrup. Stir, then add the tequila and triple sec. Add water to fill the glass to the top. Pour everything into a shaker and shake. Strain into a fresh glass filled with ice and enjoy. If you're feeling adventurous, take it straight, in a martini glass.

BLENDED Variation

Instead of shaking, simply add everything to a blender and blend until smooth.

YIELD: 1 serving

COFFEE CHILE TODDY

Ursula told us, "Lately I have been inspired by reusing the items in our kitchen we would normally throw away. This drink is a play on a classic. A hot toddy is brandy, lemon, and honey. One day I had a really bad sore throat and had used all my lemon juice, but I still had the rinds. I used them to make this delightful toddy with your Coffee Sauce. Soon my sore throat was gone."

- Rind of one lemon
- 1 teaspoon honey
- 2 ounces whiskey
- ½ teaspoon Coffee Sauce (page 104)

1. Squeeze the lemon rinds into a pint glass, drop the rinds into the glass, add the honey, and fill the glass with warm water. Stir and let steep for 1 hour. Then discard the rinds, transfer the lemon-infused water to a pot, and heat.
2. Pour the whiskey and Coffee Sauce into a mug. Top off with the hot lemon infusion and enjoy.

YIELD: Serves 4–6

FRIED BANANAS (*PISANG GORENG*)
WITH PINEAPPLE HABANERO SYRUP

This spicy dessert came about accidentally. The day we were working on spicy fruit syrups, we also happened to have some bananas browning on the counter. Instead of taking the usual action of freezing the bananas for smoothies, we fried them in generous amounts of butter. And the Pineapple Habanero Syrup was just sitting there, waiting for its opportunity — it was a lightbulb moment.

- 4 bananas
- 3 tablespoons butter
- ¼–½ cup Pineapple Habanero Syrup (page 109)

1. Peel the bananas and cut each in half crosswise. Slice each of these into halves lengthwise.
2. Melt the butter in a skillet over medium heat. Carefully lay the bananas in the pan and allow them to brown, about 3 to 4 minutes. Riper bananas have a lot of sugar, so be careful that they are caramelizing, not burning.
3. Turn the bananas over and fry them on the other side for 1 minute. Then remove the pan from the heat and allow the bananas to cool for a minute, then pour the pineapple syrup over them. The syrup will cook lightly in the hot pan and mix with the caramelized butter. Serve warm, spooning the syrup over each portion.

Kirsten's Banana Story

When I was six years old, my father's work in anthropology moved our family to the village of Ari on the tiny island of Ambon, part of the Moluccas in Indonesia. The local banana, *pisang Ambon*, is the banana that became America's grocery-store banana.

As an honored guest of the village, I was gifted a banana tree, which is not really a tree but a plant grown from a rhizome (kind of like an iris) that can live for decades. The plant produces one flower which becomes a bunch of bananas. At the age of six, it is very difficult to accept that the whole "tree" must be cut down to retrieve the bananas. It would die back anyway, and I was told that the little shoots on the side would become a new plant, but I believe I was placated only by many plates of my favorite dish — fried bananas. On the island of Ambon, fried bananas are traditionally made with green bananas, but don't let that limit you — any stage of ripeness is delicious.

YIELD: About 1 quart

CHOCOLATE–CRANBERRY MOLE ICE CREAM

This ice cream is fruity and crazy creamy, with a hit of chocolate and chile. It does not have a standard cooked-custard base, because we began making it when we had an abundant supply of fresh raw milk, and it seemed a shame to cook it. This recipe is just as tasty with pasteurized milk — but be sure to use whole milk, and don't skimp on the cream.

- 1 egg
- ⅓ cup plus 1 tablespoon sugar
- 1 teaspoon vanilla extract
- 1⅞ cups heavy cream
- ½ cup whole milk
- ¾ cup Chocolate-Cranberry Mole (page 136)
- ¾ cup pitted whole dark cherries, fresh or frozen

1. In a large bowl, whisk the egg until well blended. Whisk in the sugar and vanilla.
2. Add the cream and milk, whisk briefly, and then stir in the mole and cherries.
3. Churn in an ice-cream maker according to the manufacturer's instructions. Eat immediately for a soft, creamy ice cream, or freeze for an hour to harden.

Christopher's Ice Cream Story

Ice cream socials were still around in the Midwest when I was growing up, and I hope they still are. Walking up to one, you could tell that it was going to be a good one by the number of big wooden freezers being carefully tended by the old guys (who knew their stuff) and how many tables were bowing under the weight of homemade cakes and pies. As a kid, I apprenticed for years as an ice cream maker, first by dropping handfuls of ice into the sides of the spinning tumbler, and then, when I was strong enough, cranking on the handle until my arms felt like they would come off.

I remember when those newfangled motorized models began to infiltrate with their bright plastic tubs and grating noise. My grandpa Jud would have none of it — ice cream needed to be tended, fretted over, and made by hand. I'm less of a purist and admit to being in love with our bright red Cuisinart ice-cream maker. I guess I'll let our grandkids push the button when they apprentice.

YIELD: About 1½ pints

PERSIMMON GINGER SORBET

For weeks we'd been trying different versions of a nondairy ice cream for this book — including a spicy avocado ice cream that was met with comments like, "Well, it's good, but it tastes like frozen guacamole." Then we went to a neighborhood gathering where we were gifted a flat of three different varieties of very ripe persimmons. Naturally smooth in texture, they seemed perfect for a spicy sorbet.

Gingery and delightfully warming, this sorbet is rich, with a velvety texture — all while being probiotic! Use any variety of persimmons, but make sure they are fully ripe. Hachiya, the large, bright orange ones, must be completely soft — so soft you think it is too late because it looks like there is runny syrup inside the skin, which has started to blacken. The squat fuyu persimmons are less astringent and can be eaten as soon as the flesh feels soft.

- 1½ pounds persimmons (4 or 5 large ones)
- ½ cup sugar
- 2 teaspoons finely chopped Fermented Ginger Pickles (page 78)
- 2 teaspoons brine from the ginger pickles
- Juice of ½ lemon

1. Carefully peel the persimmons. Combine the flesh with the sugar in a blender or food processor. Process until very smooth.
2. Place the mixture in a bowl and stir in the pickled ginger, brine, and lemon juice. Chill in the freezer for about an hour, or until the mixture is very cold.
3. Churn in an ice-cream maker according to the manufacturer's instructions. Eat immediately for a soft, creamy sorbet, or freeze for an hour to harden.

NOTE: *We attempted to back off on the sugar, as the persimmons are so sweet on their own. Some sugar is needed for good texture, though — it's part of the science of freezing. The sugar keeps the water from freezing too much and creating crunchy ice crystals.*

Fermentation Doctor

It's inevitable that sometimes, despite your best efforts, something will go wrong — or will appear to have gone wrong, even when your ferment is still doing fine. Here are some common and less common sights, diagnosed.

WHEN BRINE LOOKS LIKE SNOT

We know that nothing seems okay about gooey, viscous brine surrounding your ferment. Although, honestly, you will hardly ever see gooey brine (in all our fermenting, we have encountered it only a handful of times), it is a normal result of the bacteria eating their way through the starches and creating acidity. In our experience, this condition is more likely to occur when a ferment is fermenting very slowly because of cool temperatures. If you check your ferment and come across a glutinous brine but all other indications are good, just tuck that ferment back in place, move it to a slightly warmer spot, and give it another week or so.

BULGING LIDS

Despite everything we've been taught about bulging cans, a bulging lid is okay. The rules of canning are very different from the rules of fermentation. The pressure on the lid just shows that there has been a lot of lactic-acid bacteria activity, and the ferment went too long without being burped. If you find yourself staring at something like this, carefully open it over a sink or bowl, as there will be some bubbling. (Remember making a volcano with baking soda and vinegar?) Is it safe? To eat, yes. To open, yes — just be careful.

LAVA FLOW

This ferment is very active. There were 2 inches of headspace in the jar, and the ferment had been quiet until day 6. Then it started to leak. We stirred it down, and an hour later we walked into this. It happens. It's okay. Just discard the overflow and stir down what remains.

SCUM ALONG ZIPLOCK

This mash is perfectly fine. The bag is doing its job of keeping the mash submerged under the brine. The yeasts and scum along the sides of the bag will be removed with the bag. When fermentation is complete, wipe the sides of the jar and remove any bits that might be sitting on the ferment, and then transfer the ferment to a new container for storage.

(continued on next page)

MASH SEPARATION

This ferment should be burped and shaken to remove air pockets and keep the mash under the brine (see Curing Note, page 32).

MOLD

This thick paste ferment developed a little dot of mold, even under a one-way valve lid. When you see mold, simply remove it, along with the surrounding ferment. This could have been avoided with the use of a cartouche (page 39).

CLOUDY BRINE

This bubbling brine is cloudy, which means fermentation is happening just as it should (see page 183).

SEDIMENT

This white sediment, more obvious on red and other dark ferments, is a normal part of fermentation (see page 183). It is harmless.

KHAM YEAST

This yellow pepper paste developed a layer of Kahm yeast despite an airlock lid. But it's no reason for concern. You can leave the yeast where it is until the fermentation period is over. When the ferment is ready, remove the yeast and wipe down the sides of the jar with a paper towel. Transfer to a new container for storage. (See page 31.)

BLUE GARLIC

This is rare but harmless. Overnight this rempah turned a blue-green hue. There are no green veggies in it — it was the garlic. According to the September 2004 issue of *America's Test Kitchen Newsletter*, "Under acidic conditions, isoallin, a compound found in garlic, breaks down and reacts with amino acids to produce the blue-green color. Visually, the difference between garlic cooked with and without acid can be dramatic, but a quick taste of the blue garlic proved that the color doesn't affect flavor."

Acknowledgments

We have been touched by the support and kind words from all of you — our readers. We truly thank each of you for enjoying our work and taking the flavors, the fun, and the knowledge out to your families, friends, and communities.

We want to thank our own family for their continued love and support. This time around, the tasting support could feel a little dangerous. Thank you to Jakob, Lydia, Dmitri, and Lyra, who might well be the youngest hot sauce taster ever. Ariana, you were here for it all — the seemingly endless months of spicy meals, beginning with the experiments and, if that wasn't enough, the repeats and variations, not to mention the capsicum-laden peppers piled on every kitchen surface. Some days it was a lot to take, but you always had a good sense of humor about it. Thank you!

Nicole and Kelton, thank you for all the help with fine tuning the recipes, both here on the farm and in Boulder. A big thanks to Kirsten's mom Nadine, who braved many hours of teary pepper prepping and long, tongue-numbing tasting sessions. You always asked what else you could do to help, and we thank you for everything. Helen Bartels, we thank you again for sharing your mother's kitchen wisdom. And Ursula Raymond, thanks once again for sharing your talent for inventing cocktails.

Mary Alionis and Vicki Hames, thank you both for your unwavering support in terms of the stars of this book — the peppers and the plants that grow them.

Who doesn't need the support of a retired professor and microbiologist who is always willing to patiently explain the science of lacto-fermentation, our complex microbiome, and how it all ties together to make us healthier? Thank you, Dr. Arthur Ayers.

We want to do a special shout-out to folks we have met since *Fermented Vegetables,* who contributed in small ways by adding richness to this book: Marcus McCauley, Lisa Murphy, Dominique Fevry, Brian Layman, and Ed Currie for sharing their stories and recipes. Northwest potters Hadar Iron (crocks and serving bowls) and Josh Ratza (fermenting weights) for contributing their work to the photo shoot. And Nathan Elkins, of Ghostpepper Farms, who shipped freshly picked ghost chiles to spice up the photo shoot.

We want to thank all the wonderful folks at Storey (those we have met as well as the ones behind the scenes) who have supported us and continue to encourage us through this wild fermentation journey. Lastly, a big thank you to our editor, Hannah Fries; art director Michaela Jebb; and photographer Lara Ferroni. It was delightful working closely with each of you and we are so very much aware that a book is truly a sum of all of the people who put their time and energy into it.

Index

Page numbers in *italic* indicate illustrations and photographs.
Page numbers in **bold** indicate charts and tables.

C

G

H

I

J

K

L

M

N

O

P

Q

R

S

T

V

W

X

Y

Z

ROUND OUT YOUR FERMENTING REPERTOIRE

with more recipes from Kirsten K. Shockey and Christopher Shockey

Get to work making your own kimchi, pickles, sauerkraut, and more with this colorful and delicious guide. Beautiful photography illustrates methods to ferment 64 vegetables and herbs, along with dozens of creative recipes.

"***Fermented Vegetables*** will inspire and guide you. A multitude of recipes utilizing fermented foods from 'crocktails' to desserts — yes, fermented desserts — round out this excellent resource."
ACRES USA

"Sweet, savory, briny, salty, tangy — all your favorite flavors are here, folded neatly into gorgeous food photos and easily replicated with clear, simple recipe instructions."
FOOD NETWORK DISH

"Full of appetizing and useful recipes for more than just the typical krauts and kimchis, offering up a relish tray of dishes that you'll find yourself using every day."
PUNK DOMESTICS

"A hefty guide to the reemerging art of fermentation … perfect for the fledgling *fermentista*."
PORTLAND MONTHLY

Join the conversation. Share your experience with this book, learn more about Storey Publishing's authors, and read original essays and book excerpts at storey.com. Look for our books wherever quality books are sold or call 800-441-5700.